TRADING GAZES

TRADING GAZES

Euro-American

Women Photographers

and Native North Americans,

1880–1940

Susan Bernardin

Melody Graulich

Lisa MacFarlane

Nicole Tonkovich

with an Afterword

by Louis Owens

RUTGERS UNIVERSITY PRESS

NEW BRUNSWICK, NEW JERSEY,

AND LONDON

Frontispiece. Kate T. Cory, Old Oraibi, ca. 1905–1912. Courtesy Museum of Northern Arizona, Flagstaff. MS–208 #75.1944N. Kate Cory Photography Collection.

Library of Congress Cataloging-in-Publication Data

Trading gazes : Euro-American women photographers and Native North Americans, 1880–1940 / Susan Bernardin . . . [et al.]; with an afterword by Louis Owens.

    p.   cm.

   Includes bibliographical references and index.

   ISBN 0-8135-3169-1 (cloth : alk. paper)—ISBN 0-8135-3170-5 (pbk. : alk. paper)

   1. Indians of North America—Pictorial works—History.   2. Women photographers—North America—History.   3. Photography in ethnology—North America—History.   I. Bernardin, Susan, 1966–

E77.5 .T73 2003

970′.00497—dc21

2002070503

British Cataloging-in-Publication information is available from the British Library.

Manufactured in Canada

To the memory of Louis Owens

CONTENTS

ILLUSTRATIONS

PREFACE

In many ways, we've written this book under conditions that mirror those under which many nineteenth-century women writers and artists worked. We live in Utah and New Hampshire, New York and California: our collaboration has been fundamentally shaped by our geographical dispersal. Although we have access to technological advances that have made our working together quicker and easier than they could have imagined, nonetheless our project is marked by the span of the continent we straddle.

We began in the summer of 1998, when Melody enticed us to put together a panel for the Western Literature Association Conference in Banff, Alberta. The promise of a gorgeous location, gracious hosts, and congenial colleagues made that an easy sell. Listening to each others' papers, and to the comments of a knowledgeable and astute audience, made us realize how the different stories we were telling revealed central issues in the history of the North American West; in the history of photography; in women's and gender studies; and in the ongoing negotiation, both theoretical and material, over race and representation. Another panel at the American Studies Association Conference later that fall convinced us to write a book together.

Although we've often wished for a week together in some conducive location, not since those original conferences have the four of us been in the same place. Although some might see this as a feature of our own time, these were common circumstances for our turn-of-the-century subjects. We learned what the women in this book knew: what it meant to have collaborators, audiences, and publishers in distant locations. Mary Schäffer lived and worked in Banff but published in New York and Philadelphia; Jane Gay divided her time between Washington, D.C., and Idaho; Kate Cory maintained connections with both the Hopis and her family in Illinois; Grace Nicholson's business transactions took her from Pasadena to the Peabody Museum in Cambridge. Like us, each of them was deeply aware of other readers, in other regions, looking at her work with other sets of eyes. Their many contemporaries, both Euro-American and Indian, also saw their manuscripts travel across country, shaped by editors, friends, ethnographers. It seems somehow appropriate—if occasionally frustrating!—to have followed their lead.

Our writing process, too, had nineteenth-century antecedents. The postal photographic clubs that flourished throughout the turn into the twentieth century enabled far-flung practitioners to share prints, techniques, and aesthetic strategies. A Massachusetts photographer might pack up a set of prints and mail them off to a colleague in Pennsylvania, who would write a lengthy comment, appreciating some elements of the work and criticizing others. The entire package would head off to yet another colleague, perhaps in Delaware or Connecticut, and so on. Months later, the packet, now considerably thicker and perhaps a bit dog-eared, would arrive home, making material a kind of virtual photographic workshop. So too with us: we wrote the introduction, for example, in sections and in stages, relaying it back and forth, not across the mountains, but across different e-mail and word-processing protocols, relying on a series of comments that piled up like geological strata to help us harmonize our different voices, writing processes, and backgrounds. And just as our predecessors relied on a network of delivery services and energetic couriers, so did we—except ours included Federal Express, university computer services, and our local internet providers.

Finally, like our nineteenth-century forebears, we too have found the journey eased by serendipitous encounters and deepened by growing friendships. Our profession gives us few opportunities to collaborate on such intimate terms. More often, our research and writing are structured as solitary activities. To have had the chance to experience another way of writing has been one of the challenges, and the gifts, of this book. In a sense, then, we too have traded gazes.

ACKNOWLEDGMENTS

Much of the work that resulted in *Trading Gazes* was done in museums and archives. We thank the following: the Cumberland County Historical Society for permission to reproduce images from its collections; Humboldt State University Special Collections for assistance with photographs taken at Hoopa Valley Reservation; Idaho State Historical Society for permission to reproduce images from the Jane Gay Photograph Collection; the Huntington Library for permission to reproduce images and quote from unpublished materials in the Grace Nicholson Collection; the Museum of Northern Arizona, Flagstaff, for permission to reproduce images from the Kate Cory Photography Collection; the National Anthropological Archives, Smithsonian Institution; the Smithsonian American Art Museum and the National Museum of the American Indian, Smithsonian Institution, for permission to reproduce images; the National Archives; the Newberry Library for permission to reproduce an Emma Freeman photograph; *News from Native California* and the National Park Service for permission to reproduce a map of northwestern California; the Peabody Museum of Archaeology and Ethnology at Harvard University for permission to quote from unpublished material from Grace Nicholson's correspondence; the Pusey Library at Harvard University for permission to quote from Alice Fletcher's correspondence; the Schlesinger Library on the History of Women in America, Radcliffe Institute, for permission to reprint images and quotations from Jane Gay's *Choup-nit-ki;* the Sharlot Hall Museum, Prescott, Arizona, for permission to reproduce images and quote from unpublished materials in the Kate Cory Collection; the Smoki Museum, Prescott, Arizona, for permission to quote unpublished captions from Kate Cory's photograph album; the Whyte Museum of the Canadian Rockies Archives and Library for permission to reproduce images and quotations from the Mary T. S. Schäffer and Mollie Adams Fonds.

We would also like to thank the following museum curators and archivists for their special help: Richard Tritt of the Cumberland County Historical Society; Marie-Hélène Gold and the staff at the Schlesinger Library on the History of Women in America; Carolyn Bowler of the Idaho State Historical Society; Joanne Cline and Sylvia Smith of the Smoki Museum for sharing their knowledge and for their generous help; Mary Tahbo of the Museum of Northern Arizona for help in understanding how a contemporary Hopi views Kate Cory's photographs; Joan Berman from Humboldt State University Special Collections for sharing her interest in Grace Nicholson and in other women photographers in Humboldt County; Erin Chase, rare-photograph curator at the Huntington Library, who unfailingly and generously provided expert (and generous) assistance with Grace Nicholson's photographs; Viva Fisher and Susan Haskell from the Peabody Museum for their gracious assistance with the Nicholson correspondence; Lars Krutak of the National Museum of the American Indian Repatriation Office for sharing his own research on repatriation involving photographic evidence; John Powell from the Newberry Library; Peter Palmquist, whose meticulous research on and encyclopedic knowledge of western women photographers were invaluable for Susan Bernardin's research; Don Borden and Elizabeth Cameron from the Whyte Museum of the Canadian Rockies Archives and Library for sharing their knowledge of Mary Schäffer's life and work, for information on Byron Harmon and other Banff-area photographers, and for graciously and promptly answering innumerable queries on everything from local history to Canadian law to the intricacies of obtaining permissions; and Claude Roberto and Diane Lameroux of the Provincial Archives of Alberta.

We thank those who provided research assistance. They include Sarah Rudd and Matt Burkhart, Utah State University; and Melisa Klimaszewski, Deborah Tokars, and Christine Peters, University of California, San Diego. Invaluable help in manuscript preparation came from the following people: Sabine Barcatta and Alan Barlow, Utah State University; and Jake Mattox, editor extraordinaire, University of California, San Diego.

All the collaborators involved in this book thank Leslie Mitchner of Rutgers University Press for her ongoing faith in this project. Nicole Tonkovich thanks the Schlesinger Library on the History of Women in America for travel funds; the Hellman family for generous fellowship support; and the faculty senate of the University of California, San Diego, for research monies. She also extends thanks to Elizabeth Jacox for her unparalleled intellectual generosity in sharing her extensive research. Finally, she thanks her colleagues—Susan Larsen, Marta Sánchez, Stephanie Jed, Kathryn Shevelow, and Michael Davidson—who provided helpful commentary and support.

Lisa MacFarlane would like to thank Barbara Steinberg, Art Library, University of New Hampshire; Gary Sampson, Doug Prince, and Lisa Nugent, Photographic Services, University of New Hampshire, for sharing their technical expertise and knowledge of photographic history; and Siobhan Senier, University of New Hampshire, who generously read and commented on portions of this manuscript. Marc Bousquet helped compile permissions and provided technical assistance. The work on Mary Schäffer is the better for their help. In addition, Lisa MacFarlane would like to thank the College of Liberal Arts and the Graduate School, University of New Hampshire, for financial assistance in researching this project; and she is especially grateful to the Center for the Humanities, University of New Hampshire, for providing subvention funds and a leave of absence during which the Schäffer chapter was written.

Melody Graulich would like to thank the people of the Hopi Nation for allowing scholars to reproduce photographs from the nonrestricted files of the Museum of Northern Arizona.

Susan Bernardin gratefully acknowledges the stories and assistance offered by Leaf Hillman, director of natural resources of the Karuk Nation. He was the first person to show her Nicholson's photographs of Karuks. She also thanks Violet Super, Jeanerette Jacups-Johnny, Terry Supahan, and Phil and Sue Sanders, all of whom have gifted her with stories and insights about the Klamath and Karuk region. Jeanne Perkins shared personal knowledge of Nicholson's years in Pasadena. Susan Bernardin is also indebted to Ira Jacknis for his knowledge of early California Indian anthropology and photography and to Marvin Cohodas, whose study of Grace Nicholson's patronage relationship with Elizabeth Hickox informed much of the research on Nicholson. Faculty Grants-in-Aid and a Faculty Research Leave from the University of Minnesota provided much-needed time and resources for this project. Many thanks to John Hitchcock and Elizabeth Prose, both for their friendship and for their readings of Nicholson's photography. Finally, Susan Bernardin thanks Julie and Michael Patterson-Pratt for lending strength when it was most needed, and her husband, David Craig, whose grace, patience, and faith kept her on the trail.

TRADING
GAZES

EMPIRE OF THE LENS

Women, Indians, and Cameras

I n July 1908, Grace Nicholson, a basket trader, amateur ethnologist, and photographer, made the first of several purchasing expeditions among the Karuk in northwestern California. Equipped with a camera, she was eager to record the authenticity and origin of her purchases. In a photograph taken by her business associate, Carrol S. Hartman, she and an elderly Karuk woman, known to her as Snappy, or Emma, sit together on the ground, seemingly oblivious to the camera's eye (fig. 1). At first glance, the women's postures and body language suggest a relation of equality, trust, and closeness, a relation made visually striking by their dramatically different clothing and features. Yet a phrase in the trader's travel diary suggests the inequities of the encounter: she noted that she was able to "secure her [Snappy's] picture without any trouble."[1] The resistance Nicholson may have anticipated from her informant is conditioned by the Euro-American occupation—physical, scientific, cultural, and visual—of the space these two women inhabit. They share this common ground only briefly, framed by the photographer's gaze. A closer examination suggests that, as documentary verification, this image is most notable for what it does not show: the featherband Snappy sold to Nicholson. The absence of the visible sign of the transaction that brought them together raises questions about other stories and material objects also absent from the vast archive of Indian photographs in the late nineteenth and early twentieth centuries.[2]

Little-known photographs such as this one expose the complex stories of unconventional, well-educated middle- and upper-middle-class women such as

1. Carrol S. Hartman, *Emma Telling Grace Nicholson about Featherband,* 1911.

Reproduced by permission of The Huntington Library, San Marino, Calif., Album C, page 28.

Nicholson, who fulfilled personal and professional aspirations by working or living in Native communities. The four photographers we write about here—Nicholson (1877–1948), who worked with the Karuk and other northern California tribes, and her near contemporaries, Jane Gay (1830–1919), who spent four summers among the Nez Perces in northwest Idaho; Kate Cory (1861–1958), who made her home among the Hopis in northern Arizona for seven years; and Mary Schäffer (1861–1939), who was a neighbor of the Stoney in Alberta—inhabited multiple and at times conflicting roles. They were tourists, artists, and writers; ex-officio documentary photographers, amateur ethnologists, and collectors; and brokers to museums and private collectors. Hundreds of their photographs, now largely unknown, chart a continuum of encounters, from close relationships to fleeting interactions, with Native peoples of the U.S. and Canadian Wests.

Like other New Women of their day, Gay, Cory, Schäffer, and Nicholson came from prosperous families, had been well educated, and did not follow the conventional patterns of marriage and child-rearing that had characterized the lives of their mothers and grandmothers. Eager for adventure and achievement, willing to risk reputations, and careless of comfort, they headed into new territory. Western life among the "uncivilized" helped them to reject the constraints and capitulations of middle-class Victorian womanhood and domesticity: to trade a parlor for a tent, a gown for a beaded jacket, a ball for a Snake Dance, a bath for a rain barrel. As they pursued new occupations in the arts or social sciences and revised older feminine roles in tourism and art patronage, they turned to Native peoples, cultures, and values to reinvent themselves. At age fifty-eight, after having worked as a teacher, a dead-letter-office clerk, a nurse, and a writer, Jane Gay set out to learn the new craft of photography so that she could document her friend Alice Fletcher's ethnographic projects. For four summers, these two friends rode a Pullman "palace car" across the continent to the Nez Perce Indian Reservation. Here, where the temperature on a summer afternoon often exceeded 108 degrees, they lived in tents and clapboard shelters, drove rickety wagons over dirt roads or hiked mountainous terrain, and facilitated the allotment of land to the Nez Perces. Gay made over four hundred images of the allotment process.

Intending only to tour the Far West on a vacation from teaching painting at Cooper Union School of Design, the forty-four-year-old Kate Cory got off the train at Canyon Diablo in 1905 to visit the Hopis and never used her return ticket, spending seven years on the mesas and the rest of her life in Arizona. Living on the second floor of her Hopi landlady's house, she said, "gave [her] a new point of view," expressed in the over six hundred remaining negatives of her work. Three thousand miles to the north, Mary Schäffer horse-camped across the still-remote Canadian Rockies, reveling in "the emancipation from frills, furbelows, and small follies"; her confession that the "mountains had thrown a glamour" over her remind us that Euro-American women's deeply complicated turns toward the Native were transnational in scope. Finally, Nicholson's move to southern California in 1901 for health reasons linked white women's embrace of western locales to broader cultural currents more often associated with literary males who found in "wild" terrains their "west cures."[3]

Our title, *Trading Gazes*, evokes and acknowledges the history of often unequal exchanges in "trading posts" throughout the West and points to the interchange that was taking place among cultures in a frontier contact zone. We explore the asymmetries of power that made these images possible in their own moment and that have preserved (or obscured) them for our own age. White women working or living within Native communities frequently initiated trades—of gifts, goods, services, objects, and knowledge—that resulted in what we have now come to see as the alienation of the cultural and intellectual property of Indian nations. At times, they mediated exchanges in which tribal concessions were traded for supposed political benefits. Their photographs were integral to these relations: sometimes they gave prints to tribal members; more frequently, they circulated their work in private albums, magazine articles, public lectures, travel books, and as a part of museum collections and displays.[4]

Today, the photographs these women took serve as complex and sometimes contradictory markers of cultural exchange. Some grace the walls of tribal museums: Cory's photographs have hung on the walls of the Hopi Cultural Center. Others, like those of Gay and Schäffer, enrich archival collections and state historical society libraries. Reviewed from new perspectives, these photographs bear witness in contemporary times: under legal provisions such as the Native American Graves Protection and Repatriation Act (NAGPRA) (1990), items like Snappy's featherband, long out of sight but not out of mind, may be eligible for repatriation. Donated to the Peabody Museum by one of Nicholson's wealthy clients and for over a century part of its permanent ethnographic collection, the featherband and its provenance might now be documented by a photograph first intended to establish its authenticity to a buyer or collector. Ironically, perhaps, *Emma Telling Grace Nicholson about Featherband* chronicles both Karuk survival and the ways in which contemporary Native nations continue to reshape the archive of Indian photography.

Yet these photographs, like those made by women teachers, government employees, and missionaries, remain largely absent from official or public photographic archives. Often characterized as amateur, they do not follow the conventions of content, framing, and pose used by the men engaged in the "grand endeavors" of scientific, anthropological, or aesthetic photography.[5] Their makers, although sometimes sponsored by governmental or educational agencies, were generally unaffiliated and marginal to official undertakings. These photographs constitute a counter-archive, inviting comparisons with other images of indigenous peoples from the nineteenth and early twentieth centuries. They re-turn our attention to the circumstances under which such images were made and ask viewers to mark their own complicity in interpreting them.

In *Trading Gazes* we explore this counter-archive of images produced by Gay, Cory, Nicholson, and Schäffer. Tracing the intersecting histories of these women and their Indian subjects, we consider their place in the larger histories of Native peoples and in Euro-American westward expansion. We investigate how gender and race may affect access to political and cultural power and thus result in different kinds of writing and photography. We consider the contexts in which these women's photographs and texts have been received: at the moment of their production in a specific interaction between photographer or writer and subject; as they were collected into albums, travel books, and memoirs, or into more culturally capacious museums and archives; and, in the larger sense, as they become parts of the histories of tribes and nations. We explore the ways in which these photographs sometimes record acts of violation and dispossession, but we include no images of ceremonial practices or sites. Instead, the photographs featured in *Trading Gazes* direct us toward the successes and failures, inevitable contradictions and compromises, of intercultural understanding during a watershed era of U.S. and Canadian Indian history.

PHOTOGRAPHY IN THE WEST

Since photography's early moments in the mid-nineteenth century, American Indians have been favored subjects. Photographs recorded unfamiliar landscapes and Native peoples, placing figurative borders around space undefined by Western cartography. For North Americans who pushed west throughout the nineteenth century, photography became a way to take inventory of the land and to frame its contentious history into a readily digestible narrative of inevitable white expansion. As Susan Sontag says, photography allows "people to take possession of space in which they are insecure."[6] Photographs chronicled the domestication of Native peoples and, at times, their resistance to such incursions. Those images that were circulated codified ways of seeing Indians that furthered expansionist policies. At the same time, photography registered a lament for a vanishing wilderness and its indigenous inhabitants, recapitulating the familiar story made explicit in Frederick Jackson Turner's "The Significance of the Frontier in American History": that American development was predicated on the presence of and then dominance over what Turner and his generation believed to be "free land," of which "the Indian" was an intrinsic natural feature.[7] From the 1860s to the 1920s, increasing numbers of white Americans participated in this visual dispossession, both as active agents and as viewers.

Contradicting the myth that the late nineteenth-century West in both the United States and Canada was populated largely by cowboys at home on the range and by women homesteaders and schoolmarms, Wallace Stegner and others have demonstrated that after the Civil War, and particularly after the completion of the transcontinental railroad, the West attracted numerous well-educated professionals, whose activities were integral to the area's development.[8] Among the best known are Clarence King and John Wesley Powell, both heads of the U.S. Geological Survey (a division of the Department of War), whose purpose was to survey western lands for railroad lines, mines, and commercial development, and whose crews included artists such as Thomas Moran and photographers such as William H. Jackson and John Hillers, later a staff photographer for the Bureau of American Ethnology under Powell. Interested in advancing scientific knowledge, in naming, mapping, and rationalizing western resources, and funded by a government devoted to integrating western lands into a national grid of economic and social power, they included the western Indian tribes among their objects of study. These professionals acknowledged, although sometimes only obliquely, the intellectual, economic, and social interconnections among land (geology and geography), peoples and culture (ethnography and history), and representation (art and photography). Their projects helped to generate a vast archive of Indian images.

Nineteenth-century photographs of Indians combined documentary impulses with aesthetic devices. Following the example of scientists and explorers, photographers made sense of and rationalized information, and communicated it to a predominantly eastern audience. From artists and writers, they borrowed representational conventions to elicit appropriate emotional responses from their viewers. The combination legitimated white conquest in political, evolutionary, and moral terms. In field records and geological-survey materials, in boarding-school records and studio portraits, photographs illustrated an allegorical narrative of the eventual conquest and extinction of tribes, making Indian presences and absences part of the visual discourse of the expanding nation. The camera helped government officials "manage" Indian policy, as suggested by terms associated with photographic practice—to take, to develop, to capture, to shoot, to frame.

The commingling of ethnographic and romantic visual vocabularies pervaded every genre of Indian photographs. The camera followed the conventions of landscape painting, bringing romantic visions of the untamed wilderness to bear on scientific documentation. Majestic paintings of western scenery, such as Albert Bierstadt's *The Rocky Mountains* (1863), used the pictorial conventions of the sublime—a domesticated foreground, with peaceful Indian encampment, giving way to impenetrable mountains glowing with divine favor—to justify westward expansion and political and cultural dominance in accordance with the ideas of Manifest Destiny.[9] In the narrative this painting suggests, Indians peacefully departed the land so that whites could take it over. The photographers who accompanied the initial railroad surveys borrowed from this tradition as they trained their cameras on the resource-rich trans-Mississippi West. When Bierstadt joined King's 1871 U.S. Geological Survey, one of his colleagues was Hillers,

2. Unknown illustrator, *Photographing an Indian Delegation, in Bell's Studio, for the Government,*
Frank Leslie's Illustrated Newspaper 53 (10 September 1881).

Courtesy Clements Library, University of Michigan.

who pictured Indian territory in Christian and nationalist terms, as his photograph of a southwestern rock formation entitled *Navajo Church* (1882) suggests.
Conflating the land with its inhabitants, their images represented North American Indians, like mineral deposits, as an inherent part of the landscape to be mar-
veled at, then mapped, contained, possessed, and removed by the expanding
nation.

Scientific and aesthetic norms also determined how photographers who made
portraits of Indians approached their work. Like paintings, official photographic
portraits of groups of tribal leaders who traveled east to negotiate treaties with
government officers were staged, using props and backdrops (fig. 2). Such stiffly
posed tribal leaders can be described only as costumed, whether dressed in top
hats and carrying umbrellas or bedecked in the feathers, fringes, and blankets
that may or may not have been their authentic attire but that signified "Indian" to
white viewers.

At the same time, as Elizabeth Edwards suggests in "The Resonance of Anthropology," the conventions of Indian photographic portraiture echo the anatomical visual studies produced by early anthropologists. The use—or entire
absence—of backdrops, as well as captioning practices, emphasized Indians'
anonymity and otherness. Portraits of Native subjects were often identified solely

by taxonomic captions of tribe and gender.[10] In this they resembled other pictures made of cultural materials—still lifes. Artfully lit and arranged before unobtrusive backdrops to focus the viewers' attention on their aesthetic appeal, baskets, pots, weapons, and clothing were removed from the contexts of their daily use and renamed as "artifacts" for museum collections. In the process, they were stripped of tribal connections, of their rich contexts of intelligibility and meaning. Their meanings for white viewers were often stabilized by interpretive text that foreshadowed tribal extinction, most famously in captions such as Joseph Kossuth Dixon's *Sunset of a Dying Race.* Such photographs, says Edwards, "become a metaphor of power" in which "ideas of both [the] scientific and the aesthetic operate simultaneously, the nuances of meaning shifting according to the contexts in which the photographs 'performed.'"[11]

These two strands of photographic practice thus develop differing but complementary narratives. Documentary photography records vanishing "savage" Indians for anthropological study while the aesthetic/sentimental approach identifies "civilized" Indians as ready for assimilation, a policy aimed at extinguishing tribal structures. In the postbellum period, these tensions manifested themselves in popular portraits of a parental figure, usually dressed in traditional clothing, with a child dressed in conventional "white" attire (fig. 3). Paired "before-and-

3. Unknown photographer, *Indians from Southern Alberta*, n.d.
Courtesy Provincial Archives of Alberta, Edmonton, OB 9249.

4. J. N. Choate, *Chiricahua Apaches Dressed in Native Garb as They Arrived from Ft. Marion, Florida, Nov. 4, 1883.*

Reproduction courtesy of Cumberland County Historical Society, Carlisle, Pa.

after" shots implied that exposure to Euro-American culture through "benevolent" pedagogies would transform "wild" Indians into "civilized" citizens (figs. 4 and 5). As a premium to new subscribers, Carlisle Indian School's *Indian Helper* offered "two PHOTOGRAPHS, one showing a group of Pueblos as they arrived in wild dress, and another of the same pupils three years after, or . . . two photographs showing still more marked contrast between a Navajoe [*sic*] as he arrived in native dress, and as he now looks, worth 20 cents a piece."[12] In the circumstances of their production and in their subsequent uses, these photographs complemented the work of government agents such as Alice Fletcher, who was engaged in dividing reservation lands into 160-acre farms to be given to newly minted Indian citizen-farmers. Such images illustrate what John Tagg calls the "benevolent, transcendent gaze, the gaze of the camera, and the gaze of the paternal state."[13]

Portraiture produced by studios and boarding schools found its ironic double in prison photographs. Government officials and scientists turned to the camera as a way to "capture" Indian subjects for regulation, preservation, and assimilation. Famed anthropologist Franz Boas took head shots and made cranial measurements of Indians in a Victoria, Vancouver Island, prison in 1888 as part of the well-established scientific practice we might now call "racial profiling."[14] The carceral associations of the camera were equally literal for the first Diné (Navajo) subjects of photography while they were imprisoned at Bosque Redondo in New Mexico from 1864 to 1868 and for Nez Perce chief In-mut-too-yah-lat-lat, or Joseph, whose likeness was taken in 1877 and circulated by F. J. Haynes as Joseph was being transported to an Oklahoma prison following his unsuccessful uprising (fig. 6). Patricia Penn Hilden calls such prison photos "signifiers of conquest, captivity, ownership."[15]

The camera can portray, obscure, or erase symbols of power, sometimes in the same image, as demonstrated by a famous photograph of captive subject Goyathlay (Geronimo) and his band taken en route to prison in Florida following his surrender in 1886 (fig. 7). By presenting Geronimo as simply one among a group of Apache prisoners, the photographer decenters his formidable power as a resistance leader. The angle of the camera lens further diminishes the threat posed by Geronimo and the other Apaches by placing them below the looming presence of a train car, that preeminent symbol of westward expansion. Framing this scene are several shadowed figures leaning against the train steps and crouched under the train—armed U.S. soldiers whose placement in the image's background does not obscure the guns they casually hold and who thus visibly call

5. J. N. Choate, *Chiricahua Apache Group Four Months after Arriving at Carlisle*, ca. 1884.

Reproduction courtesy of Cumberland County Historical Society, Carlisle, Pa.

6. Unknown photographer, *Portrait of Chief Hinmaton Yalakit (Thunder Rolling in the Heights), Called Chief Joseph, in Native Dress, 1877.*

Reproduction courtesy of National Anthropological Archives, Smithsonian Institution, Washington, D.C.

attention to the violent underpinnings that made this image possible.[16] Like the photographs of Geronimo in which handcuffs were purportedly erased during processing, this image represents the photographer's effort to veil what Theresa Harlan has called the "unseen" in Indian images from this era—"the presence of foreign occupation and the experience of being watched and recorded by the penetrating stare of the invaders." The image thus participates in a complex game of hide and seek, of invisibility and visibility.[17]

Collectively, then, pictures of Indians inscribe the various ways Native peoples were removed from geographical, cultural, and familial matrices; they conceal, even erase, the agents of that removal. Even the photographs themselves were removed, rarely remaining in the locales of their making, as Carolyn Marr points out: "Photographs . . . were eagerly sought by non-Indians . . . [and were] taken away—to libraries, and museums, or postcard galleries—and seldom seen by the people photographed."[18] The export of photographs of Indians to distant metropolitan centers further limited Native peoples' access, ownership, and control for several generations. The paradox of Indian photography in this period, then, is its literal and metaphorical inscription of removal.

As Indians became more restricted in their geographical movements, more controlled by government and benevolent societies, the numbers of whites who could engage in the rituals of Indian removal increased. Technological advances such as the railroad and the Pullman "palace car" allowed field matrons (who were sent to the West by the Indian Service to train Indian women in white middle-class domestic practices) and government agents such as Fletcher or adventurous tourists such as Schäffer and Cory to traverse the continent with relative speed, safety, and ease. Advances in photographic technology opened the field to those who previously could neither afford nor physically manage the task. Early photographic technologies were cumbersome, expensive, and time-consuming. The delicate, large, glass plates of the collodion process yielded stunning panoramic views in precise gradations of black and white as well as studio portraits in which the photographer controlled the pose, the expression, the costume, and the backdrop. But these same processes demanded considerable support: equipment, mules and wagon for transport, a portable darkroom or tent, and assistants to arrange the backdrops, costumes, and poses and to help with the complex chemical processing. At mid-century photographers carried equipment weighing

7. A. J. McDonald (?), *Goyathlay (Geronimo), Chiricahua Apache (third from right, front row) in Front of the Train Taking a Chiricahua Apache Group from Ft. Sam Houston, Texas, to Ft. Marion, Florida, 1886.*

Courtesy National Museum of the American Indian, Smithsonian Institution, Washington, D.C. P07009.

"from 50 to 70 pounds [that] often required a large steamer trunk to hold the necessary paraphernalia: glass plates and lenses, a heavy wooden tripod, at least two cameras with their plate holders, a dozen or so plates, solution bottles, [and] a heavy glass tank for sensitizing." Wet-plate processing involved eight discrete steps. Photographers—or their assistants—had to know how to "make collodion, coat, sensitize, and develop a print, construct the silver bath . . . [, and] print, tone, and fix the prints."[19]

After 1880, however, a quick succession of technological developments made photography decidedly less cumbersome and specialized. Dry-plate technology, celluloid film, and smaller cameras with lenses whose exposure times could be mechanically controlled opened the practice of photography to amateurs. In 1889, Kodak introduced a handheld camera, costing just $25, already loaded with paper film. All one had to do was point and shoot, as the ads promised. When the film was used up, the manufacturer developed the prints, reloaded the camera, and sent the finished photographs and camera back to the customer. Kodak marketed this camera in ad campaigns aimed at women. "Kodak girls" were featured in magazine ads and roamed public venues such as the 1893 World's Columbian Exposition, demonstrating the ease with which anyone could make images of themselves, their possessions, their leisure activities, and their travels. These more portable cameras made possible the snapshot and the candid, informal images associated with the domestic and feminine, as well as with spontaneity, leisure, and tourism. By the end of the century, even those lacking sophisticated training in photographic technique could train their eyes on, and capture, "vanishing Indians."

Once captured, Indian images could be removed and displayed to ever-widening audiences. In 1880, the halftone process allowed magazines and newspapers to print photographs directly rather than to rely on engravings adapted from photographic originals. This innovation transformed how photographic images were disseminated and consumed, fueling the explosion of magazine journalism in the United States during the last decades of the nineteenth century and, in turn, creating a demand for ever more photographic images as illustrations. Photographers of Indians took full and varied advantage of magazines' distribution networks and wide readership. Photographers on assignment with the governmental surveys of the 1870s and 1880s provided images for documentary and scholarly reports as well as to magazines promoting locales newly accessible to tourists. Frank Hamilton Cushing published copiously illustrated accounts of government-sponsored anthropological expeditions in the *Atlantic Monthly, Popular Science Monthly,* and *Century Magazine.* Their appeal exceeded the communication of information; artful poses underscored the presumed exoticism of Cushing's Zuni subjects. Photographic images sold as postcards allowed those who could not rush west to purchase their own last glimpse of the vanishing Americans, diminutive images of America's past. In all these venues, photographs served as "social currency," exchanged among the cognoscenti, deposited as raw data in federal archives, and invested as cultural capital; they underwrote imperial expansion, funded scientific inquiry, and lured investigators, visitors, and sightseers to western destinations.[20]

No location more perfectly epitomized the collaboration of Indian photography with narratives of assimilation and national expansion than the exposition, a crucial confluence of popular culture, science, and governmental policy. At the New Orleans World's Industrial and Centennial Cotton Exposition of 1885, Fletcher exhibited photographs showing the transformation of Omahas from "savagery to civilization." For the exhibit she prepared for the Bureau of Indian Affairs, she had ordered her photographer to take views of models "dress[ed] in old-time costumes and . . . showing their past customs."[21] These she balanced against images of Omahas enjoying the benefits of allotment and assimilation. Chicago's Columbian Exposition of 1893 shaped the public's perceptions of Indians and Indian policy through photographs in venues ranging from the Midway entertainment district to the Bureau of Indian Affairs and boarding-school exhibits to the Anthropology Building. Images of Indians circulated widely at the fair: the Peabody Museum at Harvard bought "before-and-after" photos taken of Indian students at Hampton Institute;[22] fairgoers purchased anthropological photographs of Kwakwaka'wakw (Kwakiutl) participants at the fair as souvenirs.

The pedagogical and ideological uses of exposition photographs may have culminated with the Paris Exposition of 1900, where Frances Benjamin Johnston's highly aestheticized photographs documented for an international audience the nation's success in assimilating its racial others through the work of establishments such as the Hampton Institute. Impressed by Johnston's photographs, Carlisle Indian School's Richard Henry Pratt hired her in 1901 to make a similar set of images documenting the success of his school in assimilating Indian students (fig. 8). Created and circulated in the service of a range of often conflicting agendas—from boarding-school boosterism and assimilationist rhetoric to ethnographic salvage and tourist spectacle—such images attest to photography's role in consolidating Indians as visual territory.

As industry and agriculture expanded west, driving Indian peoples onto ever shrinking reservations, their disappearance indeed seemed inevitable to Euro-American readers, who followed a succession of Indian defeats in print: the Modoc Wars of 1872 and 1873 and the massacre at Wounded Knee in 1890 were illustrated in dispatches to the popular press, as were the culminating military victories over the Lakotas and the Apaches in the 1880s and 1890s. Nostalgia for the "vanishing Indian," long a feature of East Coast representations, reached an apex by the turn of the century. This belief in certain extinction added urgency to documentary and aesthetic enterprises alike. In yet another irony, while white audiences lamented the "disappearance" of Native peoples, Indians were more available than ever in print. While the rapidly growing fields of ethnography and

8. Frances Benjamin Johnston, *Carlisle Indian School, Ninth Grade*, ca. 1901. Reproduction courtesy of Cumberland County Historical Society, Carlisle, Pa.

anthropology often focused on western tribes and used photographs to represent cultural differences, numerous commercial photographs also sought to "document" cultures presumably soon to be assimilated into the expanding United States, a belief suggested by the title of Edward Curtis's much copied image *The Vanishing Race* (1904).

But Curtis's soft-focus technique and the trunk of costumes he carried with him from which to dress some of his subjects cannot be called documentary. Like their antebellum counterparts, his photographs combine ethnographic conventions with a desire to create aesthetic images that fulfill viewers' expectations about cultural difference. Shots by Curtis, Adam Clark Vroman, Frederick Monsen, and many others seemed to suggest that tourists should hurry west because Indian cultures were on the wane, forever changed by white contact. Infused with what Renato Rosaldo has termed "imperialist nostalgia"—mourning the loss of what one has helped to destroy—such photographs encapsulate a cultural sentiment of longing that resulted from the military defeat and containment of Indians on reservations.[23] But the vanishing of Indian peoples and their cultures was overstated: the many shots of ceremonial occasions—most visibly the Hopi Snake Ceremony—demonstrate that many tribes continued to follow their ceremonial calendars, despite having to "share" their public observances with unwelcome spectators.

Although turn-of-the-century technological advances had transformed photography from an unusual into a ubiquitous occupation, and the venues and audiences for photographic display had increased dramatically, the visual conventions governing its practice remained strikingly similar to those of its early days. White Americans were saturated with a visual pedagogy that conflated romantic and ethnographic values and validated the results of white westward expansion. By the last two decades of the nineteenth century, photographs told a widely accepted story about the fate of North America's Native peoples.

WOMEN, INDIANS, AND THE CAMERA EYE

By the 1870s and increasingly thereafter, ostensibly vanishing Indians made room for white women—and their cameras—in the North American West. These women often perceived the Far West as offering them, in Mary Austin's words, the chance to walk off "society-made values" that confined women to domestic locations and pursuits.[24] But the very nature of Anglo-Indian interaction for white women presupposed the confinement of Native peoples: on reservations, in boarding schools and in prisons, as wards of the state, as prisoners of war, as anthropological specimens, and as objects of governmental policies designed to assimilate them. Individual white women may have had mutually satisfactory and even supportive relationships with individual Indians; however, those relationships were conditioned by the many layers of Indian removal described by and facilitated by the camera. Austin's goal of walking off society-made values in the West would happen in a West where Indians were being coerced into accepting those values as a precondition for their survival.

As Indians were confined to smaller and smaller geographical spaces, the opportunities for white women in the region expanded. Some accompanied husbands, fathers, and brothers to farm and mine, to work for railroads and banks, to run stores and schools and churches. Others were unmarried and willing, even eager, to build lives independent of traditional family. Some, drawn to the romantic visions of the West that suffused the public spaces of magazine articles, postcards, ethnographic exhibitions, and Wild West shows, participated actively in disseminating those visions. Inspired by the West's presumed differences from the more decadent East, these women created and sold art and literature, encouraged tourism, and lobbied for governmental policies of domestic and civic reform. Others found employment with agencies associated with the new branches of social science or in the bureaucratic structures designed to manage Indian populations; still others, trained in newly developing professional fields open to women, pursued scientific research. Even if they worked in areas understood to be womanly pursuits, they embraced these occupations with a zeal fueled by efforts to professionalize teaching and to apply the insights of academic sociology to missionary efforts and social and reform work.

Marriages provided many women with independent opportunities, sometimes in fields that were accepted as feminine (in literature, for example) and sometimes in new and unorthodox endeavors (like ethnography). Helen Hunt Jackson and Mary Hallock Foote went west in the 1870s with engineer husbands and used their experiences to further literary and artistic careers. Jackson's trip resulted in *A Century of Dishonor* (1881) and *Ramona* (1884), while Foote published numerous sketches of Indian women laborers in Mexico in *Century Magazine*. After accompanying her husband on geological surveys throughout the West, Matilda Coxe Stevenson was hired by Powell in 1879 as "volunteer co-adjutor [assistant] in ethnology" on her husband's expedition to New Mexico.[25] Her work with Powell resulted in *Zuni and the Zunians* (1881), the first of her many publications. A generation younger, Schäffer discovered her attraction to the Canadian Rockies while assisting in her husband's fieldwork. Charles Schäffer was a well-respected amateur botanist, his wife the silent partner whose hand-colored lantern slides of alpine flora won both of them acclaim. After he died, she embarked on her own quite public career promoting the Canadian Rockies as a tourist destination through her essays, lectures, books, and photographs.

Unmarried women also found that social sciences provided new careers. As companion and ex-officio photographer, Jane Gay accompanied Alice Fletcher, a government anthropologist, as Fletcher implemented the Dawes General Allotment Act among the Nez Perces in Idaho; Gay served as unofficial documentarian of the expedition. Their records demonstrate how contradictory governmental and scientific agendas frequently become entangled: governmental policy meant to force Indian life into Christian and white patterns, while ethnography demanded that Indian tradition be studied and recorded. This paradoxical agenda was mirrored in Fletcher and Gay themselves: on the one hand, the presence in the field of two unmarried middle-aged women was unorthodox; on the other hand, it was oddly logical, for the social sciences, especially anthropology and ethnology, had from their beginnings welcomed the labor of women helpmeets.

Similarly contradictory assumptions about gender facilitated women's participation in professional social sciences: their presumably natural nurturant abilities fitted them to study the infancy and development of humankind; their womanly patience and tolerance for repetitive and detailed work qualified them to collect ethnographic "data that seemed to be rapidly disappearing."[26] Likewise, social science investigations simultaneously "invited and constrained research on the relations between the sexes."[27] According to Kamala Visweswaran, although such research established that gender roles were not biologically determined, it did not alter the hierarchical relations between the sexes because it also presumed that differentiated sex roles were an evolutionary achievement, a necessary part of a highly developed (that is, white Victorian) civilization. Such conflicted agendas about gender characterize the work of all the women we study here. Fletcher, for example, was fascinated by Omaha matrilineal kinship yet apparently remained unfazed that the Dawes Act, which she sponsored, was designed to offer citizenship to Omaha men but to disfranchise Omaha women and would, in

Visweswaran's words, "radically alter women's role in transmitting inheritance rights within matrilineal societies."[28]

Scientific research and the implementation of governmental policy were not the only agendas of women social scientists and civil servants. The conventional association of women's work with charitable enterprises allied them with larger projects aimed at the rescue, support, governance, education, and reform of American Indians, a process that Deborah Gordon terms "matronization."[29] Whereas Fletcher and a few other women stepped into roles heretofore reserved for men, other women interested in reform and social science served as field matrons. Grace Nicholson encountered many such women during her trips to Native communities throughout California. In their prescribed roles as exemplars of white middle-class femininity, participants in the Indian Service's Field Matron Program (1890–1938) were sent to western Indian communities to train Indian women—often considered the main obstacles to federal and "humanitarian" assimilation efforts—in the domestic arts.[30] In transmitting the domestic practices and values of middle-class U.S. culture, field matrons reinforced the gender pedagogy of Indian boarding schools, while serving as gatherers and "translators of cultural meanings for white administrators who needed information to supply welfare services."[31] They also served as economic liaisons between Indian communities and the dominant culture, evidenced by the many letters Nicholson received from matrons trying to sell baskets for women under their "charge."

Women anthropologists and social service workers turned to ethnography and to the West as a way of rebelling against conventions that foreclosed feminine achievement and independence. As Gordon has suggested, "In search for different ways of being white and female," they "looked to Native Americans and Native American women for the reconstruction of themselves."[32] Also seeking escape from domestic confinement, artists ironically romanticized, as Lois Rudnick has pointed out, "the roles that women played in pre-industrial societies, where they contributed to household and community economies through their work within well-defined separate spheres. Their concept of domesticity included spiritual and aesthetic expression."[33] In her search for a more expansive life, Kate Cory perceived in Hopi culture her desire for the integration of art and everyday domestic life. One of her initial, but conflicted, stages of reconstruction can be seen in an unattributed image, very likely a self-portrait, taken in her rented house on the Hopi mesas (fig. 9). Wearing a skirt and high-necked blouse, the uniform of the New Woman, Cory poses in front of a loom with a partially completed blanket, her own. Her pose is common in the standard archive of American Indian photographs. Her acquaintance, the great Hopi-Tewa potter, Nampeyo, sometimes claimed to be the most photographed American Indian woman, practiced her art at "Hopi House" at the Grand Canyon for tourists with cameras during the years Cory lived at Oraibi. Yet Cory's image reverses, for

9. Unknown photographer, Kate Cory in Front of Her Loom, ca. 1905–1912.
Courtesy Sharlot Hall Museum, Prescott, Arizona. Kate Cory Collection, #PO299P3P.

instance, Curtis's *The Blanket Weaver—Navajo* (1904) (fig. 10). Unlike most Indian weavers, Cory faces the viewer and turns her back on the art. Her notes
point out that she never became a skilled weaver and eventually gave up the practice. Like the blanket in her portrait, her acquisition of Native American skills—
artistic and domestic—remained uncompleted.

Cory anticipates the later group of writers and artists who moved to New Mexico after World War I and who, according to Rudnick, found in the Southwest a
"New World whose terrain, climate, and indigenous peoples offered a model of
ecological, spiritual, and artistic integration to an alienated and decadent western
civilization."[34] Mabel Dodge Luhan, for example, hosted a famous salon in New
Mexico, where her ties to Taos Pueblo allowed artists and writers such as Mary
Austin and Georgia O'Keeffe to make use of the aesthetic possibilities of the
southwest landscape and Native cultures. Of course, this world-view is replete
with imperialist assumptions, as Rudnick suggests: "The Anglo expatriates' hunger for spiritual and psychic renewal often blinded them to the more unpleasant
social, political, and economic realities that surrounded them," particularly the
exploitation of racial minorities.[35] As "collectors," affluent women like Luhan
defined new roles for themselves as consumers and brokers of American Indian
art and "artifacts."

10. Edward Curtis, *The Blanket Weaver—Navajo*, 1904.

Courtesy Philadelphia Museum of Art. Purchased with funds from the American Museum of Photography, 1971. 1971–117–21(33).

Many women devoted themselves to collecting American Indian "objects" at the turn of the century. Some, like Gay, Fletcher, and Nicholson, helped build ethnographic collections at established knowledge-producing institutions and museums. Nicholson also profited from her occupational connection, however, selling other Indian "curios" at her highly successful gallery in Pasadena. Other wealthy white women—among them Amelia Elizabeth White, Mary-Russell Ferrell Colton, Millicent Rogers, and Mary Cabot Wheelwright—established museums to house the Indian cultural items they collected, museums Susan Brown McGreevy has called "intensely personal statements." As McGreevy has pointed out, women collectors such as these abandoned "Eastern sociopolitical ideologies" and "achieved prestige and recognition that would not have been possible in their cities of origin." "Indeed," she adds, "most were viewed as eccentric—at best—by friends and relatives in the East."[36] Viewed as eccentric by both easterners and her Arizona neighbors, Cory helped found the Smoki Museum in Prescott, which owns a number of her paintings of the Hopis and her photograph album. With her friend Sharlot Hall, territorial historian and founder of the Sharlot Hall Museum in Prescott, she provided ethnographic information, no doubt using her photographs, to the "Smoki Tribe," a group of white residents who tried to "preserve" Indian dances by staging their own versions, provoking Hopi protests.

Similarly, Mary Schäffer "shopped," as she put it, among the Stoney and Métis whom she met on her annual horseback camping trips around Banff, purchasing clothing and artwork.[37] She often used these items in her everyday activities; a favorite beaded jacket (fig. 68 in Chapter 3) was apparently a frequent part of her riding habit. Over her thirty years in Banff, she accumulated a small but significant collection that eventually found its way to the Whyte Museum of the Canadian Rockies in Banff, which also owns her photograph collection.

Today these same museums often provide researchers, scholars, and, ironically, tribal members themselves, with data that are invaluable for reconstructing tribal lives and traditions destroyed by centuries of cultural looting. The museums these women founded "redefined the boundaries of institutional power structures," as McGreevy points out; and many of these women had close personal relationships with members of the tribes whose photographs they took and whose cultural patrimony they collected. Yet it is important to recognize that the "personal statements" that became museums were ghostwritten by others, the collectors' freedom the result of centuries of unequal economic and cultural exchange.[38]

In the memoirs, magazine articles, and narratives produced by western and westering women in this era, references to cameras and picture-taking abound. Josephine Kemp's article "Photographing in the Hopi Land," published in a 1905 issue of *Camera Craft*, recounts her participation in the "well-populated" "photographer's row" at the Hopi Snake Dance ceremonies.[39] Far from the tourist spectacles assailing Indians in the Southwest, Mabel Reed and Mary Arnold, field matrons among the Karuk in northern California from 1908 to 1909—the period of Nicholson's business forays in the region—recalled that their buckskin bag "packs a Kodak and all the money we possess."[40] Writing of her experiences "kodaking the Indians" in the same region of northwestern California fifteen years later, Mildred Ring claims that, "in many respects, I believe that being a woman has proven an advantage."[41] Being a woman "proved an advantage" for Julia E. Tuell, who served as a teacher alongside her husband on several reservations in the early twentieth century, including the Northern Cheyenne reservation in Montana and the Sisseton-Wahpeton reservation in South and North Dakota. Although a few of the photographs she made of countless friends and acquaintances found their way into print, most of them remained in her family's possession until the publication in 2000 of Dan Aadland's *Women and Warriors of the Plains: The Pioneer Photography of Julia E. Tuell*.[42]

Indeed, by century's end, photography had much to recommend it as an occupation for women: it could be easily learned; it could be practiced in private and used to document domestic relationships; and it was understood to be a craft and not an art and thus was consistent with other "womanly" pastimes such as needlework and china painting.[43] Moreover, photography provided a way for women to break out of kitchens and into laboratories to study chemistry and optics, to leave parlors and head into the mountains to do fieldwork. As the documentary and aesthetic coalesced in photographs of Indians, female and male preserves converged for women photographers. According to Naomi Rosenblum, "By 1900, some 3,500 women were listed in the census as professional photographers, an increase of over 400 percent since 1870."[44]

Unlike the majority of professional photographers, whether men or women, Schäffer, Gay, Nicholson, and Cory did not work out of homes, studios, or salons but traveled and lived in areas of the trans-Mississippi West still considered to be "uncivilized." They did not identify themselves primarily as photographers but used the camera as an adjunct to other pursuits, principally to document their encounters with others. In their work, documentary and romantic agendas coexisted. Fletcher decided as early as 1883 to buy camera equipment to aid her in her ethnographic work among the Plains Indians; six years later, she hired Gay to document her work among the Nez Perces. Nicholson knew that a camera was essential to document the "authenticity" of the items she collected and sold. Cory used her photographs of the Hopis as material for her ethereal paintings. Schäffer began her photographic career recording plants and flowers for botanical publications; so skilled did she become that in 1900 she was solicited for Frances Benjamin Johnston's series on "Foremost Women Photographers."[45]

But in spite of the increasing numbers of women entering the field, the archive of late nineteenth- and early twentieth-century Indian images against which we read the photographic production of Gay, Cory, Nicholson, and Schäffer is an androcentric one. As Lucy Lippard observes, "The photographers whose names we know are virtually all white men."[46] Alfred L. Bush and Lee Clark Mitchell's monumental *The Photograph and the American Indian* contains the work of some sixty-five photographers who were active before 1930. Of these, only two are women. Paula Fleming and Judith Luskey's *Grand Endeavors* showcases the work of fourteen important men who made images in the western United States but includes only two, relatively unknown, women.[47] Nor have women photographers emerged centrally in interpretive studies and cultural histories such as Leah Dilworth's *Imagining Indians in the Southwest.* Dilworth explores how the photographs of Curtis, Vroman, and others represented Indian life at the turn of the century as "spectacle" to be consumed in "ethnic tourism"; although she discusses the work of women writers and anthropologists, she does not consider women photographers. Only two women who photographed Indians in this period have received sustained scholarly attention. At the turn into the twentieth century, Gertrude Käsebier produced an archive of domestic art photography and took studio portraits of Indians who were her "invited guests." Barbara Michaels has written Käsebier's biography; Laura Wexler considers Käsebier with other women photographers who employ the "imperial gaze." Laura Gilpin, a well-trained professional who worked a generation later than our four women, is the subject of Martha Sandweiss's *Laura Gilpin: An Enduring Grace.* Both Käsebier and Gilpin figure largely in Judith Fryer Davidov's *Women's Camera Work.*[48]

Why do women photographers of American Indians receive so little attention? They are often ignored as "amateurs," and their work is generally difficult to access, held in out-of-the-way archives or small regional museums. Cory's negatives were lost for many years and were rediscovered in cardboard boxes around 1975 on a shelf in the Smoki Museum, while Gay's were stored in the attic of the Lapwai mission house for nearly a century before being donated to the Idaho State Historical Society. As Lippard suggests, women often "took up photography on their own, [and] had less access to adventure, money, and publicity."[49] Although Gay, Cory, Schäffer, and Nicholson were comfortably middle class, none of them received any kind of official or unofficial sponsorship for their photographic production. Their work does not appear in the standard aesthetic histories, for they did not affiliate with any formal photographic studio, group, or tradition. For the most part, they even fall outside the network of women photographers studied by Davidov in *Women's Camera Work* as an alternative lineage to the masculine genealogy of traditional photographic histories such as Alan Trachtenberg's *Reading American Photographs.*[50]

We have not sought to establish, nor have we assumed, that women "see" differently from men, but we are not surprised to find that the lives of our four women influenced their frames of reference, angles of vision, and access to subjects if only because, as women of the nineteenth century, they conceived of their concerns as different from those of their male counterparts.[51] In some ways their work falls into familiar thematic patterns central to American Indian photography—with a focus, for instance, on material culture and traditional life—yet their photographs often seem to lack the "serious" photographic techniques of the "masters," fitting comfortably in neither the documentary nor the aesthetic archives of western photography. As Nicole Tonkovich suggests about many of Gay's photographs, their images sometimes initially seem "banal" and, like many women's diaries, require contextual reading and analysis that probes beneath their surfaces.

We have been, and continue to be, challenged by the possibility of using these images to narrate new stories, both of Native peoples and of the women themselves, in ways that neither demonize nor lionize them. Taken together, the stories of these four women complicate our understandings of the West, of photography, and of late nineteenth-/early twentieth-century cultural history. Their work and their lives in different regions of the West, at times spanning a quarter-century, represent a range of Indian-Anglo interactions. Their stories, like their images, often lack the high drama of other western myths that celebrate the grand at the expense of the subtle, the heroic at the expense of the domestic, and that focus more on the expansive sweep of history than on the details of everyday living.

11. E. Jane Gay, *Photographer,* after 1893.
The Schlesinger Library, Radcliffe Institute, Harvard University, Cambridge, Mass.

The photographs produced by the four women who are our focus here demand a critical engagement with images of indigenous peoples, with the circumstances of their making, and, for many viewers, with their own complicity as viewers and consumers of photographs. One of Jane Gay's few self-portraits demonstrates this critical nexus of camera, subject, image, consumer, and viewer (fig. 11). Enclosed in a circular format (a consequence of the paper film Gay was using, but still a conscious choice on her part) rather than the standard rectangular, Cartesian frame, this image shows a figure sitting, back to the viewer, apparently in the act of preparing a profile self-portrait. The image's tondo form suggests the photographer's intent of resisting the linear, the square, and the frontal gaze, while its content—the ambiguously gendered subject, the very act of portrait making—suggests that she sought to explore the power of the camera to create the illusions of gender and of presence.

Like *Emma Telling Grace Nicholson about Featherband,* Gay's self-portrait directs us to the themes we consider in *Trading Gazes.* Few scholars of nineteenth- and early twentieth-century photography have looked in a sustained fashion at the photographic and textual productions of Jane Gay, Kate Cory, Grace Nicholson, and Mary Schäffer. It is as if these women had turned their backs to us, or we to them. Yet Gay's turned back is paradoxically inviting. It suggests an alternative relationship with the usual structures of empire and institutional power. Like many of the images produced by these women, it seems to claim a kind of domestic privacy. As does this portrait, which refuses to engage our gaze, their work now asks us to look at them looking, making us as viewers more self-conscious about the acts of voyeurism entailed in any study.

PHOTOGRAPHIC MEANING

In approaching the work of Gay, Cory, Schäffer, and Nicholson, we have been attentive to two related concerns of contemporary studies of photography. On the one hand, we attend to iconography: the biographical and immediate conditions under which our women worked, the technologies that enabled their images, the process of developing, printing, and distributing their work, the network of circumstances and relationships that led to the recorded moment, the visual vocabulary that created meaning for contemporary photographers, subjects, and viewers. On the other hand, we are also interested in iconology: how photography as a medium continues to convey and shape shifting meanings. The images these women made are not only representations of specific historical moments but also objects in their own right, with discrete histories that have structured—and continue to structure—relationships between Indians and Euro-Americans over time and space. Iconography refers, in short, to our reconstructions of the broad and deep contexts of the images; iconology allows us to offer our own, new, readings of them, a task made possible by the photograph's continuing importance and our own positions, interests, and commitments.[52]

In investigating iconography, or context, we have remained aware that, as John Berger and Jean Mohr put it, photographs are "irrefutable as evidence, but weak in meaning."[53] Frequently, in an effort to stabilize or limit their meanings, photographs are supplemented by words—added as captions, as interpretations, as narrative, or even inserted into the image itself. Still, a finite meaning may remain elusive because stories, whether public history, private memory, oral tradition, or popular culture, are equally artificial constructions; their meanings can be recovered but can also be imposed or even fabricated. A chilling example of the oscillating meanings of images and their accompanying narratives is offered by Laura Wexler in her discussion of a pair of photographs of three Indian girls at Hampton Institute made by an anonymous photographer in the 1880s. Taken fourteen months apart, these images, like the Carlisle set in figs. 4 and 5, were intended to show the salutary effects of white and "civilized" activity on the dark and "primitive" bodies of children dispossessed of their homes, families, clothing, customs, and languages. Hampton's nineteenth-century donors (and Carlisle's as well) presumably saw progress and reform in such poses, the smooth assimilation of Indian youth into their appropriate positions within white society, and the triumph of Christian nurture over racialized nature. Wexler, however, reads doubly, attending both to the children's investment in their Hampton education and to their resistance to it. In the image, she sees the result of what

she calls "tender violence": the care given the girls, ostensibly with their improvement in mind, nonetheless injures them and therefore exists along a continuum of violent acts perpetrated on Indians in the nineteenth century.[54]

Some scholars, such as James Faris, insist that any photograph by a white person of an Indian person not only depicts asymmetrical power relations but also solidifies the racial and gender hierarchies that produce it, that reading sympathy, empathy, resistance, or collaboration into the relationships between a Euro-American photographer and her subjects constitutes sentimental wish fulfillment on the part of the critic.[55] By contrast, we, like Wexler, find a productive and fascinating ambivalence in many of the images we discuss here—an ambivalence that is exposed by our iconographic, or contextual, readings. Nez Perces, for example, understandably did not welcome—and indeed often resisted—the intrusions of Alice Fletcher and her new policy of allotment. Yet they and Fletcher were part of a larger and equally flawed narrative, a policy intended as a compromise among white greed, the nation's ostensibly irresistible progress, and Native rights. And even this explanation does not exhaust the complexity of the issue because dissent characterized all parties involved in the process. Some whites were eager to extinguish Indian land titles immediately; others advocated a hands-off policy. Nez Perces who saw assimilation as the best solution to a difficult dilemma lived among others who advocated adhering to traditional patterns of tribal life. Some Nez Perces were eager to receive title to their lands so that they could sell them; others were forced to sell because they were not able to farm the hilly and rocky terrain. Given such complexity, any image of the allotment, whether enhanced by eloquent narration or standing alone, offers only a partial representation, capturing a brief moment in a long, complex, and contentious process.

We realize as well that an effort to construct a contextually thick description remains unequal to the resonance of photographic images themselves, an almost magical power often recognized by viewers.[56] Attending to an iconologic reading of such an image can help us understand why our response to it exceeds its own history. It can help explain, for instance, Lucy Lippard's powerful reaction to a remarkable and seductive photograph of Sampson, Leah, and Frances Louise Beaver that Mary Schäffer captioned *Sampson Beaver, His Squaw, and Little Frances Louise* (fig. 12). Although Schäffer's caption suggests to a contemporary reader a dismissive, hierarchical, and even racist estimate of its subjects, Lippard is intrigued by the calm and friendly faces smiling into the camera, which make the photograph "a microcosmic triumph for social equality as expressed through representation." Even as she discovers more information about Schäffer and her life in Banff, her relationships with her Indian subjects, and her investments in Euro-American cultural institutions and values, Lippard cannot completely dismiss her initial reading. Fully aware of the way photography has been used to "imagine Indians" as a vanishing romanticized race, of its role as "propaganda,"

12. Mary Schäffer, *Sampson, Frances Louise, and Leah Beaver*, 1906.

Courtesy Whyte Museum of the Canadian Rockies, Archives and Library, Banff, V527–NA 124, Mary Schäffer Fonds, captioned *Sampson Beaver, His Squaw and Little Frances Louise*.

and having "insisted that white people need to surrender the 'right' to represent everybody," Lippard nevertheless finds that Schäffer's image presents a "classic visualization of what anthropologists call 'intersubjective time.'" It "commemorates a reciprocal moment (rather than a cannibalistic one), where the emphasis is on interaction and communication; a moment in which subject and object are caught in exchange within shared time, rather than shouting across history from their respective peaks." For Lippard, Schäffer's photograph provides "the illusion of seeing for ourselves, the way we never *would* see for ourselves, which is what communication is about."[57]

Like Lippard, we are led to imagine the interaction the photograph implies between photographer and subject and also the interactions between viewer and photograph. The continuing presence of the photograph, its existence as an object through the passage of time, allows it to perform doubly: it can both record an encounter and bring that encounter into question, making it available to other readings, other uses, sometimes through resistant readings, sometimes through parodies, and sometimes through outright challenges, as the final section of this chapter makes clear. We seek to understand how these images resist history or, rather, help us to resist readings of history that are too familiar and to narrate different and more complex histories.

Our method is, like our understanding of the photographs, multiply exposed. We weave together several narratives. We consider the initial moment that the photograph records, note the tension between that moment and the long histories that brought the participants to that encounter, and consider the contexts in which the photographs and texts were collected into individual albums or into regional and national museums and archives, always interested in the counterarchive these women provide.

Thus, although the photographs taken by Schäffer, Gay, Nicholson, and Cory are part of the imperial iconography we associate with nineteenth-century westward expansion, they are also iconologic, available for new readings. As such, they call on us to uncover what Davidov calls "sub-versions," whole new archives of texts and images that ask us to linger over paradoxical and idiosyncratic details.[58] As well, they point to the continued processes by which Native peoples have collaborated, resisted, parodied, and reclaimed the territory so copiously captured by nineteenth-century photography.

CODA: AN INDIAN WITH A CAMERA

In a 1903 pictorial essay, self-described camera fiend Horatio Stoll details his "amusing" experiences trying to outwit Indians in his quest to take pictures in northwestern California. Stoll's article is hardly unusual in its dismissal of Native residents who angrily resisted his efforts to "snap" them, yet he offers this unexpected conclusion: "It is interesting . . . to speculate how long an Indian, armed with a camera, would be permitted to snap interesting specimens of our summer girls at the beach, our crack golfers at Presidio links, or our humped bicyclers at the Golden Gate Park. . . . Not many, if ever, for his camera would be snatched from his hand and trampled underfoot by some indignant individual before he succeeded in walking even half a block."[59]

Dramatically reversing the terms of visual encounter that permeate the rest of Stoll's essay, this wryly imagined scene anticipates the critical stances today of Native artists who use photographs and performance pieces to comment on and reappropriate the long tradition of Euro-American photography of Indians; in doing so they offer contemporary viewers new contexts in which to read images like those produced by the women we study here. Writer/photographer Tom King's ambitious project "Medicine River Photographic Expedition" has led him across Canada and the United States to meet and take pictures of countless Native peoples. In trickster counterpoint to Curtis's peripatetic photographic journeys in search of the "authentic" Indian, King travels with his own trunk of props —Pocahontas wigs, Lone Ranger masks, plastic arrows—as part of a strategy

13. James Luna, *The Tribal Identity,* Panel 3, "Before College," 1996.
Courtesy of James Luna.

Louis Owens calls "writing back with a camera."[60] He playfully yet seriously derails the salvage paradigm governing many photographs of Indians in the Curtis era, while salvaging the camera as a weapon against the persistently romantic, exoticizing vision of indigenous peoples in the United States and Canada. James Luna's four-panel photograph *The Tribal Identity* (1996) follows the conventions of before-and-after images in Panels 1 and 2, historical re-creations shot in black and white. In Panels 3 and 4, Luna satirically reverses the order, suggesting that tribal identity can be reclaimed (figs. 13 and 14).[61] The "the" in the title asserts a resistant, pan-tribal coalition, as Ralph Rugoff suggests. Yet the obviously "posed" quality of Panel 4 also resists "cultural police seeking to locate the 'real Indian.'"[62]

The work of such artists, as well as of writers such as Gerald Vizenor and Jolene Rickard, who see in photographs "the compression of multiple realities," suggests how iconology, the exploration of a photograph's contemporary resonance, provides us with significant new ways of interpreting historical photographs.[63] In analyzing photographs of that most-photographed California Indian, Ishi, Vizenor focuses on his elusiveness and resistance, while Jimmie Durham discovers in Geronimo's expression in *Geronimo at the Wheel* (1904) that, "no matter what had been taken from him, he had given up nothing."[64] Through his subversive reading of an 1897 photograph made of the Indian Industrial School football team in Battleford, Saskatchewan, Cree artist, curator, and critic Gerald

McMaster transforms an image intended to document assimilation into one announcing a defiant and resistant identity. Contemplating how the initials of the Industrial School embroidered on the students' sweaters marked them as the school's own, McMaster rereads those same initials through the inadvertent message they convey to him: "I was amused by the rapid fire repetition of the letters IS, IS, IS, IS, which appear not as acronyms but as statements of being. . . . The verb constitutes a claim to identity."[65] Read in this way, the photographs defy their taker's intentions and reverberate with contemporary perspectives. We seek in Gay's, Cory's, Nicholson's, and Schäffer's photographs similarly conflicting, culturally shifting views: within the frame of photographs forged out of implicit or explicit participation in narratives of primitivism, of salvage, of assimilation are other ways of reading those images that edge or occupy the same space.

As Native peoples, Vizenor and Rickard, King and Luna, are particularly concerned with showing that images can be wielded as a powerful tool in their varied assertions of cultural, political, and artistic sovereignty. Because photographs taken of Native Americans by Euro-Americans in the late nineteenth and early twentieth centuries often reveal more about the needs and desires of their image makers than those of their subjects, these photographs risk reinforcing what Vizenor calls "terminal creeds"—static, deadening representations of Indian identity and culture.[66] Instead of viewing Indian photographs as taxidermy, we too are concerned with demonstrating that photographs have lives that cannot be contained by the historical moment, by their producers, or by the iconography

14. James Luna, *The Tribal Identity,* Panel 4, "After College," 1996.
Courtesy of James Luna.

that shaped their production. This chapter began by suggesting the unintended life histories of photographs such as the one of Nicholson and an elder Karuk woman, histories still in the making amid ongoing struggles over sovereignty. Historical photographs of Native peoples, housed in the very museums that contain Native cultural patrimony, have now been used to document and forward repatriation claims advanced by Indian nations, such as the Tlingit and Kwakwaka'wakw, a topic that is discussed much more fully in Chapter 4 and the Afterword.[67]

At the same time, photographs once intended to commemorate a vanishing people are now literally placed by Native peoples in new contexts and put to new uses both in tribally owned museums and sponsored exhibits and as family and community photographs, thereby turning the trope of the vanishing Indian back on itself. An enlarged copy of a Nicholson photograph featuring a Karuk ancestor of Panámniik General Store owner Ginny Larson hangs on the store's wall in Orleans, California, while Hopis have hung Cory's photographs in their Cultural Center. Yet efforts to reclaim archival images still meet with some difficulty: some of Gay's photographs, for example, are housed across the country from the Nez Perces, while Nicholson's photographs of Karuk have had to be bought back by their descendants from institutions such as the Smithsonian and the Peabody. The use and meaning of these images shift depending on their context and audience, as we discuss more fully in each of our chapters.

In exploring the lesser-known images produced by four Euro-American women, we strive, as do the contributors to Lippard's *Partial Recall,* "to fill in the blanks left by incomplete and mythologized histories."[68] Yet we know, as well, that the history of Anglo-Indian "relations" cannot "be unraveled through the photograph alone," as Rickard declares.[69] As outsiders to the cultures encountered by these women, we acknowledge that our readings of their photographs will remain partial, offering pieces of the story that can be fully narrated only by the descendants and relations of those pictured in them. Luci Tapahonso suggests that different ways of seeing inevitably shape how "insiders" and "outsiders" read photographs. In an essay accompanying Skeet McAuley's photographs of contemporary Diné and Dinétah, she sees what many cultural outsiders cannot: "the photographs document a people in transition, a culture in change, and yet cannot document the deep rootedness in history, the strong ties of language and songs, or the enduring hope in the eyes of the people."[70] Similarly, Louis Owens's photographic essay, "Blood Trails," directs us to the stories beyond the frame of photographs by knitting together family narratives from threads of stories and a trunk of recently discovered photographs whose occupants are not always known. His family's history, deeply complicated by its placement within a larger history of forced removals and dispersions of mixed-blood and Indian peoples, reveals itself in part through photographs of peripatetic lives that belie the images' framed and frozen moments. Deftly merging text and image, Owens transforms static poses into a story in motion, a story rooted in what Vizenor calls "survivance."[71] In a similar spirit, we offer this book to suggest histories and stories set into motion, as the images made by Cory, Nicholson, Schäffer, and Gay continue to take on new meanings and directions in the eyes of their different beholders in changing historical moments.

In dealing with this counter-archive of photographs, we have encountered several problems concerning titles and captions. Many of these images are untitled and not dated. Others, titled by their makers, have been recaptioned subsequently by owners, editors, compilers, or the makers themselves. Moreover, most of these titles do not identify their Indian subjects by name. In some cases, this information has been provided by other scholars. In some cases, we ourselves have learned the names, sometimes in captions. In some cases, museums, following requests by tribal nations, have requested that we not publish names.

Each of us has encountered a slightly different configuration of these problems, and each of us deals with them differently. We all include complete information about the current owners of the images and acknowledge their permission to reprint. When we have verified that the name of an image is the photographer's own, we present it as the title (in italics). When the name of an image has been added by a subsequent owner or when there are significant discrepancies in the titles, we indicate this. When such captions but not titles are available, we do not use italics for the identifying phrase. When titles are missing entirely, we use the caption "untitled" and add descriptions in the text. We occasionally add clarifying comments, estimates of dates, and names of people.

We have pursued these rather arcane distinctions for several reasons. In many cases, when the photographer's title differs from that given the image by a later person or agency, we have learned that the maker's title is more accurate and is certainly indicative of the relationships of the photographer and her subjects. As well, because much of our work focuses on the power relationships inherent in naming, we have taken care to allow those to whom the images belong to determine their "correct" designation.

**SUSAN BERNARDIN,
MELODY GRAULICH,
LISA MACFARLANE, AND
NICOLE TONKOVICH**

Where we Camped.

CHAPTER ONE

"LOST IN THE GENERAL WRECKAGE OF THE FAR WEST"

The Photographs and Writings of Jane Gay

During the summers of 1889–1892, two women friends "of a certain age" (that is, well past fifty), Jane Gay and Alice Fletcher, left the comfortable home they shared in Washington, D.C., where, during the winters, they hosted a salon that included Washington socialites and intelligentsia, and boarded the "palace car" of a train for Uniontown, Idaho.[1] There they went into the field, Fletcher to oversee the allotment of land to the Nez Perce Indians under the provisions of the new Dawes Severalty Act, and Gay to photograph her activities. Gay also wrote witty and acerbic letters to friends in the East that told of the pair's adventures. Among her correspondents was Captain Richard Pratt, head of the Carlisle Indian School, who soon arranged to publish Gay's letters to him as a semi-regular feature in *The Red Man*, the school's official newspaper.

Unlike the work of other expedition photographers who were her near contemporaries, Gay's images of the Nez Perce allotment have never been broadly circulated. Her role in the expedition was as Fletcher's companion, camp cook, and ex-officio photographer. When the allotment was complete, Gay did not compile her photos and letters to present to Washington policymakers, as had the principals in the Fortieth Parallel Survey, Clarence King and his official photographer, Timothy O'Sullivan, some twenty years earlier. She left more than four hundred glass-plate negatives in Idaho in the attic of the Lapwai Presbyterian mission house, where they languished until 1963, when they were donated to the Idaho State Historical Society. Back at home, Gay assembled an elegant, handmade, two-volume scrapbook consisting of 181 of her photographs and a

15. E. Jane Gay, cover, "Where We Camped," after 1890.

selection of her letters, which were recopied into the scrapbook. These albums were eventually deeded by her niece to the Schlesinger Library on the History of Women in America in 1951. The Schlesinger also holds several small, handmade photo albums, including one titled "Where We Camped." This album includes images Gay made in Idaho and apparently is the germ of her larger scrapbook project (fig. 15).

Although Gay's photographs are accessible to scholars, her work is seldom included in more generally circulated collections such as Paula Richardson Fleming and Judith Lynne Luskey's *Grand Endeavors of American Indian Photography* or Alfred L. Bush and Lee Clark Mitchell's *The Photograph and the American Indian*. Banal in an era of spectacular landscape photography, domestic rather than exotic, Gay's images challenge the commonplaces of nineteenth-century ethnographic and survey photography. They do not feature costumed Indians posed with weapons, baskets, or pottery; rather, they show Nez Perces in western attire plowing and harvesting their crops. They do not frame spectacular landscapes; instead, they present curiously flattened vistas of settled towns, fenced farms, or river bottom lands. They do not depict intrepid explorers perched precariously on jutting outcroppings; rather, they capture men and women engaged in the quotidian and domestic activities of surveying and allotting land.

Not all of Gay's correspondence has been collected and reprinted. About three-fourths of the letters she transcribed into her albums have been collected by Frederick Hoxie and Joan Mark, Fletcher's biographer, in a volume illustrated with thirty-eight of Gay's photographs. This book's title—*With the Nez Perces: Alice Fletcher in the Field, 1889–1892*—indicates how completely Gay has been erased from the record of the Nez Perce allotment. Much of her work, it seems, has been "lost in the general wreckage of the far West"—a phrase Gay herself used to describe what happened to white New England men who "went Native" in Idaho.[2]

Such a loss is a serious one, for Gay's photographs and writings offer an important unofficial account of the Nez Perce allotment. Her work shows that the aim of the Dawes General Allotment Act—to transform supposedly savage Indians from nomads into citizen-farmers—was an impossibility. Gay's charming, opinionated, and highly readable letters from the field make apparent the incoherent and sometimes openly contradictory aims that undergirded the new Dawes Act, exposing this highly touted policy, which had been drafted and promoted by her friend Alice Fletcher, as seriously flawed. The Nez Perces were neither savage nor uncivilized, nor did they unanimously welcome allotment.

Gay's letters document the divisions among the Nez Perces and the often contradictory positions taken by those who were responsible for the Act's implementation. They show that, when confronted with the hard facts of western terrain and the social consequences of imperial legislation, even "civilized" women such as Gay and Fletcher manifest such contradictory desires and act so inconsistently that they seem to embody different personas. When she is speaking of herself and her friend as agents of the government, seeing through imperial eyes, Gay calls herself "the Photographer," and her friend "Her Majesty," titles that name their official functions. When she writes of them as women involved personally and professionally in projects underwritten by sentimental and charitable affiliations, she refers to herself as "the Cook" and to Fletcher as "the Allotting Agent." When she focuses on their mutually supportive relationship as friends sharing the challenges of living and working in a new and often hostile environment, she calls herself "the friend," and Fletcher "Miss F." Finally, when she wishes to hail absent supporters of the Dawes Act, asking them to recognize their complicity in allotment, she calls the women "you" and "I." The identity of "I," however, remains ambiguous, a way of refusing the imperial certainty that bankrolled their expeditions. These multiple identities suggest that the policies that had been promoted as models of progressive benevolence were suspiciously flawed, contradictory, and incoherent.

In a similar fashion, Gay's self-conscious and ironic photographs point to the gap between abstract policy and its concrete application. Neither heroic nor documentary nor romantic nor sentimental (although Gay experimented in each mode), they challenge photography's claims to documentary realism, often by parodying the conventions of realism through emphasizing the banal. The most interesting of these images foreground the complicity of image making and image taking with U.S. enterprises of imperial expansion in the late nineteenth-century West. Thus, exposing the flaws of the Dawes Act to the well-meaning but detached proponents of allotment, who were comfortably ensconced in their eastern parlors, Gay's images and texts demand that they forsake their idealism and consider the law's material consequences for specific lands and real people.

THE DAWES ACT AND THE AIMS OF ALLOTMENT

By the mid-1880s the U.S. government's policy of containing Indians on vast western reservations was in crisis. To settlers and entrepreneurs demanding access to more land for farms, towns, railroads, highways, and mines, the reservations seemed unnecessarily generous, a waste of valuable land and resources. In the face of such expansionist fervor, self-styled friends of the Indian sought to protect reservation lands from white encroachment by advocating a comprehensive plan to secure Indian lands to their individual owners.[3] Thus in 1887 Congress passed the Dawes General Allotment Act, popularly, if not ironically, known as the "Indian Emancipation Act."[4] Designed to appease both expansionists and Indian advocates, it mandated that reservation lands be deeded to individual Indian owners, who, in turn, would receive full U.S. citizenship. However, the federal government would hold allotted lands in trust for at least twenty-five years, during which time their owners would remain wards of the nation—apprentices, as it were, in the process of "[learning] to treat [this land] as real estate."[5] Undeeded land would be sold to the U.S. government, which would, in turn, open it to development, investing the profits in tribal improvements.

A unilateral U.S. intervention into the sovereignty of Indian nations, the Dawes Act was, from its inception, a contested measure.[6] Opponents presciently characterized it as a land grab: "the baldest, the boldest, and the most unjustifiable" "of all the attempts to encroach upon the Indian."[7] They claimed that its positive effects would be limited: because most arable western lands had already been homesteaded, it was unlikely that Indians, whom they understood to lack inclination, tools, and training, would succeed in farming the substandard land that remained. They argued that the advantages promised by the Act were provisional because the much-vaunted citizenship would not be effective for a quarter-century, when the government's trusteeship would expire and the land would become alienable. Many of these objections proved to be valid. In fact, in contemporary legal practice, "the problems of Indian land tenure caused by allotment are [so] complex . . . [that they] form a separate and specialized body of jurisprudence important to the field of Indian law."[8] These problems include the "fractionated" status of allotted lands (individually owned plots interspersed among tracts of land owned by non-Indians), the Act's lack of foresight in providing land for subsequent generations, and the virtual erasure of tribal sovereignty through the disposal of all territorial land held in common.[9]

In 1887, however, the immediate benefits of the Dawes Act seemed to outweigh its risks. Its proponents emphasized that it would mitigate the worst abuses associated with prior federal policies of Indian removal and the reservation system. It would create as federal policy a procedure for allotting lands to individuals—a policy that had already been implemented on several Indian reservations.[10] It promised to protect at least some of the current reservation lands from squatters by giving Indian owners title to their own land and making putatively excess Indian lands available to what was seen as an irresistible and divinely ordained national expansion. Extending citizenship to Indians, Dawes supporters argued, would ensure the equal rule of law and enable Indians to "[cast] off . . . savagism" by eliminating tribal identities, lands, and sovereignty, eventually yielding complete assimilation.[11]

THE NEZ PERCES AND THE BEGINNINGS OF ALLOTMENT

U.S. expansion into Nez Perce territory had followed familiar lines. The arrival of Protestant missionaries in the Northwest had exacerbated differences among the more than forty loosely affiliated Nez Perce bands. Missionaries demanded that their converts discard traditional dress and hairstyles, forgo ceremonial observances, and cease to speak their native tongue. Local ecclesiastical leaders often took sides as well in more earthly disputes over political issues such as reservation boundaries. White settlers followed the missionaries, claiming the rich interior farming and grazing lands of the Oregon Territory and agitating for Indian containment. Accordingly, in 1842, Federal Indian Agent Elijah White insisted that the various Nez Perce bands unite themselves under one head chief with whom whites would negotiate. All Nez Perces, however, did not accede to this arrangement.

Thirteen years later, Isaac Stevens, who served simultaneously as governor of the Washington Territory and as territorial superintendent of Indian Affairs, and who was also (and not coincidentally) a principal of the survey for the northern route of the Pacific Railroad, called a council of the various Northwest Indian groups. He hoped to broker a treaty that would force the Indians to make additional land cessions so that he could persuade eastern investors that the railroad could be routed safely through the Northwest. Several Nez Perce groups attended this council, but only Hallalhotsoot, or Lawyer, then the putative head chief of the pro-white Nez Perces, signed the treaty, which reduced Nez Perce territory from 13 million acres to about 6.5 million. The minimal cash reimbursement promised by the government in exchange for the land came late and was never paid in full.

In 1860, white prospectors who had illegally entered the Nez Perce Reservation discovered gold. By 1862, mining activities had brought nearly twenty thousand illicit intruders onto Nez Perce lands. A new treaty, whose ostensible purpose was to protect Nez Perces from these incursions, ceded the mining areas and gold deposits to the United States. Like the earlier agreements, this treaty was not unanimously supported by all Nez Perce groups. Antitreaty groups, thinking to withdraw themselves from the binding negotiations conducted by accommodationist leaders, dissolved their connection with the protreaty Nez Perces, incorrectly assuming that they thus would not be bound by any treaty signed by Lawyer. According to historian Alvin Josephy, this contested and "fraudulent" treaty, which reduced the reservation to "784,996 acres[,] . . . slightly more than 10 per cent the size of the old one," and which gave white developers right of way to "build public roads, ferries, and inns anywhere they chose on the Indians' land," also created two irreconcilable groups of Nez Perces.[12]

The best known antitreaty Nez Perce was Hin-mah-toe-yah-laht-khit, or Chief Joseph, as he is now popularly known. Joseph was the political leader of several Nez Perce bands who resisted confinement within the new reservation boundaries, choosing to remain on their lands in the Wallowa Valley.[13] In 1877, pulled into a war sparked by local white-Indian tensions, he and his followers successfully eluded U.S. troops under the command of General Oliver Otis Howard.

After being pursued for five months over more than a thousand miles of mountainous terrain, the antitreaty Nez Perces capitulated. Contrary to the terms of the surrender, which promised that they could return to the reservation, the resisters were confined in prison camps in Kansas and Oklahoma. During their detention, Joseph became a well-known spokesman and an articulate protester of this treatment. Finally, in 1885, just four years before Fletcher and Gay arrived at the Nez Perce Reservation, he and his followers were allowed to return to Idaho. Upon their return, the group refused to live with the protreaty Nez Perces, settling instead at the Colville Reservation. Their well-publicized return confirmed the federal government's opinion that Indian resistance in the Northwest was effectively contained.

In an era when whites had little to fear from Indian uprisings, Joseph's story and his image enjoyed a wide popular circulation. A portrait of the hero, taken as the prisoners were en route to Oklahoma Territory and circulated by F. J. Haynes, "quickly became a best seller all over the country."[14] Most of the era's representations of Joseph follow the conventions established by this photograph, a close-up bust image that emphasizes the heroic and worn nature of the leader's striking face, for Joseph is posed against an empty backdrop. His clothing still suggests traditional attire, but he carries no weapons and does not wear the feathered headdress later photographers, such as Edward Curtis, included in their portraits of him. Although a hero, the Joseph captured by this image does not represent a threat to white viewers.

Gay's only image of Joseph, by contrast, suggests the domestic politics that continued to divide Nez Perce groups after the conclusion of the so-called Joseph War and captures the complex trajectories of power Fletcher would negotiate as she pursued the allotment project.[15] *Chief Joseph with Alice C. Fletcher* shows Joseph standing contrapposto in the middle of a field at the foot of forested hills (fig. 16). He looks to his left at Fletcher, who is turned in profile. A third figure, James Stuart, a Christian Nez Perce who worked as Fletcher's interpreter, kneels at the left, also in profile.[16] To those wishing to see the allotment as a success, this image might suggest that Joseph is now a peaceful man. Unarmed, clad in everyday western attire, he stands at ease in land that could be his, should he capitulate to the terms of allotment. Stuart's posture, which provides symmetry for the pictorial composition, suggests his respect for this legendary hero.[17]

Gay's inclusion of these three within the same frame suggests Fletcher's inevitable success as an agent of civilization. Yet this placid image, like others of Gay's allotment photographs, also contains elements of strife, embodied in the triangulation of power among the standing Joseph, who occupies the visual center of the image; Fletcher; and the kneeling Stuart. The stability of the triangle is disturbed by the direction of the gazes—Fletcher and Joseph trade gazes, engaging each other as potentially equal combatants; Stuart's gaze is averted from both, undermining the idea that he might be kneeling in respect. His disengagement

16. E. Jane Gay, untitled, ca. 1890.

Idaho State Historical Society, Boise, Id. 3771, titled *Chief Joseph with Alice C. Fletcher.*

suggests his allegiances to the protreaty Nez Perces, who had not univocally welcomed Joseph and his followers on their return. Joseph's posture also belies his tractability: as Gay wrote of him, "It was good to see an unsubjugated Indian."[18] His refusal to be confined on the reservation is supported by the photograph's context. Unlike Gay's many other field photographs, this one contains no fences; it suggests Joseph's refusal to be contained within artificial boundaries, as does the lightened, overexposed sky immediately behind his head.

This image is one of several that suggest the fractious situation into which Fletcher found herself thrust on her arrival in Idaho. On the Nez Perce reservation, Christian-identified groups separated themselves from those who followed traditional religious ways. Those who chose to support white government administrators were heartily distrusted by more traditionally minded parties. James Stuart, for example, had been threatened with death by traditional Nez Perces because he agreed to work as Fletcher's interpreter.[19] Over and against all the Nez Perce groups stood the white settlers, eager to claim reservation land. Gay's *Retracing a Former Survey* contains those tensions, offering to the uninformed

17. E. Jane Gay, *Retracing a Former Survey,* ca. 1889–1890.
Idaho State Historical Society, Boise, Id. 63–221.24, titled *Allotting Land to Nez Perces.*

viewer an apparently neutral view of an orderly, rational civil process (fig. 17). The image shows nine figures, eight of them male, including four Nez Perce surveyor's assistants mounted on horses. To the left, Fletcher consults with William Caldwell, a prominent white stockman and settler, and Abraham Brooks, a Nez Perce not affiliated with the surveying party.[20] Caldwell and Fletcher jointly hold a paper. A man, probably Stuart, kneels, facing Fletcher and visually disengaged from the other Nez Perces in the frame. Edson Briggs, the expedition's head sur-

veyor, stands at the image's center holding his surveyor's rod, with his back to Fletcher, Caldwell, and Brooks. The other Nez Perces warily watch the trio.

The *Jane Gay Photograph Collection Catalog* misleadingly captions this photograph *Allotting Land to Nez Perces.*[21] Such a description suggests that the group is united in the purpose of laying out lands for the possession of potential citizen-farmers. Gay's title—*Retracing a Former Survey*—clarifies the issue and suggests the tension in the scene.[22] At the time this image was made, Fletcher had not yet begun to allot land. She was, rather, retracing the lines of the 1863 survey in an effort to clarify which of the white settlers who had claimed boundary lands had supportable claims. Fletcher's attire—black coat, gloves, and hat—gives her a physical weight equal to the other masculine principals in the scene, but her position at the image's far left suggests her necessary separation from the divided loyalties that fracture the main group. Caldwell, whose hands clutch Fletcher's plat book, had lived illegally on the reservation since 1865 and was notorious for stealing Nez Perce cattle and grazing his herds on Nez Perce land without tribal permission. Caldwell's "cattle business" had allegedly attracted the "financial interest" of Nez Perce Indian Agent Charles E. Monteith.[23] Thus supported by a federal agent, Caldwell would have been a powerful opponent of Fletcher with an active interest in seeing that her new survey justified his claims.

At Caldwell's back stands "Blind Abraham" Brooks. His presence in this image testifies to another source of tension—that among the various groups of Nez Perces now thrown together on the reservation. Brooks had served as a scout for General Otis Howard, Joseph's pursuer in the Nez Perce War.[24] Wounded during that conflict, he carries a white cane that marks his literal blindness. It suggests a figurative blindness as well, a misplaced loyalty that has now allied him with Caldwell, a man who had profited from illegally using reservation land. As a prosthesis, or aid to seeing, Brooks's cane echoes Briggs's surveyor's rod. The question remains whether the scientific aid to vision, the surveyor's rod, will fulfill the same function of betrayal as that suggested by the cane in "Blind Abraham's" hand. Gay, a great partisan of Briggs, has placed him in the center of the photograph, a position that attests to the importance of his unimpeachability. His posture supports this implication: his back is turned to Caldwell's and Brooks's negotiations with Fletcher.

COMING INTO THE COUNTRY

What drew Gay and Fletcher, women well past middle age, into this maelstrom of political infighting on the high plains of northwestern Idaho? Jane Gay, it seems, sought adventure—a more challenging way to support herself than as a clerk in "the penitentiary," as she called the Washington, D.C., Dead Letter Office, where she had worked for well over a decade.[25] New opportunities for advancement seemed to present themselves when she reencountered her childhood friend, Alice Fletcher, who had recently returned from her fieldwork among the Omahas of Nebraska. Distressed at her former friend's "appearance of exhaustion [after] a summer in the field," she volunteered to accompany Fletcher on future trips as her ex-officio photographer, cook, and companion.[26] Her offer accepted, Gay set about immediately to teach herself photography.

To have embraced a new career at the age of fifty-eight was characteristic of

Gay, a woman described by her niece as one who "*could . . .* do everything better than anybody."[27] An expert cabinetmaker, seamstress, gardener, and gourmet cook, she had been a teacher and headmistress of schools for girls in Tennessee, Georgia, and Washington, D.C.; she also reportedly worked as governess to Andrew Johnson's grandchildren and as a nurse during the Civil War.[28] A long-time resident of the capital and a "lady well known in the Army and in Washington society," she had had ample opportunity to observe political folly at close hand.[29] At the conclusion of the Civil War, under the pseudonym Truman Trumbull, she published a 340-page mock-epic poem lampooning the conduct of the war; it was entitled *The New Yankee Doodle: Being an Account of the Little Difficulty in the Family of Uncle Sam.*[30] It is reasonable to assume that, as a writer, she chose to join Fletcher and use the experience as the basis for a photographically illustrated popular account of her adventures among the Indians, as had Frank Hamilton Cushing, a friend of the pair, several years earlier in *Century Magazine.*[31]

Like her friend, Fletcher had never married. She had been a successful public lecturer on American antiquities, an ethnographer, an allotting agent to the Omaha and Winnebago Indians, and an Indian advocate centrally involved in drafting the Dawes General Allotment Act. Unlike Gay, however, Fletcher was not seeking adventure or change. Returning from Nebraska, she had hoped to begin to publish her Omaha research under the sponsorship of F. W. Putnam of Harvard University. Her plans were interrupted, however, by her appointment as allotting agent to the Nez Perces.[32] A heightened sense of duty prevented her from declining the appointment, but her subsequent relations with the Nez Perces were colored by her reluctance to postpone her scholarly plans. She saw the Nez Perces primarily as the objects of federal policy. Only after two summers in the field did she begin to see that their culture deserved the same kind of intellectual engagement as that of the Omahas, whose music and ritual continued to fascinate her. The sooner she completed the allotment, the more quickly she could return to her studies with Putnam.[33]

Gay's informal snapshots of Fletcher nooning during a long summer day of allotment capture the contradictions entailed in Fletcher's work (figs. 18 and 19). Her attire suggests a costume—or uniform—of Victorian duty and respectability. Supremely impractical for field work, her black dress, corset, flowered bonnet, gloves, and handbag establish her claim on femininity and her identity as an agent of the benevolent discipline underlying the logic of a law designed to force Victorian ideals on the Nez Perces. Her costume reminds us that Fletcher was a woman quite literally occupying a man's field, driven by the wish to please her masculine mentors and to prove that, even though a woman, she would produce rigorous work.[34] At every moment, she had to demonstrate both masculine purpose and feminine unimpeachability.

The settings of these two images of Fletcher carry similar messages. Fletcher does not join her surveying party for the noontime meal—she considered their

18. E. Jane Gay, *Alice Fletcher,* ca. 1889–1892.

19. E. Jane Gay, *Nooning,* ca. 1889–1892.

food to be "so heavy."[35] In fig. 18, she sits uneasily on a rocky hillside, flanked by a water dipper and an open picnic basket that likely holds food prepared for her by Gay. In *Nooning* she perches on the seat of an unhitched wagon that rests unevenly on a dirt road. The fence and building beside the road seem to predict the eventual results of her allotment work; the uneven ground suggests the futility of her attempts at evenhandedness. At the left, the horses that have pulled her loaded wagon are being fed and watered by an unidentified man. As always, the work of men and animals is relegated to the background, while Fletcher shares the foreground with possessions that mark her status and separate her from the land, her workers, and the Nez Perces who are the object of her efforts.

IMPERIAL EYES: "HER MAJESTY" AND "THE PHOTOGRAPHER"

Technologies of imperialism brought Gay and Fletcher to Idaho: they traveled at least part of the way on a railroad line owned by the Northern Pacific, whose right-of-way had occasioned the first reduction in Nez Perce lands. They brought with them the tools of imperial enterprise: surveying equipment, ledgers, plats, maps, and cameras. They produced knowledge—including Gay's photographs and letters and Fletcher's ledgers, deeds, genealogical tables, reports, and correspondence with Washington, D.C.—that enabled the containment and consolidation of the Nez Perces. Even their attitude was imperial. Their purpose was not to study the Nez Perces nor to befriend them. They necessarily saw the Nez Perces as needing civilization: land, fences, western dress, food, and wood-frame houses. Unlike their male anthropologist counterparts who sought to insinuate themselves into tribal structures as participant observers, Gay and Fletcher lived separately from the Nez Perces, usually in government buildings, missionary cabins, or tents pitched on the lands of Christian Nez Perces. Even their Sibley tent, whose conical shape echoed that of Nez Perce tipis, bore the clearly legible stencil "A.C.F. United States Special Indian Agent June 28, 1889."[36] As well, their dress and behavior seemed part of an effort to demonstrate that even under duress white women remained civilized: Gay's photographs and letters dwell on the details of picnic baskets, boiled eggs, canned tomatoes, frying pans and Dutch ovens, corsets, umbrellas, and lace collars.

Gay's awareness of the imperial aims of the expedition is apparent as she writes of the pair's activities, representing each woman in the guise of several different personas that accord with the colonizing roles each plays. For example, throughout the letters, Gay irreverently refers to Fletcher as "Her Majesty." According to her niece's memoirs, Gay perhaps first chose this device as a joke based on Fletcher's physical resemblance to Queen Victoria.[37] The comparison exceeded the physical. Often at the mercy of governmental agencies who should have supported her but did not, Fletcher, like the queen, was a figurehead. Like the queen, she could never show doubt but had to steadfastly embody

20. E. Jane Gay, *Photographer Fatigued*, after 1890.
The Schlesinger Library, Radcliffe Institute, Harvard University.

the government and its policies. And, like the queen, she was the visible embodiment of colonial power.

Gay's persona as the Photographer balances Her Majesty. In a typical back-to-the-camera pose, the Photographer leans against a tree, in dress and in posture the mirror opposite of Her Majesty (fig. 20). Slouch hat and jacket seem well-fitted to the conditions of wilderness Idaho; the short hair, supremely practical for the dry climate, suggests an ambiguous gender; although Gay apparently posed for this photograph, the Photographer is gendered male. The Photographer is an ironic, detached, and philosophical observer. If Her Majesty's refuge is the law, the Photographer's are irony and platitudinous philosophy: "He never allows himself to be flustered; it interferes with his profession. He is a philosopher. . . . He asserts, . . . 'True philosophy is to keep cool and take things as they come.'"[38] The pose invites reader and viewer to share the point of view both of the photographer and of the Photographer and thus also to question the conditions under which these apparently documentary images were made. This photograph, for instance, could be called a self-portrait. It is highly realistic but certainly not documentary, as it was made several years after the fact, in controlled conditions.[39]

Although armed with technology and the law, Fletcher's expedition did not proceed without difficulty. The records produced by these women document their unremitting efforts to maintain imperial detachment and objectivity. Fletcher, a dutiful woman, a reformer, a friend of the Indian, and a government agent, sought to resolve the contradictions she encountered by producing rules, regulations, and directives to cover the gaps in the existing law. Gay, however, seems to have recognized early on that the gulf between the ideals of allotment and its physical application could not be bridged. As the years passed, her letters and photographs make the fissures ever more apparent. Her letters suggest that she used the technologies of imperialism as a potent antidote to Her Majesty's pretensions: "while Her Majesty [holds] diplomatic conversations" with the Nez Perces, the Photographer makes a visual record of the procedures and captures the "determined expression of resistance" on obdurate Nez Perce faces.[40]

Within the first week of their arrival, it became apparent to Fletcher that the documents she had been given did not accurately describe the land she was to apportion. On June 5, 1889, she wrote the commissioner of Indian Affairs:

> I would respectfully report that having spent some days looking over the land upon this reservation in the vicinity of the Agency and seeking information from Indians and White men concerning other parts of the same, *I am inclined to think that the estimates hitherto made concerning the proportion of agricultural land upon this reservation have been exaggerated.* The valleys, or creek bottoms contain the only land which is strictly agricultural, and these are all narrow and quite limited in extent. The bench land rising above the bottoms in some localities will grow small grain under the most favorable circumstances, but without irrigation no vegetables can be raised or sure crops of any kind secured.[41]

Yet even in the face of what she saw and reported, Fletcher held fast to her faith that rational procedures could turn the Nez Perces into farmers and bring them into an equitable relationship with the whites who threatened to overrun their land. Thus her first act was to verify and correct the lines of the 1863 survey. Although this act stabilized reservation boundaries, it did not unequivocally benefit the Nez Perces, for Fletcher wanted not only to exclude white squatters but also to correct property lines within the reservation. To Washington she wrote:

Since all the monuments have been set up and I could see how the Indians have run their fences, roads, and laid out their fields, it is clear that nearly every person must be more or less changed. It would be impossible to give them their land as they now occupy it and to discribe [sic] the tracts according to any subdivision in the legal survey, the fields cross the lines in every direction, frequently circling in and out of different lots. I have talked with a few of the more intelligent and they admit the necessity of "straightening out their land" but there will be bitter opposition from others. I have requested the Surveyor to measure the fields that are the most irregular in form, that I may be able to make a fair and equitable exchange of land and adjustment. *Fences must be moved, and where the lay of the land will permit it, the roads changed.* . . .

No time will be lost . . . as we are in a dense atmosphere of smoke from burning forests in the mts. East and North of us. The sun is invisible and we can see but a few rods distant. It is very trying to head and eyes. All this part of the country is the same way & the solar instrument is useless. The needle cannot be used here.[42]

I have quoted Fletcher at length here because her official communications so perfectly illustrate her commitment to procedures of rationality, her troubling confusion of motive, and the simple resistance of the climate and terrain to her aims. It is clear that she wishes to be fair and has at heart what she understands to be the best interests of her clients. Yet she dismisses those who disagree with her methods (by implication) as less intelligent, scanting the fact that the disorderly arrangement of Nez Perce properties demonstrates that they had already begun, without governmental interference, to build houses, plant gardens, farm arable land, and lay out townships and roads. But because they were not precisely aligned with the Cartesian coordinates of Fletcher's new survey, they all "must be moved . . . and changed," even in the face of logical Indian protest and despite the smoke from forest fires that clouded the vision of people and machine alike.

The "tender violence," to use Laura Wexler's apt phrase, entailed in the process that Fletcher describes as simply "moving" and "changing" is apparent even in two-dimensional representations.[43] Much of the topography of the Nez Perce Reservation is mountainous and rugged, riven by deep valleys and declines. Although some of the high plains are suited for farming, much of the land is not. But the inexorable logic of allotment demanded that the three-dimensional land adapt to the Cartesian surveyor's grid and that existing farms, which followed the land's contours, conform to the surveyor's logic.

Gay offers an extended and ironic commentary on this process by frequently using fences as an element of photographic composition. A useful device for delineating picture planes, the fences carry symbolic energy as well. They mark the boundaries of the tidy farms resulting from allotment. They are echoed in the lines of apparently tractable Indian subjects arranging themselves for Gay's photographic convenience. An untitled image—apparently a representation of three generations—shows two Indian women with a young boy between them seated

21. E. Jane Gay, *Some Allottees*, ca. 1889–1892.
Idaho State Historical Society, Boise, Id. 63–221.220, titled *Mounted Indian Men*.

in front of a split-rail fence.[44] The fence crowds close to the elder woman in the image, whose lap is spread with a fringed blanket, suggesting her ties to a traditional past. The younger woman, farther from the fence, wears a large lace collar and dark dress and sits on a blanket-covered chair. Her arms protectively enclose a young boy dressed entirely in western-style clothing, including high-buttoned boots. Similarly, *Some Allottees* shows ten Nez Perce men on horseback, some carrying rifles and at least one aiming a shotgun. Any suggestion of danger, however, is neutralized by the men's orderly position in front of a split-rail fence (fig. 21).

Fletcher's rational efforts were manifestly illogical, as Nez Perces did not hesitate to point out. From Gay's letters, which present multiple perspectives on the process of resurvey, we learn that Nez Perces offered their own resistances to Fletcher's straitening: they "often destroy[ed] the Surveyor's corners as soon as his back [was] turned and [made] corners of their own." Gay presents this activity as their logical response to governmental inconsistency. Because the 1863 survey was incompletely and inconsistently carried out, they expected nothing more from Fletcher's work. Confronted with her benevolent and rational explanations, they answer, "How is it? The Government made my fence; you say it is all wrong. Are there two Governments? and which is right? We will keep the land as it is; by and by another Government will come along and pull up our fences again."[45]

22. E. Jane Gay, *Carrying the Baby*, ca. 1889–1892.
Idaho State Historical Society, Boise, Id. 63–221.138, titled *Nez Perces*.

Gay's interest in the civilly disobedient responses of the Nez Perces is apparent in her photographs as well if one is willing to look beyond Western logics of Cartesian structure and aesthetic judgment. Images that initially seem amateurish and banal also document resistance. For example, in several of Gay's images of groups of Nez Perces the contents exceed their frames. *Carrying the Baby* is typical: the image's central figures are sharply in focus, but the photograph's margins fail to contain other unruly, out-of-focus subjects, including the baby at the extreme right (fig. 22). Sure signs of the amateur who is still struggling with the lengthy exposure time, these images, when they are reproduced, are often cropped of such extraneous information in an effort to align them within the neat margins of knowledge-making projects or to fit them into the tidy categories of nostalgic memory. Gay herself, for example, cropped *Carrying the Baby* to include only the figures of the woman and baby who occupy the extreme right-hand section of the larger image.[46] Yet she was always aware of the violence in this process, comparing such cropping to the Dawes Act's central assumption that the "excess" lands of the reservation could be profitably trimmed off and sold to white entrepreneurs, as one of her letters makes clear:

> An Indian has just been in to complain that the Government has given the N.P.R.R. [Northern Pacific Railroad] a right of way across his little farm, cutting out the very heart of it. One can forsee [sic] that before many years, under the pressure of the encroaching white man's civilization, all the little valley gardens of the Nez Percé will be destroyed by the railroad lines and the Indians driven back from the water courses; and when one considers that all their little agricultural endeavors and their homes are upon these streams where alone gardens can be made, it is not difficult to conceive of the suffering which will follow this sort of opening up of the Reservation. One grows sick of seeing wrongs for which there is no practical remedy. There are plenty of *theoretical* ones, evolved in the brain of good, helpless people whose pure souls could never conceive the extent of the evils, of which they strive to devise means to trim off the outer edges—the edges which they see or hear about.[47]

Significantly, in Gay's image, the baby occupies one such edge, foreshadowing the outer edges of future problems that the Dawes Act had not anticipated. Would Nez Perce women and children receive equal portions of land? And how would Dawes ensure the availability of more land for subsequent generations?

Gay's attention to this process suggests that she recognized precisely the violence entailed in survey, deed, and photograph. Of Fletcher's office, where the Dawes Act was explained, she writes: "The Special Agent has set up a blackboard in the office. It is the blackboard used long ago by the Missionary and, over the ghostly substratum of gospel texts, lessons in elementary surveying are given and sections are drawn and quartered and driven like wedges into the Indian brain by the Interpreter."[48] The cloudy surface of the blackboard echoes the smoky atmosphere that plagued the surveyors. Its palimpsest-like texts bring into a genealogical lineage the benevolent enterprises of missionary activity, education, and allotment, demonstrating how the Christian ethics—particularly submission and benevolence—underwrite the presumptions of paternalism and overwrite traditional behaviors. The allotment entails reeducation, violent and torturous. That the Chimewa-educated Interpreter, James Stuart, is himself complicit in this process only completes the irony of the situation.

Gay does not reserve her critique for Fletcher's methods alone, however. Her landscape photographs make it apparent that she was aware of the documentary uses of such images and of the resemblance of her visual prostheses to those used by the surveying team. *South Fork of Clearwater River* shows Fletcher standing in a sunken area of land in the foreground, looking toward Stuart, who is closer to the river's edge and who points to the right (fig. 23). The background is divided by the slope of a tree-covered mountain. Although a precise representation of the terrain it shows, this image resists the conventions of survey photographs such

23. E. Jane Gay, *South Fork of Clearwater River*, ca. 1889–1892.

Idaho State Historical Society, Boise, Id. 63–221.57a, titled *Clearwater River.*

as those made by Timothy O'Sullivan two decades earlier. The mountains along the Clearwater are as toweringly spectacular as any along the Snake, O'Sullivan's subject; yet the purpose of Gay's image is not to emphasize the impassible features of the terrain, as O'Sullivan's did, but to show its suitability for domestic uses. Hence, she emphasizes the flatlands along the river, which Fletcher had designated as "the only land which is strictly agricultural."[49] Gay's scrapbook caption informs us that the sunken area in which Fletcher stands was "made by ancient dwellings."[50] Fletcher is included not to indicate scale but to flatten the terrain. Fore-, middle-, and background occupy nearly the same picture plane, for the image lacks an identifiable object in the foreground against which an illusion of the depth and three-dimensionality might be constructed. Perhaps Gay lacked the inclination to seek out spectacular angles of vision or the equipment to alter the landscape to produce the three-dimensional effect that was so popular in the stereographic images of the era and that informed landscape photography as well.[51] Her approach, by contrast, emphasizes to viewers that they hold, view, and consume an artifact as two-dimensional as the survey it documents.

Several other camp photos show Gay's continuing insistence on exposing the limits of maps, plats, and surveys. *Johnny,* an image of one of the chainmen who accompanied Fletcher's surveying party, places her Sibley tent center, but the tent and its accompanying temporary structures are crowded by trees, shrubs, and underbrush (fig. 24). Fletcher, almost invisible on first viewing, sits writing in the shade of a lean-to shelter at the right rear; in the foreground stands a Nez Perce member of her party, hatchet in hand. From the photograph's composition, it is clear that Fletcher's comfort depended on the work of just such workers, who enabled her to maintain a tenuous but determined hold on civilized domesticity while surrounded by encroaching nature, which was elided by maps.

Not all the Nez Perce Reservation was uniformly forested or riparian. Much of Gay's correspondence, in fact, emphasizes arid, desolate spaces. She wrote of *Fourth of July at Kamiah:* "The Photographer tried to get a picture of the people as they sat on the yellow grass in the glare of the mid-day sun, but it came out painfully hard and contrasty. Photography in a semi-arid country is not a cheerful occupation at the best, when one considers the water required in the process and the fact that one often is obliged to take one's own bath in a pint of the precious liquid." [52] Indeed, this image is not one of Gay's best—dozens of standing and sitting Nez Perces form two or three ragged lines. Parts of the image are overexposed and parts are underexposed. The lines of undifferentiated subjects do not yield identifiable individuals; the viewer is simply reduced to counting as a way of extracting literal meaning from the image. In the process of such census taking, we are reminded of our complicity in the general project of allotment and

24. E. Jane Gay, *Johnny*, ca. 1890.
Idaho State Historical Society, Boise, Id. 63–221.105, titled *Nez Perces.*

25. E. Jane Gay, *The Damp Thermopylae*, ca. 1890.

Idaho State Historical Society, Boise, Id. 63–221.209, titled *One of Alice Fletcher's Survey Camps (Camp Thirsty)*.

of the informational gap between census and population, map and territory. *The Damp Thermopylae* also aptly attests to the difficulties of "photography in a semi-arid country" (fig. 25). The shadows suggest it was taken near noon. The image is marred by high contrasts and light leaks at its edges; the streaks of light and dark that track diagonally across the picture suggest that Gay struggled to develop it in an insufficient amount of liquid. This is a painful and uncomfortable image. Everything and everyone—the tents, the wagons, the people—are off-plumb. Members of the surveying party are scattered aimlessly over the barren ground. The fence at upper left divides the survey party from "civilization," as represented by an inviting clump of trees and a long house.

Regardless of the extremity of the conditions, each photograph of Fletcher in camp contains a reassurance that this woman carried civilization with her. *The Damp Thermopylae* shows us Fletcher, fully clad and wearing her flowered bonnet, headed toward the wagon that carried her supplies. Regardless of the field's desolation, a house is near. Similarly, *Family Umbrella* associates Fletcher, dourly staring into the camera, with possessions signifying civilization (fig. 26).[53] Edson Briggs and Fletcher sit at a table in the noonday sun. An umbrella, tied to a tripod, shades them, while Nez Perce chainmen rest on the ground nearby. Briggs sits on a sack of grain slung over a ladder; Fletcher occupies the wagon seat that has been removed for her. A skillet, washboard, bucket, and other camping gear dominate the right foreground. The umbrella was a favored object of humor in many early pictorial representations of Indians—like George Catlin's *Pigeon's Egg Head (The Light) Going to and Returning from Washington,* where it is used to mark their supposed pretensions to civilization (fig. 27). Here it loses that invidious overtone and suggests instead a woman concerned for her complexion. Lashed to the tripod, the umbrella forcefully connects Victorian womanhood and imperial expansion. Although Fletcher may look momentarily uncomfortable in the wilderness, one never doubts that she is a lady who can, and will, use the nearby wagon to return to more civilized surroundings.

Gay treats the Nez Perces more equivocally, frequently emphasizing their incomplete assimilation by suggesting their ties to the land and to natural phenomena while posing them in proximity to signs of civilization: crossing bridges, sitting on stairs, standing in the doorways of houses and in front of fences. Whether in natural surroundings or fully demonstrating their civilized accomplishments, her Nez Perce subjects look uncomfortable, off balance, or temporary. For example,

26. E. Jane Gay, *Family Umbrella (Camp Blazes),* ca. 1890.
Idaho State Historical Society, Boise, Id. 63–221.11, titled *Camp Sunday.*

27. George Catlin, *Pigeon's Egg Head (The Light) Going to and Returning from Washington,* ca. 1837–1839. Smithsonian American Art Museum, Gift of Mrs. Joseph Harrison, Jr. 1985.66.474.

her portrait of the sisters Harriet Stuart and Annie Parnell Little honors many of the conventions of Victorian portraiture (fig. 28). Both seated women wear high-collared dresses with neck pins. Their hair is tied with ribbons; both are tightly corseted. Harriet Stuart, sitting in an ornamented straight chair, holds an open volume on her lap. Annie Little's book, covered with her clenched left hand, is closed. Both women, apparently familiar with the conventions of portrait photography, look directly at the camera, although Harriet's head and body are turned slightly to her left. The image seems an especially apt portrayal of the benefits of allotment and education because both women had attended Carlisle Indian School; Harriet was the wife of Fletcher's interpreter, James Stuart, an alumnus of Chimewa Indian School.

Yet this image lacks certain items usually included in parlor portraiture. In place of the curtained, pillared, or scenic backdrop (a convention Gay followed in other instances), this photograph uses the rough wooden planks of a poorly painted building. No oriental carpet covers a polished wood floor: here, the chairs rest on hard-packed dirt. These omissions suggest that Gay or her subjects (or all of them) were uncomfortable with the illusion of domestic probity, an interpretation borne out on the body of Little: her address to the camera, although direct, seems troubled; her serious face betrays doubt—or perhaps simple discomfort, for she sits on a low, backless stool. Her clenched left hand embodies the tension that keeps the contrasting details of this image—Victorian dress and posture, wooden planks and barren ground—in delicate balance.

Two other striking images, taken at a mission-sponsored Decoration Day celebration, demonstrate Gay's awareness that Dawesian civilization might not be universally welcomed by and beneficial to its clients. In *Nez Perce Children,* eleven young girls dressed in Victorian garb, wearing boater hats, and carrying American flags and flowers, pose uneasily on a rocky hillside (fig. 29). The angle of the hill is so steep and the perspective so flattened that one wonders how the children managed to stand still for the picture. In content and setting, this image resembles that of Fletcher's solitary noontime picnic, where she also perches uncomfortably in rough terrain. But Fletcher emerges from the natural surrounding, her face precisely in focus, her grip on civilization and individuality sure. These little girls, apparently boarding-school students, are not future Fletchers. Uniformly dressed in dark frocks and boater hats and squinting at the photographer in the bright sunlight, they are nearly indistinguishable from one another, their faces and bodies blending with the brush and rocks of the hillside.

These same children appear in another photograph taken on the same occasion, which Gay explained in her letters. *Decorating Graves at Lapwai* forcefully demonstrates that the civilized behaviors with which Fletcher and the missionaries

28. E. Jane Gay, untitled, ca. 1889.
Idaho State Historical Society, Boise, Id. 63–221.83d, titled *Lapwai Nez Perce.*

29. E. Jane Gay, untitled,
ca. 1889–1892.

Idaho State Historical Society, Boise, Id. 63–
221.340b, titled *Nez Perce Children*.

before her sought to overwrite Nez Perce culture entailed erasing tradition and replacing it with meaningless—or, worse, outright violent—ceremonial observances.[54] Gay's narration draws attention to how this moment of photographic time is the (il)logical culmination of larger historical process, local minutiae, and misplaced idealism. She exposes the layered ironies entailed in making the Nez Perces—or any Indian group, for that matter—into wards of the nation. "On Decoration Day we happened to see the procession of school children going out to decorate the graves of the soldiers *who slew their fathers in the Joseph war*. . . . The procession limped disjointedly along, the children doing their best to keep step with no fife or drum, but singing 'John Brown's body lies a-mouldering in the grave' and bearing aloft, tied to a fish pole, a diminutive flag. . . . The little girls placed the wreaths they had made upon the solders' graves."[55]

SENTIMENTAL HEARTS: "THE ALLOTTING AGENT" AND "THE COOK," "MISS F." AND "THE FRIEND"

The tone of Gay's account of the Decoration Day festivities is one of restrained outrage, suggesting in its brevity that to say more would result in an unseemly criticism of the aims of the expedition of which she was a member. Such emotion, uncharacteristic of Her Majesty and the Photographer, is given fuller expression in two other personas, the Allotting Agent and the Cook, who embody the contradictions of sentimental discipline entailed in the Dawes Act. The intent of Dawes was to legislate the nation's "domestic dependents" into patterns of living that conformed to dominant models of family, work, and citizenship.[56] The framers of Dawes, including Fletcher, were aware that such ideals entailed extreme change. This violence, they felt, was regrettable but would ultimately benefit their recipients. Fletcher insisted, for example, that the law be applied regardless of whether a tribe had voted for its implementation, saying, "The work must be done for them whether they approve or not."[57] A particularly effective example of such sentimental discipline was Fletcher's trademark family registry—a realignment of Indian kinship systems designed to bring them into accord with white genealogies through which property was legally passed. As she deleted all signs of prior systems of land division from the map of the reservation, she also overwrote Nez Perce kinship with a linear, documentable, and patriarchal system of her own devising, one that would discipline the complexities of Indian kinship to match the sentimental structures of the patriarchal family.[58] Fletcher's record books show the care with which she recorded both an Anglo and a Nez Perce name for all allottees, estimated their ages, and documented their fathers, mothers, brothers and sisters, spouses, children, uncles and aunts.[59]

Gay's camera seems to offer the ideal complement to such acts of genealogical alignment. Historically, both portraits and paintings of family groups documented the close connection of family, possessions, and inheritance of property. The advent of affordable and accessible technology made photographic practice available to women; popular journalism urged women to learn the camera craft so that they could record the growth of their families and trace the inheritance of their physical characteristics.[60] A commonplace of family photography, in fact, has always been the family group, posed with its possessions on the front steps of the family home or in front of the family's new car, for example.

Thus we might expect to see Gay, as the official photographer, using her lens to document the families Fletcher inscribed into her official records. Several photographs seem precisely to do this. Gay favors the house, the door, the porch, and the stairs as frames for groups of Nez Perces who apparently constitute families. Yet without captioning and lengthy written explanation, these images simply show people in front of houses. Longstanding conventions of sentimental pose encourage the viewer to read the image as that of a "family." It might be more accurate to describe these pictures of subjects of assorted ages and sexes as ambiguous, disorderly, and impenetrable records that suggest the difficulties and inconsistencies of a program that, on the one hand, promised to make of the Nez Perces members of Uncle Sam's family and, on the other, had no intention of accepting Indians as racial equals. *Nine Pipes' Widow and Sisters,* for example, shows four women and two girls standing in front of a log cabin (fig. 30). A dog lies at

30. E. Jane Gay, untitled, ca. 1889–1892.

Courtesy Idaho State Historical Society, Boise, Id. 63–221.98, titled *Nine Pipes' Widow and Sisters, Kamiah*.

left front, partially out of the picture frame. The women, dressed in western-style clothing, seem stoic, immobile. A middle-ground fence separates the cabin from a tipi and another house visible in the background, inviting the viewer to read this image as a documentary record of allotment's success. However, smaller details suggest that after Gay's shutter closes, this group will quickly scatter. The children's faces are blurred, tracing their inability to stand still even for the brief moment required for Gay's camera; the woman at far right faces the camera, but her body is twisted to her left, suggesting her connection with the other structures in the photograph.

This image documents the initiation of these women as possessive individuals: a group—a family group?—standing on the stoop of a cabin—their home? Read against Fletcher's Washington correspondence, however, the visual record demands a reinterpretation. This is a fractious group, long engaged in a bitter legal battle over the ownership of the cabin and the property on which it sits. Nine Pipes had been killed four years earlier by a Nez Perce policeman.[61] Upon his death, his property had been claimed by and legally awarded to his sister. In the eyes of the Indian agent, Charles E. Monteith, Annie "was not legally married to

Nine-pipes [*sic*] and could not have the land." [62] Fletcher intervened, petitioning Washington to reverse the local court's decision and to award the property to the widow and thus to her daughter, the legal heir under U.S. law. That Nine Pipes's sister might inherit the property seemed to violate every norm of sentiment and law that Fletcher knew.

In these instances, when the imperial fantasies of Her Majesty are buttressed by sentiment, Gay writes of Fletcher as a different persona, "the Allotting Agent." Well-intentioned and intellectually committed—although frequently puzzled and discouraged—the Allotting Agent takes seriously the responsibility to act on behalf of the Nez Perces. Unlike Her Majesty, the Allotting Agent occasionally seeks legal loopholes through which humanitarian aims can be accomplished. These sentimental impulses did not result in unequivocal good however. Benevolent impulses, for example, led Fletcher to give allottees the best and most fertile sections of land, which contained access to water. Thus, many of the allottees received their 160 acres literally in severalty—in several widely separated parcels.

The Allotting Agent is paired with the Cook, one of Gay's personas, whose attitudes often demonstrate the ideological bases of sentiment in religious and regional prejudices. The most outspoken and the least enlightened member of the party, the Cook embodies the contradiction between the sentimental stereotypes easterners might have of "the noble savage" and the concrete difficulties entailed in achieving any kind of genuine cross-cultural understanding. The Cook approaches "the Indian problem" as a Yankee housekeeper, not unlike Harriet Beecher Stowe's Miss Ophelia in *Uncle Tom's Cabin*. Like Ophelia, she is intellectually committed to ideals of reform—in the Cook's case, to improving the lot of "the Indian." Like Ophelia, she is nevertheless outspoken about her dislike of people of color. The Cook distrusts Gooey, the camp's Chinese cook, whom she sees as a threat to her eminent domain. She distances herself from the Nez Perces, whom for the most part she sees as subintelligent, lazy, dirty, and undeserving of the attention lavished on them by Fletcher, who "sits in aggravating persistency, listening to the stupid, advising the vicious, stiffening up the weak, forgetting to rest. . . . There is not an Indian with hair so long and blanket so dirty but can claim her attention, be she ever so faint with hunger and the Cook ever so impatient." [63]

The ambiguities of the Nine Pipes case, with its absent father and several would-be heirs, might be seen as emblematic of the troubled familial relations that characterized Nez Perce allotment as well. In the largest sense, the federal government had long fancied itself a father to its "domestic dependent" Indian tribes. These children, it should be emphasized, did not possess the rights of inheritance and citizenship that were the legacy of natural children. Their relationship more closely resembled that of adoptees—wards of the nation. [64] Fletcher, as Her Majesty, was a maternal figurehead. Gay's habit of referring to

Fletcher alternately as Her Majesty and the Allotting Agent marks the difficulty of Fletcher's position, which seemed to require that she fulfill the administrative and majestic functions of a regent and the sentimental duties of a Victorian mother who habitually referred to her Indian clients as her "children."

On a smaller scale, the allotting group itself assumed a familial structure. Surveyor Briggs functioned as the ad hoc father. His New England background and his imperturbability made him a mainstay for Fletcher and Gay: as broker, mediator, go-between, and fall-back, he intervened—sometimes physically and often humorously—in difficult situations. This division of labor gave to Fletcher the maternal and feminine duties. Within this family, Fletcher seems to have determined to teach, guide, and instruct the members of her surveying crew—many of them Nez Perces who had graduated from Carlisle Indian School—in exemplary individuated behaviors. Gay humorously recounts Her Majesty's initial efforts to "fill another gap in their education" by "teach[ing] the chainmen the ethics of partnerships."[65] Meddling in their customary practice of sharing provisions, she "appeared one morning at the boy's [sic] camp with four little blank books in her hand and took an account of stock. . . . She soon found that her plan could not be retroactive: [characteristically] she had to start anew." Here Gay ceases to refer to Fletcher as "Her Majesty" and continues:

> But the Special Agent gave each chainman a little book and showed him how to keep his account of all the money he expended for the general good and at the end of the month she said there must be a settlement and she would show them how that should be done. Then she inquired as to the diet of the men and disapproved of canned currant jelly as of a suspicious quality and of *pate-de-fois-gras* [sic] on account of its expense, and ended by sending Harry to Mt. Idaho to buy provisions, giving him a list of such things as were best for health and strength. [This done,] the Special Agent has the radiant look she always wears on the accomplishment of an unpromising task.[66]

In this account, the divided functions of Her Majesty and the Special/Allotting Agent become clear: when sentiment intervenes, Her Majesty disappears and the Allotting Agent takes over. But it is also clear, at least to the contemporary reader, that the ministrations—or meddling—of the Allotting Agent may not be entirely beneficial—or welcome.

In this ad hoc family, Gay plays an oscillating function. In her masculine guise as the Photographer, she sometimes disagrees with Briggs's leadership and judgment but most frequently occupies an avuncular position of benign detachment from such family fracases. As the Cook, however, she becomes a feminized domestic employee subject to Fletcher's will: at best a partner, more frequently a helpmeet, and at worst a subordinate. As with the Allotting Agent, her sentimental interventions often have disastrous results. For example, as the Cook cleans out some cupboards in the pair's cabin, she comes upon "several nests of mice."

[One of the mice, a] sturdy mite of a beast had showed fight in defense of her young. The admiration of the Cook for any sort of pluck took the form of protection. "We can't have you here, but I'll fix you a nice little home in the shed," she said to the mouse. And this she did,—removing the inch-long babies very tenderly into a cotton-lined box and feeling quite comfortable in her mind after it was done. . . .

A week later, in moving a tall broken nosed pitcher on the top shelf, the Cook discovered the valiant mother-mouse and her eight little ones, lying stiff and cold in the bottom. The creature had brought them back, one by one, dropped them into the pitcher and then followed, herself. . . .

"That's what you get," said Briggs, "for trying the Indian policy on a new species."[67]

This anecdote turns the logic of allotment against itself. Using the language of feminized sentiment, it appeals to the readers' charitable impulses; the logic of its metaphor, however, points to disturbing consequences, which cannot be ignored because interpreted by a masculine authority. Because the incident is focalized through the Cook, however, it cannot be construed as a direct critique of Fletcher's actions.

Although Gay's writings and photographs evidence a fascinating degree of awareness of the ideological difficulties of allotment, her race and class privileges result in a selective blindness. Among the members of the comprised family of allotting co-workers were, for example, "real" families whose presence is virtually ignored by both Gay and Fletcher. Briggs, the surveyor, sometimes traveled with his wife and child.[68] Mrs. Briggs puts in a shadowy appearance in only one of Gay's photographs, *Camp with Briggs and Wife* (fig. 31). This image resembles a candid snapshot. It shows a camp whose tasks seem to be clearly divided along gender lines, an arrangement that is echoed in the vertically split picture plane. On the right Briggs kneels, studying papers propped on a makeshift desk; Stuart stands near the surveyor's tripod. Laundry hung out to dry on bushes divide them from Alice Fletcher and Mrs. Briggs, both wearing bonnets, who sit in the lower left-hand corner of the image, sharing a conversation or a meal. Fletcher's back is to the camera, and Mrs. Briggs is taken profile. The title leaves ambiguous the complex domestic relations here—"and wife" might refer to either of these women.

James Stuart's wife, Harriet, as well as the wives and children of the Nez Perce chainmen, also accompanied the party at times.[69] Gay made only one image of Harriet Stuart, the formal portrait discussed above, apparently to illustrate the civilized potential of Carlisle-educated Nez Perces. The relative lack of images of Harriet Stuart in the *oeuvre* may be explained by the rather disapproving way she is discussed in Gay's fourth letter. "We returned to Squirrel's camp to find that James had just come from Lapwai, with Harriet, his wife; our first intimation that when we hire an Indian, in any capacity, his wife is included in the bargain; where he goeth, she will go—if she pleases,—but no marital bond is strong

31. E. Jane Gay, untitled, ca. 1889–1892.

Idaho State Historical Society, Boise, Id. 63–221.5, titled *Camp with Briggs and Wife.*

enough to take her against her own will."[70] These silences, blanks, sidewise re-marks, and omissions suggest the strength of the normative family structure in determining how Gay and Fletcher alike saw their duty to the Nez Perces.

The relationship of these women to one another was absolutely central to how they went about their work. Friendship initially brought them together after an apparent long separation. Theirs followed the pattern of other "Boston mar-riages," or feminine companionate partnerships of the era. Gay, in particular, had lived with a series of women, beginning with Catherine Melville, with whom she kept school in Knoxville, Tennessee. In 1883, she traveled to Europe with Hen-rietta Bradley, one of her students. Upon their return, they moved into the Bradley home, where Gay was given a special room for her carpentry tools. Fol-lowing their return from Idaho, Fletcher and Gay shared a home for a number of years until Gay moved to England in 1906, where she lived with Dr. Caroline Sturge until her death in 1919.

My purpose here is not to speculate on the nature of the bonds that united these women. Clearly, they shared strong emotional, if not physical, attachments. I wish rather to discuss the sense of commitment characteristic of this relation-ship, for the third set of personas Gay employs in her letters spotlights how cen-tral were friendship and devotion to these women's determination to complete the task of allotment. Although this pair of personas, known as "Miss F." and "the friend," appear infrequently in the letters, they mark the personal dimensions inherent in any so-called objective and documentary undertaking. Fletcher's obsession with duty and her competitive drive dominate her official reports, obscuring the possibility that she doubted either the efficacy of the allotment or her ability to complete it. This facet of her character is revealed only infrequently, when Gay writes of Miss F., an idealist who is subject to disappointment. Miss F. appears, for example, en route to the second year's allotting duties, when the pair stops in Nebraska to check on the success of Fletcher's allotments there. Miss F., according to Gay's account, "had in mind the people she had left struggling to comprehend the new conditions she had brought upon them. They were babes suddenly raised to their feet and told to walk and her heart had ached for years that she had not a thousand hands to hold out to them. She had at last an opportunity to give them a lift. A fund of some $10,000 had been diverted . . . [to] help many to get on their feet." Gay compares Miss F.'s idealism to that of "a happy hen brooding a lot of helpless chickens, some of them with the bits of shell still sticking to their pin feathers." However, Miss F. did not accurately foresee that her Omaha charges had their own ideas about how to use the money. Rather than buying houses and farming implements, they elected to distribute the money equally among the group. Gay writes, "In the evening of the first day, I saw a disconsolate, puzzled hen. Her progeny were all ducks and had taken to the water. . . . The Omahas are full fledged and, in some sort of way, are paddling themselves in their sea of trouble."[71] Miss F.'s reaction is to "[turn] away, convinced that the only way she could help her old friends is the only way the government cannot sanction."[72] Such small hints of doubt and frustration, so inappropriate for a government agent and her staff, humanize the two women, highlight their emotional support of each other, and suggest that the strength of their friendship was a key factor in their persistent returns to Idaho over the course of four grueling summers to finish the work they had been assigned to do.

RESISTANT BACKS: "YOU" AND "I"

The most interesting—and most overlooked—facets of Gay's narrative personas, however, are "I," the first-person narrator, and the "you" this narrator creates. "I" is perhaps best captured in Gay's self-portrait (fig. 11 in the Introduction), whose gender is ambiguous and whose pose invites us to look over the photographer's shoulder and share her/his perspective. At the same time, in this image Gay is the object of two camera eyes—one within the picture plane that is controlled by the photographer and one that is invisible and that has produced this image. In the letters, "I" is sympathetic with the Nez Perces and willing to admit that his/her conventional notions have been modified by his/her experiences in northwest Idaho. S/he is also subject to the gaze of her/his readers and is determined to make that relationship apparent.

"I" and "you" appear most frequently in sections of Gay's *Red Man* columns that she did not transcribe into her scrapbooks. Her apparent intent was to use these personas to invite Pratt and his readers to imagine themselves in the situation encountered by Fletcher. They might, in the process, come to realize the irrationality of allotment. For example, the initial *Red Man* column directly addresses readers as "you," inviting them consider the extent of their knowledge of the details of the Dawes Act: "Do you know anything about allotting Indians?" the narrator asks, then immediately answers, "Not unless you have yourself tried."[73]

A second "you" participates in these accounts as well. In the earliest *Red Man* columns, Fletcher is consistently transfigured into "you." This transformation immediately follows the passage quoted above, and the reader, who has been hailed as "you," merges with Fletcher. "You start from Washington with instructions which read easy."[74] In Idaho, you (the reader and Fletcher) stand together before the assembled Nez Perces "and with reddened cheeks and stammering tongue, you try to impress them with the advantages of this little arrangement. . . . Your cravat is tight and you loosen it. There is a stricture about the cardiac region. You . . . look along the lines of dark faces. They do not light up as they meet your gaze."[75] Thus, "you" works to produce in the reader the same identification, involvement, confusion, and detachment that Gay and Fletcher experienced, demonstrating to the reader who takes the time to think about it that he or she is also of divided intent. Otherwise, how can "you" expect that Nez Perces will be made, with the stroke of an allotting agent's pen, into singular, unified, individual U.S. citizen-farmers?

The Dawes General Allotment Act did not, however, allow for ambiguity or mixed motives on the part of either its administrators or its subjects. The Nez Perces, already divided by the difficulties of the Joseph War, were seen by Fletcher and the government as a single tribe, composed of members whose identities could be precisely mapped, documented, and inserted into the fabric of allotment. Gay's images and letters, however, point to the damage that Dawes would do and invite readers to imagine how they would react to such strictures. By multiplying and dividing the principal actors, their readers, and their supporters, she brings into question the very notion of the self-determined and mappable individual.

"You" are also included as a viewer—and co-constructor—of Gay's most complex and interesting photographs. I have already discussed her predilection for taking back-shots of her subjects. Too often employed by Gay to be a sign of amateur photography, this technique invites viewers to recognize their complicity in the activities of allotment, to be wary consumers of photographic illusion, and, as Briggs in *Retracing a Former Survey* does, to resist the intrigue that would benefit whites as a result of allotment. As *Nez Perce Women at Well—Lapwai* shows, Gay puts the viewer in the position of looking with, rather than looking at, this group (fig. 32). The women, all wearing clothing that suggests both tra-

32. E. Jane Gay, untitled,
ca. 1889–1892.

Idaho State Historical Society,
Boise, Id. 63–221.295, titled *Nez
Perce Women at Well—Lapwai.*

ditional affiliations (the blanketed shoulders) and western accommodation (the
long dresses), are separated by a post-and-wire fence from a group of tipis and
A-frame tents, toward which all of them are looking. Have they turned their
backs on civilization, longing to return to the traditional lifestyles from which
the fence separates them? If so, the separation is incomplete, and the hybrid quality of the image suggests that the assimilation Fletcher sought to effect would remain imperfect.

"TO CORRECT THE ANGLE OF VISION"

In a letter written near the end of the first summer, Gay relates the pair's en-
lightenment at discovering several acts of charity done for them by elderly, cold,
and hungry Nez Perces. Having thought themselves to be cold and hungry, Gay
wrote, "It is good to be pinched a little: it teaches charity towards those who are
pinched a good deal. . . . It takes a bit of personal experience sometimes to correct the angle of vision." [76] An image whose arrangement challenges us to correct
our angle of vision in the same way, *Nez Perce Land Allotment—Trial Lots Case at
Ed Conner's Fish Camp,* will serve as a summary to the arguments I have pursued

here (fig. 33). It reminds viewers that the photographic surface is an illusion and is limited to two dimensions; that the photographic subject has three dimensions; that for every front there is a back. In choosing this angle, Gay is not bringing us behind the scenes but is subjecting us, along with the Nez Perces, to Fletcher's deliberations. Her angle of vision also places Fletcher under double scrutiny— the Nez Perces' and the viewer's—a photographic testament to Gay's under-standing that the process of allotment is being watched by invisible whites who, although they understand the law, will do all they can to subvert it and take all the arable Nez Perce land.

33. E. Jane Gay, untitled, ca. 1889–1892.

Idaho State Historical Society, Boise, Id. 63–221.85, titled *Nez Perce Land Allotment—Trial Lots Case at Ed Conner's Fish Camp.*

The ultimate effects of the Dawes Act were stultifying. After Fletcher's allotment, Nez Perce holdings were reduced to fewer than 200,000 acres; at present, they own just over 112,000 acres.[77] Michael McLaughlin summarizes the "broad range of contemporary issues" that have resulted from this watershed legislation:

On lands subject at some point in time to Dawes Act provisions, individuals (both natives and nonnatives), private enterprises, and tribal nations involved in seemingly mundane activities such as starting or operating a small business, buying and selling goods, renting land, determining child custody, improving property, negotiating small and large construction projects, cutting timber, hunting and rec-reational activities, controlling tribal resources, or enforcing tribal laws may find themselves involved in costly and time-consuming legal situations caused by these provisions.[78]

It seems clear, then, that Gay, through her letters and photographs, was aware of the contradictions implicit in the Act, which her friend had devoted herself to im-plementing. In this multitude of personas, the "real" Jane Gay remains a mystery, a presence not quite absent from her photographs, whose traces remain a silence, a fingerprint on a badly processed negative, a long intruding shadow in the fore-ground of a late-afternoon snapshot. Such shadows, absences, and ambiguities were part and parcel of Dawes, which sought certainty: erasure of Indian sov-ereignty, deeds, and tidy parcels of land aligned along Cartesian coordinates; tidy cabins housing heterosexual, monogamous families; voting Indian citizens. Certainty, a necessary fiction of imperialism, was maintained at great effort by Fletcher, whose strivings for documentary perfection established her reputation as a pioneering ethnologist. Gay's work, I suggest, provides a counterbalance and a necessary corrective to these official accounts. Taken entirely—including the fullness of the letters she included in her scrapbooks, the accounts she published during her lifetime, and the full archive of her photographs—her work offers us a much more accurate sense of allotment and its discontents.

NICOLE TONKOVICH

CHAPTER TWO

"I BECAME THE 'COLONY'"

Kate Cory's Hopi Photographs

In 1905 Kate Cory, a well-educated urbanite and commercial artist, forty-four years old and never married, bought a round-trip train ticket for a western tour. She was inspired by her friend Louis Akin, who painted promotional scenes for the Santa Fe Railroad and intended to establish an "artist colony" in Arizona on the Hopi mesas, where Cory planned to spend a few months. Akin gave up his scheme, but Cory, as the legend goes, got off the train at Canyon Diablo, promoted by the railroad as a tourist stop, and never used her return ticket. "Louis' plan did not bring the party to the reservation," she wrote, "and thus I became the 'colony.'"[1]

Unlike other Euro-American photographers of the Hopis, Cory lived in two Hopi towns, Walpi and Oraibi, for an extended period, from 1905 to 1912; there she took hundreds of photographs, such as fig. 34, many of which suggest a warm and spontaneous relationship with individual Hopis. Although she also took posed portraits and images of ceremonies, informality characterizes what I see as her most suggestive work. As an inhabitant of the mesas, she took many candid shots. One of her most historically significant shots, for instance, was totally unstaged: an image of two men wrestling on the ground in 1906, the only known photo of the struggle between two groups of Hopis, the "friendlies," who were willing to compromise with whites, and the "hostiles," or "unfriendlies," who were opposed to white interference.[2] This struggle between adaptation—or, in its more negative implications, assimilation—and tradition is a major theme in her photographs of the Hopis—and also in her own life. Her time on the mesas

34. Kate T. Cory, Hopi man, ca. 1905–1912.

Courtesy Museum of Northern Arizona, Flagstaff. MS-208 #75.629N. Kate Cory Photography Collection.

changed her life, leading to her rejection of early twentieth-century consumer culture. Like her friend Akin, she anticipated in her life choices and work the far better-known radicals who moved to the Southwest after World War I and who, according to historian Margaret Jacobs, cast "Indian culture[s] as the dichotomous opposite of white American culture . . . [in order to achieve] a critical perspective on modern America."[3]

After leaving the mesas in 1912, Cory spent the rest of an unconventional life in nearby Prescott, Arizona, dying in 1958. Her biography is filled with gaps, although her adopted town has claimed her through local newspaper articles and oral history as a town character, an eccentric artist who lived to be ninety-seven, an icon in Prescott's ongoing boosterism. Like another "spinster," Emily Dickinson, she is regarded as having been "slightly cracked." Stories emphasize her peculiarities: she used runoff rainwater in her darkroom to develop her photographs (picking out the dead rodents); she was a vegetarian who satisfied her sporadic hunger by sticking a spoon into a can of beans left for days on the back of her wood stove; she wore ragged, decades-old clothes that prompted her church to offer her decent attire; she designed upside-down doors for her house so children could not reach the knobs; she traded her paintings rather than selling them; she lived meagerly but gave away two houses to renters. Along with her more conventional and successful friend, the poet and state historian Sharlot Hall, she is part of Prescott's local color: her salty character adds flavor to Prescott's tourist industry. These anecdotes from oral history do, however, point to more significant recurrent rebellions in Cory's life: her willingness to make do with leftovers, to recycle; her disregard for material possessions; her tendency to barter rather than buy; and her limited appetite and consumption. All suggest why the pared-to-the-bones Hopi lifestyle attracted her and what she learned from her years on the mesas.[4]

Although Akin and many others sold their images of the Hopis and other American Indians to railroads, postcard companies, and businesses such as the Fred Harvey Company, which marketed "authentic" Indian products and people, Cory gave up commercial art in Arizona and apparently never peddled her photographs. Only a few appeared in her lifetime, primarily to illustrate her own essays and much later in biographical pieces in local Arizona publications. A cropped version of fig. 35 accompanied Cory's 1909 essay "Life and Its Living in Hopiland—The Hopi Women," published in a small monthly magazine devoted to western topics, with the caption "Hopi woman preparing to cook a rabbit at an outside oven."[5] The unusual floor-level camera angle, looking up at the woman, with the eye led toward her by the bowls on the floor, the sharp contrast in the textures of the physical world, and the use of dramatic light and shadow are characteristic of Cory's best work, as is the thematic focus on the woman's everyday work.

Yet the caption, with its specific ethnographic information, is inaccurate, prob-

35. Kate T. Cory, *Piki making*, ca. 1905–1912.

Courtesy Museum of Northern Arizona, Flagstaff. MS-208 #75.894N. Kate Cory Photography Collection.

ably provided by an editor rather than Cory. The Hopis certainly ate rabbits, but the bowl beside the woman appears to be filled with *piki* bread batter, and indeed the Museum of Northern Arizona, which now owns Cory's collection of negatives, captioned this photograph "Piki making." As we discuss in the Introduction, captions are often added to photographs—by the photographer or by others—to stabilize meaning, to define for viewers what they are seeing. Cory was aware of the need to use language accurately to communicate across cultures: she wrote her own dictionary to help her learn the Hopi language and kept a detailed ethnographic diary. She originally wrote captions on the back of her prints, but museum curators are unsure who copied the captions when the prints were mounted in her album, leaving us uncertain how reliably the album records her own comments on what she photographed. Yet many captions undeniably express her voice, wit, and opinions. She captioned an image of a shepherd and his flock "I got his goats" and an image of a man in Hotevilla "Unfriendly—but a fine man." Most of her negatives have been captioned by others. In a general article about Native American photographs, Joanna Cohan Scherer ironically suggests that "you can't believe your eyes," but dilemmas interpreting Cory's photographs often result from not being able to believe the words, from others' labeling, mislabeling, and omissions, as we shall see.[6]

Cory may well have begun taking photographs as raw material for paintings such as *Hopi Maiden* (fig. 42, discussed later). A successful painter, she exhibited in the 1913 Armory Show and later sold nine of her works to the Smithsonian. She left most of her others to museums in Prescott: the Sharlot Hall Museum, which owns twenty-one paintings, and the Smoki Museum, which owns eight paintings as well as her only known photograph album, containing small, contact prints of many shots the museum curators now feel are too fragile to be reproduced. Few knew about her private photographic archive, and the significance of her photographs went so unrecognized that the over six hundred negatives, made on nitrocellulose film, that she left in the museum were rediscovered only during a renovation project in the 1970s in a dusty cardboard box on a storage shelf. Negatives for many of the shots in the album are now missing. Looking for expert advice on preserving the negatives, the Smoki Museum turned them over to the Museum of Northern Arizona (MNA); for several years the two museums disputed who owned them.[7]

In the early 1980s, the MNA's director of photography, Marc Gaede, made prints of some of Cory's negatives, which he published in *The Hopi Photographs: Kate Cory: 1905–1912,* co-written with Barton Wright and Marnie Gaede; some images were also printed as posters. Because it contains many shots of secret ceremonies, the book was, and is, controversial.[8] Like many other tribes, the Hopis have asserted their rights to their cultural property. Working with the Hopis, the MNA has now placed many of Cory's negatives in a restricted file, where they can be viewed by researchers but not reproduced. None of these shots are reproduced in this volume. In the 1990s, the Hopis also asked the Smoki Museum not to allow researchers to quote from Cory's album the personal names of now-dead Hopis. The Hopis themselves are interested in using the Cory archive for what they can discover in it about their cultural history. I first encountered her images during a visit to the Hopi Cultural Center in 1996, where some of the posters made from Gaede's prints were on display. A few years ago the tribe received a grant to put the images on a CD-ROM in order to preserve them; during the time I was doing research at the MNA a young Hopi woman, Mary Tahbo, an anthropology student at Northern Arizona University, was working on the CD-ROM.

Although photographs certainly can provide viewers, Hopi or Euro-American, with historical and ethnographic information, this chapter does not focus on the ostensible subject of Cory's photographs, the Hopis, their ways of life, or their spiritual practices. The Hopis hardly need any more outside scrutiny; as anthropologist Albert Kunze points out, "No ethnic group of comparable size has had as much attention trained on it as the Hopi Indians of Arizona."[9] Cory's archive is really about the difference between "us" and "them" or, more accurately, "the idiosyncratic me" and "the representative them." Her interest in the Hopis, their art, and their various ways of life was genuine, but she used their "difference" as a way of defining her own differences with modern, urban life while retaining many of her claims to its privileges—as symbolized, for instance, by her possession of a camera. As James Clifford and George Marcus have suggested, "It has become clear that every version of an 'other,' wherever found, is also the construction of a 'self,' and the making of ethnographic texts . . . has always involved a process of self-fashioning." [10] It is equally clear that the construction of a "self" takes place within a social context, shaped by and reflecting social and cultural concerns. Cory worked within the visual vocabulary and the assumptions about "primitivism" she inherited from and shared with her near contemporaries, images and assumptions that circulated within the consumer culture she came to repudiate, often popularized by the artistic counterculture—the colony—to which she belonged.

Yet most of the photographers of the Hopis, passers-through, never saw them as anything more than exotic spectacle. I believe that Cory "encountered" the Hopis, to borrow Judith Fryer Davidov's term, which is to say that she was profoundly changed by them. [11] One key danger in focusing on Cory's self-creation and what it can reveal to us about her time—and ours—is that images of the Hopis become yet again a space Euro-Americans colonize for self-knowledge or for self-deception. Some might argue that in this reading Hopis become props in her photographs, contained in her aesthetic vision, characters in her story. That is not my goal. For theoretical underpinning, I turn to a contemporary Hopi, Victor Masayesva, Jr., photographer and filmmaker, who has written, "Photography is a philosophical sketching that makes it possible to define and then to understand our ignorance. Photography reveals to me how it is that life and death can be so indissolubly one; it reveals the falseness of maintaining these opposites as separate. Photography is an affirmation of opposites. The negative contains the positive." [12] I read Cory's photographs as a visual autobiography filled with reflections—of self and other. They define her experience and her ignorance. They remind us of the interplay between the negative and the positive. One of the few critics to write about Cory, Lucy Lippard, describes her as "enigmatic"—and I agree. [13] As Masayesva suggests, understanding comes from accepting the interplay between opposites. Cory's life was full of them.

Produced in a contact zone, in Mary Louise Pratt's terms, a "social space where disparate cultures meet, clash, and grapple with each other," Cory's work records exchanges—both positive and negative—between peoples, as exemplified in an image of a Navajo woman who has come to New Oraibi to trade goods (fig. 36). [14] I chose this image not for its aesthetic appeal but for what it chronicles. To borrow from Nicole Tonkovich, it is one of Cory's "banal" shots, a "snapshot" of a woman shaking out goods to display or perhaps preparing to pack up her horses. The separate background buildings, with their modern windows and roof lines, are not picturesque like the mesas themselves, but they make visible physical (ex)changes in the community. Some newly Christianized Hopis settled in New Oraibi after being banished from Old Oraibi, while others who chose to move there for its proximity to schools and a store sometimes were perceived as assimilationist. [15] The Navajo woman's presence and activity record the ongoing

36. Kate T. Cory, Navajo
woman at New Oraibi,
ca. 1905–1912.

Courtesy Museum of Northern Arizona,
Flagstaff. MS-208 #75.842N. Kate
Cory Photography Collection.

historical exchanges between desert peoples, which Cory often mentions in her diary and essays. And the shot captures another kind of exchange: this image of a woman engaged in trading goods is one of Cory's most overt images of "trading gazes." The adobe wall in the right foreground clearly positions Cory, who, it seems, has been watching the Navajo woman from around the side of the building. As she leans out to take the shot, she deflects the woman's attention from her own activities to her sudden movement. The image captures both the object of her gaze and the Navajo woman's irritated return gaze. While the man in fig. 34 looks away from Cory, it's clear he does so comfortably, feeling the shy absurdity many feel when asked to pose for close-ups, but the exchange in fig. 36 reveals Cory's stealth and the Navajo woman's wariness. The images of the smiling Hopi man and the resistant Navajo woman establish the difficulty of generalizing about the gazes we see traded in Cory's photographs.

And our generalizations about Cory's work are determined by our own positions as viewers, by what others choose to show us. For *The Hopi Photographs*, Marc Gaede chose to reproduce two different images of these same people. In a posed portrait shot at closer range or cropped, the Hopi man, wearing the same shirt but without the necklace, stands with his back to a building; he faces the camera directly, center frame, brow furrowed and much of his face in shadow, gazing forward seriously toward an apparently threatening future. Cut off at the waist, the Navajo woman rides horseback on a western saddle, the buttons on her velvet shirt reflecting the sun, her eyes averted from the photographer. The image is captioned "Proudly erect, a Navajo woman attends a horse race at First Mesa."[16] Both are far more handsome shots than the ones I've chosen, but, to my eye at least, the stories they tell are more static than active, less complicated and compelling, far more familiar. Throughout this chapter, I return to some of these issues: Who has the right to control and interpret what we might regard as Cory's intellectual property and to what uses should her photographs be put? I am also concerned with why certain images are compelling to certain viewers, with what images tell whose stories. But first it is important to establish the historical context in which Cory took her photographs.

Cory arrived late to the "colony," after some 350 years of efforts to profit from, subdue, and "know" the Hopis. The first of many Euro-Americans in search of various kinds of riches to plunder, the Spanish visited the area they called Tusayan in 1540 on Coronado's expedition. Between 1628 and 1633, in search of converts, Franciscan missionaries used Hopi labor to build three churches and accompanying missions on the mesas; this mission period ended with the Pueblo Revolt of 1680, when the Hopis killed four missionaries and dismantled the churches. In 1776, another Franciscan missionary, Silvestre Escalante, referred to the mesas as a "rebellious province" that imposed "formidable penalties" for talking to the fathers about religion.[17]

As we will see, Cory's photographs attest to the Spanish presence, to the history of asymmetrical religious exchange. In her view of Old Oraibi (fig. 37), she uses a wide angle to include what appears to be a church suggestively located on the far outskirts of the community. The MNA caption is "Old Oraibi—pre 1906. The old church is pictured." During the time Cory lived in Old Oraibi, its chief, Tewaquaptewa, enjoyed telling white visitors about the great beams lying in front of his house, remnants of the Franciscan mission destroyed in the Pueblo Revolt, and showing them the deep ruts worn nearby from logs Hopis had been forced to drag to build the church.[18] In the 1890s a new mission church was built by the Mennonite missionary, H. R. Voth. (It was destroyed by a fire caused by lightning around 1912.) This image suggests how iconographic and iconologic readings can work together to reveal Cory's attention, across time, to the presence of white missionaries at what is presumed to be the oldest continually occupied town in the United States. Although claiming that "few liberties were taken in the cropping of the negatives," Marc Gaede crops the right side of the image, the church. His caption suggests that he was also attempting to present a historical view, defined by a particular moment and by a date associated with the establishment of the nation that would follow the Spanish into the territory: "Oraibi as it would have been seen by Father Garces [sic] as he entered the morning of July 4, 1776."[19]

After the Mexican War, as the United States sought to take both physical and

37. Kate T. Cory, Old Oraibi, ca. 1905–1912.

Courtesy Museum of Northern Arizona, Flagstaff. MS-208 #75.1944N. Kate Cory Photography Collection.

intellectual possession of the Southwest, the Hopis became the objects of both scientific and commercial scrutiny. John Wesley Powell visited the "Moki" mesas on one of his scientific expeditions in 1869 and published an essay about his visit in *Scribner's Monthly*.[20] The first anthropological expedition arrived in 1879, sponsored by the Smithsonian and Powell's Bureau of American Ethnology and led by James Stevenson, accompanied by his anthropologist wife, Matilda Coxe Stevenson (who used a camera to document her research), Frank Hamilton Cushing, and the professional photographer John K. Hillers. That year the Snake Dance was first recorded by Euro-Americans, who found it perpetually fascinating. The local Indian trader, Thomas Keam, published an essay on the Snake Dance in 1882, the first to be written by a Euro-American eyewitness. He immediately grasped the opportunity and, according to Laura Graves, "never let another Snake Dance pass without capitalizing on the tourist business it brought to his trading post." Even before the railroads, Keam began to market the mesas as a tourist destination by providing the Smithsonian and other institutions with items of Hopi material culture for exhibitions; he brilliantly took the "artifacts" to the tourists to entice them to visit his trading post. While the scientists who used Keam's post as a home base collected some ten thousand items from the Hopis

and Zunis between 1879 and 1882, presumably for the purposes of documenting a culture, Keam's motives were commercial: as Graves argues, he was largely
responsible for demonstrating "the salability of Hopi material culture" by selling
over eight thousand pots and other items as well as "hundreds of kachina dolls,"
which had never before been marketed.[21]

Keam's "tourist business" was facilitated by changing attitudes about the
Indians. By the 1880s, the western tribes were perceived as subdued. The Euro-
American "discoveries" of southwestern Indian ruins and the work of ethnographers documenting the histories and cultures—particularly of the Pueblo tribes
—provided the United States with an "ancient history" promoters could capitalize on, an "*old* world instead of the *new*," as one said. Once "dirty aborigines," the
Pueblo peoples could be claimed as national ancestors: as a railroad pamphlet
pointed out, long "before the Pilgrims landed upon the shores of New England
. . . the great Southwest was peopled by a race who enjoyed a high degree of civilization." Their "high degree of civilization" did not protect them from objectifi-
cation: "the most important antiquities of the United States are the aborigines."
And even while using Indians as evidence of national superiority, southwest
tourist guidebooks made few distinctions among tribes with dramatically different life-styles and histories, though their comparisons certainly maintained class
distinctions: "the Hopis, Havasupais, Apaches, and Navajos are more picturesque
than the Swiss, Irish, Serbian, or Russian peasants."[22]

As "antiquities," the Pueblo Indians were statically pictured in a perpetual past,
their future assumed to be assimilation to the dominant white culture, which
would sadly but inevitably erase the cultural differences outsiders found so intriguing. Borrowing from anthropology, Philip Deloria changes the tense but not
the meaning: "the salvaging of disappearing Native cultures required imagining
them in a precontact 'ethnographic present' always temporally outside of modernity." He suggests that the "only culture allowed to define real Indian people was
a traditional culture that came from the past rather than the present."[23] Focusing
on cultural continuity and on change, Cory's work both supports and complicates this view.

Descriptions of ceremonies as spectacle persuaded tourists to come before
they were no longer practiced. (Ultimately, many ceremonies would be outlawed.)
Words evoked their romantic picturesqueness, but photography was the medium
that could best arrest the passage of time and document both material culture and
ceremonies. Rayna Green calls the North American Indians "the most photographed people in the world"; during the period before Cory's arrival at Oraibi,
certainly the Hopis were the most photographed tribe.[24] Between 1880 and
1905, they were extensively photographed by professional photographers such
as Hillers, William H. Jackson, Charles Savage, Adam Clark Vroman, Ben Wittick
(who died from a rattlesnake bite while participating in a Snake Ceremony), Jo
Mora, George Wharton James, Sumner Matteson, Frederick Monsen, and Edward S. Curtis, as well as by ethnographers such as Matilda Coxe Stevenson and

missionaries such as Voth. As Graves points out, "In 1895 the photographer Adam Clark Vroman saw his first Snake Dance and noted there were about forty tourists . . . ; in 1897, he recorded over two hundred tourists at the Snake Dance."[25] Many of these tourists brought their own cameras: "'Snap! went all the cameras,'" wrote Nell Clark Keller in 1905.[26] Cory criticized the presumptuous behavior of outsiders; in a long passage on tourists, she concludes, "We, the white people, have appropriated most of the best seats, by some assumed natural right. . . . The camera fiend, his pockets bulging with films and his brain with possibilities[,] has perched himself and herself everywhere, deep in devices for speed, focus, etc."[27] Such a passage suggests her doubled vision: she is part of the "we, the white people," who take over, act like colonizers "by some assumed natural right," but she, who is unobtrusive, hides behind walls, is not a camera *fiend*.

As photographers and tourists increasingly disrupted Hopi life, numerous documents recorded Hopi resistance to photographers. James acknowledged that he took many shots "in spite of the opposition of the Hopis." After being told by the governor of Walpi that he "must not take photographs," Monsen commented on the "diplomacy" he practiced to get good shots; one "method" was to use three "concealed" cameras worn under his "loose coat." Both Vroman and Voth are reported to have sneaked cameras into kivas; Leigh Jenkins, director of the Hopi Preservation Office, recounts how his "grandfather helped throw Voth out of a kiva during the Wuwuchim Ceremony. They held him flopped on the kiva roof, yelling and screaming. They had to throw him out four times."[28]

Cory was possibly the first white woman invited into the kivas, but she apparently respected Hopi wishes and took no photographs. Her many ceremonial shots focus on parts of the days-long ceremonies tourists apparently did not attend; or perhaps she simply managed to frame shots to exclude them, for her archive contains only a few images filled with Euro-American onlookers. She also reports in her diary being told that she would be welcome to enter a house only if she didn't bring her camera. Individual Hopis were certainly resistant to her presence, fixing her with hostile glares, as does a young woman whose image, surrounded by calico prints, suggests the intrusion of the "trading post"—and the Euro-American gaze—into traditional Hopi life (fig. 38). (The negative for this image is damaged.)

Yet many of the images made by Cory and the other photographers support Younger's contention that it "is obvious . . . that once initial objections were overcome, numerous photographers struck up good relations with individual Hopi. Comfortable smiles and relaxed poses characterize much of the photographic record." She does not mention Cory, but she provides a historical framework for the Hopi Cultural Center's display of her images: "From the start," she says, Hopis "readily accepted duplicate prints and often hung these images on the walls of their homes."[29] Nevertheless, during the time Cory lived on the mesas, the Hopis increasingly restricted photography, and in 1915 they banned it altogether.

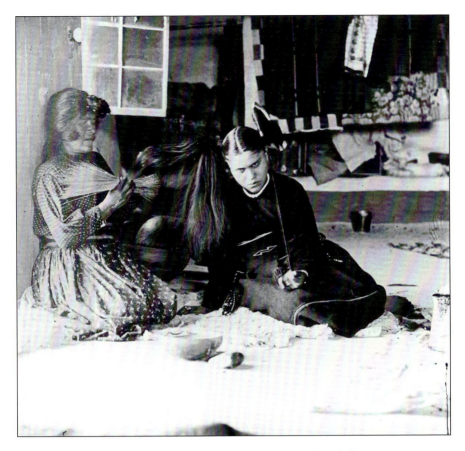

38. Kate T. Cory, *Young Hopi woman having her hair dressed*, ca. 1905–1912.
Courtesy Museum of Northern Arizona, Flagstaff. MS-208 #75.776N. Kate Cory Photography Collection.

Neither restrictions nor bans, however, could prevent the international circulation of photographs of the Hopis. In the 1890s photographs began to accompany essays published in popular magazines and ethnographic studies. Graves estimates that over "250 books and articles were written in English, German, and French about the Hopis between 1870 and 1900."[30] Railroad guidebooks published early in the century were accompanied by photographs by Vroman, Wittick, and James. Photographs were marketed as souvenirs. Keam sold photographs by Vroman in his trading post, while other Vroman images were made into postcards.

What created such an exploitable market for images of the Hopi and of other Pueblo tribes? Seen as agrarian, sedentary, and peaceful, with generally small populations inhabiting contained spaces, they never represented a threat to westward expansion, and, by century's end, they could be utilized as yet another natural resource to consolidate nationhood because of their obvious adherence to traditional lifestyles. Indeed, whites interested in the Hopis for both political and economic reasons occasionally intervened on their behalf. Partially because of Keam's lobbying of his Washington contacts, the Hopis were exempted from the Dawes General Allotment Act of 1887 and were "allowed" to live in their traditional way; unlike other ceremonies banned by the Religious Crimes Code (1900), the Snake Dance was never outlawed, perhaps largely because of lobbying by tourist promoters. Former president Teddy Roosevelt was one of the tourists at the Snake Dance in 1913. Although Roosevelt enjoyed the exotic spectacle, the Indian agents supported the Hopi ban on photography because they "believed that photographing ceremonies provided unwanted encouragement for the Indian to retain native customs and discouraged the assimilation of white ways."[31]

Cory photographed many ceremonies, but her work did not promote tourism nor did it particularly encourage or discourage assimilation. She did not sell her images. Images taken by Euro-Americans who hoped to sell their work were often intended to appeal to the Anglo gaze and to Anglo assumptions, and the fascination with the Hopis tells us about historical events occurring beyond the frame, generally far from the Hopi mesas—increasing industrialism and urbanization, assembly-line labor, spiritless modernist wastelands. The many images of Indian craftspeople suggest some of the reasons for the national fascination with the Pueblo tribes. The impulse behind such shots of Indian craftspeople at work is not only aesthetic but socioeconomic, grounded in a competitive, capitalist marketplace where workers are detached from the products of their labor. As critics such as Leah Dilworth have suggested, the many turn-of-the-century photographers offered the Indians up to Anglo consumption, to their appetite for a spiritual life apparently lived closer to nature, for an integration between work and everyday life, for a garden without machines. Cory certainly found these ideas attractive, but, for whatever reasons, her work did not enter the marketplace.

According to Younger, images of Hopis whose purpose was to attract tourists "tended to fall into two main categories: Picturesque configurations of everyday life and dramatic portrayals of ceremonial performances."[32] Cory's work often fits into these categories; some of her many images are predictable and stereotypical, while others stretch generic boundaries. Like Younger's, her work asks us to avoid generalizing from a few images, whether stereotypical or idiosyncratic, and to look at the photographer's full archive.

Younger points out two favored Hopi subjects for postcards. One was Hopi artisans, particularly the potter Nampeyo (Hopi-Tewa), who was "featured" for a time at Hopi House, which was built at the Grand Canyon in 1905 by the Santa Fe Railroad and the Fred Harvey Company and was designed by Mary Colter as a tourist attraction.[33] The other was "maidens" wearing the "butterfly" hairstyle, sometimes also called "squash blossom." Cory's interest in these subjects seems to suggest how strongly her thinking was infiltrated by the conventional visual vocabulary of her time. Yet the story is more complicated than that.

39. Louis Akin, *Hopi Weaver*, 1904.

Courtesy of Matthew Veazey.

In *Navajo and Photography*, James Faris uses "portfolios" to establish what he views as clichéd tropes of American Indian photography: "Loom" contains ten images of Navajo weavers, most resembling in some ways Curtis's repeatedly reproduced *The Blanket Weaver—Navajo* (1904) (fig. 10 in the Introduction) and no doubt thousands of snapshots taken at Fred Harvey stores.[34] Perhaps influenced by the composition of a painting by her friend Louis Akin (fig. 39), Cory produced similar generalized shots such as fig. 40. Images such as this one speak to a central conflict in studies of photography between aesthetics and politics, both approaches often historically oversimplified. With its intriguing verticals and horizontals and the parallel line between the loom and the weaver's arm, this is a lovely photograph; yet as Faris most vehemently among current critics of photography of American Indians would argue, it is stereotypical, apparently recapitulating the repeated image of the "primitive" Native artisan, faceless, generalized. (Ironically, though few Native artisans signed their work, preferring to remain "anonymous," within a few years, collectors would pay far more for a "signed" pot or basket or rug.)

Yet this apparently anonymous image also disrupts convention, records historical changes, and hints at cultural exchange. When I show this image to my students, they assume the weaver is a woman and a Navajo—and they assume they are reading ethnographically, distinguishing the cultural contexts at play in the photograph. They recognize the familiar Navajo style of rug and loom from images such as Curtis's, which saturate our contemporary culture; they may know that in Navajo culture women do the weaving, or they may simply assume that weaving, like other domestic chores, is universally women's work. If they're unsure, the weaver's bun certainly labels "her" gender.

But my students are actually reading iconologically, revealing the way cultural assumptions and knowledge, working on many levels, inform what we see.

40. Kate T. Cory, Hopi weaver, ca. 1905–1912.
Courtesy Museum of Northern Arizona, Flagstaff. MS-208 #75.819N. Kate Cory Photography Collection.

Cory's weaver is a man, performing a traditional male activity among the Hopis. Hopi men had used upright looms to weave cotton since around 800; their cotton cloth was a highly valued trade item among Indian peoples prior to white "contact."[35] In 1598, the Spanish introduced churro sheep and soon forced Pueblo peoples to herd their sheep, "knit wool socks for the use of settlers and for trade to Mexico, and weave woolen blankets." Probably it was the men who learned to knit. Crossing genders, Pueblo men taught weaving to Navajo women, probably after the Pueblo Revolt of 1680, when many Pueblos joined the Navajo to avoid Spanish retaliation. As Kate Peck Kent argues, their weaving had certainly been "'Hispanicized'" before they taught the Navajo.[36]

Cory's photographs cannot give us all this information, but they do chronicle it, and, ironically, my students intuit the long history of exchange of raw materials, practical skills, finished products, artistic traditions, the history of "trad-ing"—voluntary and imposed, pre- and post-"contact"—in the Southwest. That theme is subtly suggested in this image by the pattern, which points to various exchanges. The Hopi man has adapted the terraced Navajo design, which the Navajos themselves adapted from basketwork; Hopi designs, adapted from the Spanish, were, according to Kent, striped.[37] Perhaps he has also made some gen-der crossings, borrowing a Navajo woman's design.

Cory's weaver is a "traditional" Hopi, as suggested by his bun. Shortly before Cory arrived at the mesas, Indian Agent Charles Burton issued an order that any Hopi males who refused to cut their hair would have it cut by force. This order, along with reports of treatment of children at schools, led to a scandal precipi-tated by white supporters of the Hopis such as Charles Lummis, longtime friend of Theodore Roosevelt and editor of *Out West* magazine. Lummis published sev-eral editorials and articles; in one he referred to Burton as "the pinhead official . . . this oppressor . . . Czar over the lives of 1800 Hopi . . . that bully."[38] Burton was reprimanded but stayed on the job.

Thus, hairstyles on the mesas conveyed significant cultural and historical meaning. During Cory's years there, so-called progressive men (among the Hopi they were labeled "friendlies" by Indian agents and others) sometimes cut their hair. In fact, many of the men in Cory's archive have cropped hair, as does the man in fig. 34, while in most images leaders have longer hair. In other images, men's hair appears to be "growing out," perhaps attesting to the enforced hair cut-ting and to the man's politics. Although an image of a spinner (fig. 41) is certainly posed, one of a series of the same man taken at the same time, and although Cory is still as interested in her image's composition—its lines and textures, lights and darks—as in its subject, this shot of a man intent on spinning wool is not a fa-miliar or predictable image. Perhaps the man's position straddling shade and sun reflects the worlds he also straddles, which are visually conveyed in his cropped hair and Anglo clothes and in his skill at spinning wool, its presence in the South-west the result of encounters between the Spanish and Native peoples. Although romanticized conceptions of preindustrial labor may have influenced Cory to ex-plore the spinner's activities, she manages to see what he is doing with her own eyes and to suggest its historical resonance. Read anachronistically, her interest in weaving and hairstyles seems to indicate her recapitulation of conventional im-agery; read in the context of her time and place, it reflects one of the main themes of her archive: the interaction between tradition and change.

Yet Cory's numerous photographs of various women wearing the squash-blossom hairstyle, preliminary studies for her very conventional painting *Hopi Maiden* (fig. 43), tell another story. She apparently told a magazine writer, Harold Butcher, that she at least once prevailed on a Hopi to "dress up" in a culturally inappropriate costume and thereby created conflict among the Hopis. She "per-suaded a married woman to put up her hair [in the squash-blossom style] so that

41. Kate T. Cory, Hopi spinner, ca. 1905–1912.

Courtesy Museum of Northern Arizona, Flagstaff. MS-208 #75.865N. Kate Cory Photography Collection.

she could paint her portrait." Using stereotypical grammar, Butcher records what the woman, observed and confronted, may have told Cory: "The womans say I must not have my picture made with my hair like unmarried girl, and they are very angry with me. They say if I do not take it down they will come in and do it themselves."[39] In Cory's album, two images of a young woman are captioned "[Name deleted], unmarried girl with whorls which are never worn after marriage." Are the photographs "authentic"? The episode, the painting, and the photographs all represent a manipulative exchange between Cory and the woman and between Cory and her viewers, whomever she may have conceived them to be.

Yet by and large Cory recognized a difference between her photographs and her paintings, which were usually stylized and mythical: in *The Return of the Kachinas,* for example, a cluster of kachinas float down from the heavens toward a group of Hopis on a mesa. In contrast to Akin, she presents her weaver not as an exotic other in a loincloth but as clothed, wearing contemporary "white" clothing. Comparing the images points to the many difficulties in interpretation. Although Akin's image seems romanticized, in the summer's heat on the mesas the loincloth would seem the more sensible clothing. Perhaps Cory's weaver is

42. Kate T. Cory, Pottery firing, ca. 1905–1912.

Courtesy Museum of Northern Arizona, Flagstaff. MS-208 #75.968. Kate Cory Photography Collection.

43. Kate T. Cory, *Hopi Maiden*, ca. 1905–1912. Courtesy Sharlot Hall Museum, Prescott, Ariz. Kate Cory Collection.

dressed in winter clothing, or perhaps he is a "friendly" adapting to white culture. The temptation to "pose" her weaver in loincloth must have been great because she read differences in attitudes toward the body as evidence of how far white culture had fallen. Watching Hopi men on a ritual run in the desert, she wrote, "As they pass one cannot but admire their splendid bronze chests, broad shoulders, and well-shaped limbs, and, for the moment, well up with resentment at Mother Eve and Father Adam, . . . [who] forfeited us the privilege of living in the presence of our God-given bodies."[40]

Cory's images of human bodies producing pottery do not reinforce romanticized conceptions of preindustrial labor but instead disrupt convention. She knew Nampeyo, whose methods of work she described in her diary, and recognized her as a great artist; during a year of schoolteaching on the mesas, she taught Nampeyo's daughter (pictured in fig. 49 below). Yet I have been unable to identify any images of this celebrated artist in Cory's archive or any shots that appear to be posed. Her captions deromanticize the labor involved while providing ethnographic detail. She captioned fig. 42 "Ready to fire pottery which is done by burning sheep manure from corrals." This is no sanitized image of a handsome Indian craftsperson happily at work creating tourist trinkets. Cory sees a very individual older woman dirty from her labor, with a bag of sheep dung thrown over her back, engaged in a firing process most tourists would prefer not to contemplate. Not too happy at being interrupted or photographed, she does not perform for her audience. She looks back, and, in this exchange of gazes, she drives a hard bargain, capturing and conveying judgment of Cory's activities in her expression.

Images such as fig. 42 tell as full a story about the photographer as about the photographed. The Kate Cory we encounter today is created in the gazes we see traded in her photographs. They are a visual autobiography, telling us all we can know about the inner life of this enigmatic woman. She kept a written diary during her years at Oraibi, but it focuses on Hopi ceremonies and everyday life, telling us little—almost nothing—about her interior life. Even her autobiographical fragment, "Confessions of a Tomboy," contains nothing confessional or even particularly personal. We don't know why she left New York, why she spent seven years on the Hopi mesas, why she eventually left. Reviewers of a book she submitted in the 1940s to the University of New Mexico Press, *People of the Yellow Dawn,* commented on her absence from her own narrative: the book "was disappointing because it failed to tell more of Kate Cory—why she was there and what she did for five years." As with her photographs, Cory's writing focused on others but derived from her point of view. As another reader of her manuscript recognized, "The book in a way is a study of the Indian woman's mind. That is a natural consequence of the identity of the author [who is a woman]."[41]

The photographs, so much more descriptive and textured than her writing, reflect and reveal the "natural consequence of the identity of the author." Although an image such as fig. 44, of a Hopi woman carrying water, reflects Cory's artistic training, her obsession with form, line, and textural contrast, the shrouded subject, turned away from view, also conveys Cory's tendency to shield herself behind her apparent subjects. Politically and ethically, the photograph turns its subject, an individual woman with intelligence and agency, into an art object, aestheticizing her body and human labor, or perhaps into a projection of the photographer's personal concerns. Ethnographically, the image's generalization disrupts the project of providing specific and concrete cultural information. Artistically, its abstractions and spare formal properties anticipate the qualities Georgia O'Keeffe found so appealing in the Southwest—except that O'Keeffe, unlike her photographer husband, Alfred Stieglitz, never reduced a human body to an element of design.

The shrouded, mysterious self, with its spiritual overtones, recurs in many Cory photos, including the one I consider to be her most beautiful and evocative, which I cannot reproduce.[42] It is an image of a Hopi man, shot from below with an uphill rocky slope as background, a dark shawl enveloping his body and head. Wrapped within the shawl, against his body, he carries something. The caption in the MNA collection identifies the image as "A Hopi man carries a dead infant

44. Kate T. Cory, Hopi
water carrier, ca. 1905–
1912.
Courtesy Museum of Northern
Arizona, Flagstaff. MS-208
#75.920. Kate Cory Photogra-
phy Collection.

to the cemetery." While once again generalizing the individual man to a symbolic
abstraction, the image speaks powerfully of private pain. Yet although the shawl
shades the man's face and eyes, no doubt he, like the Navajo woman in fig. 36,
was distracted by Cory and her invasive camera. As Masayesva writes, "I would
risk generalizing. Hopis are very private, often secretive people who understand
the value of silence and unobtrusiveness."[43] Cory's image captures this "generalization" about the Hopis, at considerable cost to the mourning father. Ironically,
through her obtrusive camera, she projected her own concern with secrecy and
privacy.

Cory's candid shots of hidden or obscured selves are not always so intrusive,
serious, or romanticized. Although the MNA caption for fig. 45, "Hopi woman
putting bread in oven," leaves the baker without an identity, Cory provides her
with a face in her album caption, "My landlady [name deleted] tending the baking out of doors. Walpi." (Ironically, I cannot reproduce her name.) Formally,
Cory's eye was no doubt caught by the contrast between the lively print on her
landlady's calico skirt, the wrought iron grate with its Spanish echoes, and the
subtle textures of the hand-patted adobe walls. She captures the textures of this

woman's life. But her captions, as well as her diary and essays, also provide contexts that make the scene more revealing. She points out that among the Hopis women own and manage the houses; she also describes how women plaster the houses with their hands and maintain them. Although the landlady engages in a traditional women's activity, baking, the photograph alludes to a broader context for understanding Hopi women's activities: the traditional Hopi house belongs to the landlady, who rents out rooms to Anglos and does not wear traditional Hopi dress, yet cooks in a manner whites would see as quaintly primitive. Like many of Cory's images, "My landlady" records both continuity and change, conformity to tradition and flexibility about cultural adaptation.

What is known about Cory's background suggests that her own nonconformity was encouraged by both family and schooling. Born in 1861, she was raised in a prosperous abolitionist family in Chicago; her father was editor of the *Waukegan Weekly Gazette* and an active participant in the Underground Railroad. After a family move to New York, she and her mother stayed behind in Chicago for her to finish secondary school. In New York, she attended Cooper Union Art School, where young women were encouraged to aspire to professional lives. Mary Hallock Foote, influential illustrator of the West from the 1870s to the

45. Kate T. Cory, Landlady putting bread in oven, ca. 1905–1912.

Courtesy Museum of Northern Arizona, Flagstaff. MS-208 #75.895. Kate Cory Photography Collection.

1890s, had attended Cooper Union a generation earlier. Cooper Union students received strong training in art with a practical emphasis: it was assumed that they would need to support themselves. As part of that practical training in money-making media, photography was included in the curriculum. After graduating, Cory taught drawing at Cooper Union and practiced commercial art. She later studied at the Art Students' League. During her years in New York, Cory must certainly have encountered the influence of the Photo-Secession group of photographers, who were devoted to pictorialism, art photography, and formal experimentation. Stieglitz, their leader, founded *Camera Work,* where many published their work, in 1903, two years before she left New York.

Yet Cory had other influences in New York: two friends with whom she "shared her love of the outdoors," Ernest Thompson Seton and Grace Gallatin Seton-Thompson.[44] Ernest was a naturalist and, like Cory, an artist. Both Setons wrote books about their western tours. Ernest Seton's life fits a pattern discussed by critics such as Jane Tompkins and Gail Bederman, in which male writers and politicians made use of the image of the West and the development of the formula western to counter the perceived increasing effeminacy of turn-of-the-century men whose ties to the "primitive" had been severed by urbanization and industrialization and to construct a more "vigorous" masculinity. Seton turned to Indians. Having founded and popularized the Woodcraft Indians, a youth-development group, in 1901, he went on to cofound the Boy Scouts of America, while Grace Seton-Thompson and Cory were involved with the Camp Fire Girls. As Deloria argues in *Playing Indian,* Seton, faced like others of his generation with "the challenge of imagining an identity that was centered not so much on Europe and the legacy of the Revolution as on the angst that accompanied the crowded cities and assembly lines of modernity," believed that Indians offered "role models for American youth." Instead of consigning Indians to a "mythic frontier past," Seton "put them to far more complicated uses as manifestations of a modern-antimodern identity," in which they represented "positive qualities—authenticity and natural purity—that might be expropriated . . . as the underpinnings for a new, specifically modern American identity."[45]

Women, too, especially professional women, sought that modern American identity, and they too turned to the West and to Indians, according to Deborah Gordon, in a "search for different ways of being white and female," for "the reconstruction of themselves."[46] The West seemed to offer liberation from narrow roles—from corsets, literal and symbolic, and domesticity. Although many professional women initially went to the Southwest as moral reformers, seeking to suppress "primitive" sexuality and hoping to "uplift" Indian women, as Jacobs argues in *Engendered Encounters,* the post–World War I transplants turned to Pueblo women and "primitivism" to express "an acute critique of modern industrial life" and to redefine "womanhood, feminism, and women's sexuality."[47]

Although writing many years earlier, Cory's friend Grace Seton-Thompson also describes the West as a place of sexual liberation in her lively book, *A Woman Tenderfoot* (1900), where she plays Walt Whitman as a feminist, encouraging women to travel west "to acquire a new vocabulary and some new ideas" and inviting her reader to "come with me and learn how to be vulgarly robust." *A Woman Tenderfoot* is all about adventure and physicality; ignoring moral reform, even moving far beyond New Womanhood, Seton-Thompson ends her book with an orgasmic paean to primitivism: "I have felt the charm of the glorious freedom, the quick rushing blood, the bounding motion, of the wild life, the joy of the living and of the doing, of the mountain and the plain; I have learned to know and feel some, at least, of the secrets of the Wild Ones."[48] Perhaps the middle-aged Cory coveted that "quick rushing blood" and the release from conventionality the Setons connected with western life, where repressions could be cast off, and with "Indians," whose "secrets" provide antidotes to overcivilization.

Like Seton-Thompson and Cory, other turn-of-the-century women associated the West and "primitive" life with their desires for unconventional lives. To escape from her prescribed "rest cure," Charlotte Perkins Gilman left her locked room and her husband and moved in 1890 to southern California. One of Gilman's friends, Mary Austin, published in 1907 a story called "The Walking Woman." Burdened by responsibilities to others, an unnamed woman defies gender expectations, has a passionate affair, and then lives a solitary life wandering throughout the desert West. "She was the Walking Woman. That was it. She had walked off all sense of society-made values, and, knowing the best when the best came to her, was able to take it."[49] Although Cory could not leave behind all her cultural inheritance—indeed, her work never touches on sexuality—this epigrammatic line serves as a summary of what she wanted from the second half of her life. Like Austin, who claimed that from her study of American Indian culture and art she "learned to write," Cory appropriated from the Hopis what she needed in order to walk away from her society's expectations and to live her own life.[50]

In Deloria's and Jacobs's terms, Cory enacted, or perhaps confirmed, her modern womanhood through her relationships with the Hopis, though I don't believe she ever saw such a move, as Deloria does, as leading to "a position of cultural power."[51] She rejected the increasingly urban consumer culture of routine existence and critiqued the material culture of urban middle-class life. After a visit to a Navajo camp, she wrote, "I wondered why civilization has led us into such intricacies of equipment that much of our lives is spent in the proper care and adjustment of these timesaving implements."[52] Although she certainly did not reject the intricacies of her camera or binoculars (which she enjoying lending to the Hopis), when Cory moved to Prescott in 1912, Hopi friends helped build her first house there, a stone house based on Hopi architecture. A newspaper account reported that every household "article will be of Indian make, and not a vestige of the present civilization will be permitted in the building as far as the utility of

46. Kate T. Cory, Hopi woman in traditional dress, ca. 1905–1912.
Courtesy Museum of Northern Arizona, Flagstaff. MS-208 #75.666. Kate Cory Photography Collection.

the accommodations [is] to be considered."[53] Yet, unlike Schäffer and Nicholson and so many others who, in Molly Mullin's words, "approach[ed] the Southwest . . . as consumers," Cory was not a collector and never sold Hopi items. When a group of Hopis visited her in Prescott in 1933, she showed them some gifts she had received over the years, including a planting stick that, she said, had been given to her by a chief. After the Hopis told her it had been handed down "from generation to generation as a good omen for crops," she immediately returned it to them.[54]

Her photographs often reflect her critique of consumer culture and interest in Hopi material culture. Her caption for fig. 46 is "[Name deleted] wearing regular Hopi dress before white man spun, woven and dyed by hand." (In the MNA, this same image is paired with one of a man and is labeled "His wife?") Although the photograph performs "salvage ethnography," recording a mode of dress rapidly disappearing, as Cory comments in her essay on Hopi women, the image also points to changes in Hopi life resulting from trading with whites. On the wall behind the subject hang tools she may well have valued as the "timesaving implements" Cory finds superfluous. Unlike fig. 44, this image does not simplistically record the timeless "precontact ethnographic present"; it mediates between the past and the future. Cory's photographs vacillate between the two perspectives, often taking a naively critical view of cultural exchange and the physical symbols of assimilation, engaging in what Renato Rosaldo calls "imperialist nostalgia."[55] Using the ethnographic present to generalize, she concludes her essay on Hopi women, for instance, with this line: she "is an industrious worker, and withal a splendid specimen of primitive womanhood before whom civilization should think well and deeply in attempting to replace her ideals and customs with its own."[56] Here, as elsewhere, she anticipates later women who argue "that many traditional Indian cultures appeared far superior to modern American society."[57]

As this example suggests, consumerism has to do with the assignment of value. Cultures make meaning through material goods. "Implements" Cory took for granted and thus came to see as superfluous may well have been valued by the Hopi woman in fig. 46 as "timesaving," as helping her fulfill hopes for a slightly less "industrious" life. The traditional dress Cory finds appealing is the result of time-consuming labor, performed, as figs. 40 and 41 demonstrate, by Hopi men; yet her photographs of men weaving and spinning, with their emphasis on line and composition, implicitly suggest that weaving is an art, even a performance, not labor. Yet those very men are wearing white "work clothes" probably purchased at the trader's store.

Many of Cory's images explore the traditional labor of both Hopi men and women and its ties to cyclical patterns; she shot a predictable but beautiful series on corn, for instance, from the initial preparation of the field to planting, hoeing, harvesting, curing on rooftops (fig. 47), shucking, and piki bread making. In this series, men and women work separately but together in a mutually satisfactory division of labor, presented as natural, organic, healthful, tied to the earth, not as hard physical work. Offering an alternative to urban industrial work, such labor would allow the displaced modern to get in touch with his or her physicality, as is shown in this quotation from George Wharton James, one of many photographers of the Hopi, whose book, *What the White Race May Learn from the Indian* (1908), is yet another paean to "primitivism." "When I go into my garden to work, I put on blue overalls, a flannel shirt, and a pair of heavy shoes, and I try not to be nice. I roll around in the dirt, I feel it with my hands, I revel in it, for thus, I find, do I gain healthful enjoyment for body, mind, and soul. I owe many things to the Indian, but few things I am more grateful for than that he taught me how to value important things more than 'looking neat' and being 'nice.'"[58]

But Cory was not blinded by assumptions about idyllic primitive life, as can be seen by comparing her idealized image of the Hopi water carrier (fig. 44) with a passage from "Life and Its Living in Hopiland—The Hopi Women," where she writes, "One's pity grows, though, on watching the older women [Cory was at this time nearly fifty], on whom many of the heavy burdens seem unjustly out of proportion. The great corpulent water jar, which is full of five gallons, is a hard pull up a steep incline of half a mile or more, and many an uncomplaining little

47. Kate T. Cory, Corn crop covers the roof, ca. 1905–1912.
Courtesy Museum of Northern Arizona, Flagstaff. MS-208 #75.878N. Kate Cory Photography Collection.

groan escapes the lips at the top of the climb, if one is listening for it, but it is reckoned part of life with them, and accepted unrebelliously. It is part of 'the Hopi way,' and that is enough."[59] In passages such as this one, Cory certainly does not romanticize manual labor; rather, like the moral reformers, she sees Pueblo life as oppressive to women and separates herself from those "primitive" women who cannot or will not complain about their "plight." Yet, unlike the moral reformers, Cory did not see whites or white culture as superior. In her own life she picked and chose among cultural traditions and inheritances. Her work suggests that she saw the Hopis doing the same.

Although Cory was certainly fascinated by the material culture and ceremonies of traditional Hopi life and never advocated assimilation, she did not see the Hopis as living in an unchanging, idyllic, preindustrial, eternally harmonious community. Unlike Curtis's staged shots, her images recognize historical change. As I have suggested, she represented the presence of the Spanish in images of churches and material artifacts such as her landlady's gate, as well as the longtime exchanges between Hopis and Navajos. She noted in images and writing the conflict between groups within the Hopis, a conflict far more complex and longstanding than can be conveyed in words like *friendlies* and *unfriendlies, progressives* and *traditionalists.* Although she admired the beauty and grace of woven wool dresses, she wrote in one of her captions of a woman and child wearing machine-made fabrics, "The white man brought in his prints and calicos, more comfortable than the itchy woolen Hopi dress." Compare this pragmatic recognition that there might be practical reasons to adapt to a new style to a comment by Edna Fergusson in *Dancing Gods* (1931), who complained that the young Hopi girls who used to dance with their hair in squash blossoms "appear now in badly made calico dresses . . . from the stores."[60]

Cory, James, the Setons, Akin, Austin, Lummis, and no doubt many others were part of an avant-garde who preceded the well-known group of expatriate artists and writers who fled the East after World War I and settled in the Southwest. Like Jacobs's "antimodernists" and Lois Rudnick's "transcendental modernists," these earlier bohemians also rejected modernity and the city and looked to the Southwest to "help them to reunite body and mind and spirit and matter." Also like the later group, they were fascinated with "preindustrial communities for whom the arts were not compartmentalized" but instead were "intended to induce change in people, the land, or the climate, and to bring the listener-participant into 'harmony with the essential essence of things.'"[61] And so they romanticized American Indians; inspired by the abstraction and stylization of their arts, they often turned people into abstractions. "Every Indian woman is an artist,—sees, feels, creates, but does not philosophize about her processes," wrote Mary Austin in 1903 in a story called "The Basket Maker."[62] Although Austin philosophized about others in words, Cory did her philosophizing primarily in images.

Seeking new forms of writing and art, new ways to live, but generally isolated from the influence of organized art circles, Cory and the rest of the earlier group in many ways anticipated modernism; they might be seen as premodernists who rejected the "conspicuous consumption" described by Thorstein Veblen in 1899. Their isolation from dominant traditions led them to experiment rather than follow a shared ideology. Wealthy and well-connected, Mabel Dodge Luhan established her influential artist colony at Taos, something Akin, who died in poverty in Flagstaff in 1913, had envisioned many years earlier. Akin and Cory are largely unknown, while visitors to Luhan's house such as artist Maynard Dixon and photographer Laura Gilpin are famous.

Austin, throughout her life a political activist for Indian rights and other causes, later became part of the group in Taos and Santa Fe; members of this group, faced with the horror of World War I, believed that they could convince the modern world that "non-Anglo, nonwhite cultures had laid the groundwork for a vitalized American civilization." Although Rudnick rightly points out that the Euro-Americans' "hunger for spiritual and psychic renewal often blinded them to the more unpleasant social, political, and economic realities that surrounded them" and that, "in arguing for the importance of Hispanic and Native American peoples and cultures, . . . [they] were arguing for the importance of themselves,"[63] many of the later group became activists for a variety of American Indian causes, including water rights and land rights. Members of this group became particularly active in the Indian Arts and Crafts Movement and, in the early twenties, in the controversy over Indian dances, initiated by Circular 1665 (1921), which dramatically restricted dances. Cory also became involved in the Indian dance controversy, but in a typically idiosyncratic and quirky way.

Some years after leaving the mesas, Cory joined the Smoki People of Prescott, a group founded in 1921. Actually only men could officially be Smoki until 1931, when a "squaw" auxiliary division was created, but Cory and her friend Sharlot Hall worked closely with this group of prominent Anglo Arizonians, who dressed up as Indians and performed dances. The first dance, largely a burlesque, took place in 1921, part of a "Way Out West" pageant to raise money for the Prescott Frontier Days Association. But after 1922, when the group began to initiate members and work with Cory, they defined a more serious mission. According to Jennifer De Witt, quoting from Smoki materials, their "'sole aim' now was to perpetuate 'the Indian rites of the Southwest . . . commemorating the traditions of the early Indians.'" Participants and local residents credit this change to Cory: "Cory's experiences and her interest in promoting Native American culture were vital in the early years of the Smoki. Her critical artistic eye ensured the most authentic costuming possible. She also instructed the men in the proper performance and meaning of the dances and, on one occasion, took part in the presentation of the Hopi Flute Dance. A 1926 Smoki renegade credited her with 'guiding the organization away from a sort of parody of Indian activities' and stressing the sacred nature of the recreated observances."[64]

Meanwhile Hall, who "insisted that Kate Cory's direction lifted the ceremonies 'into an intellectual region,'" wrote the Smoki "mythology," publishing *The Story of the Smoki People,* with a cover by Cory, in 1922.[65] And yet another Prescott woman, Grace Sparkes, secretary of the Yavapai County Chamber of Commerce, saw the moneymaking possibilities and began to promote the dances as tourist spectacles, attracting hundreds every year. In 1925 Cory published her own account of the Hopi Snake Dance, perhaps originally written as instructional notes for the Smoki and entitled "A Realistic Story of the Great Hopi Indians," in *The Yavapai Magazine,* published by the Chamber of Commerce. The heading read, "Miss Cory's heart is with the Indians in their problems. She knows their wants as few white people do, for she lived many years among the Hopi People. ONLY WITH THE THOUGHT OF PERPETUATING THE SOLEMN RITES OF THE INDIAN CEREMONIES, AMONG THEM THE SNAKE DANCE OF THE HOPI, has the great idealistic work of the SMOKI PEOPLE been undertaken."[66]

Despite their "idealism," the Smoki People's activities were much criticized from their inception. Commissioner of Indian Affairs John Collier called the performances a "travesty."[67] Direct Hopi responses are unrecorded, but a resident of a rival town "referred to Indian complaints that their sacred ceremonies were 'being desecrated . . . for profit making exhibitions.'"[68] In defense, the Yavapai

Fig 48. Photographer unknown, Barry Goldwater dressed in ceremonial costume of a Smoki dancer, ca. 1940s. Courtesy the Arizona Historical Foundation, University Libraries, Arizona State University. #G–878.1.

County Chamber of Commerce suggested that the Smoki tried to re-create "in all reverence, the traditions, ceremonies and chants of the American Indians in a form that would appeal to the white man's mode of thought."[69] Later Prescott residents criticized the "ceremonies," often with humor. Calling the group's ideas "absurd, incredibly presumptuous, and in some cases, downright sacrilegious," John Hills suggested in the 1970s that "'a group of entrepreneuring Indians get together and put on their own pageant depicting and perpetuating the ceremonies, both secular and religious, of the white business man.'" Perhaps calling themselves the "Whiti People," they could substitute "attache cases for gourd rattles" and offer "ceremonies relating to annexation, city parking, industry enticement, and water prices."[70]

Fig. 48 shows one of the better known Smoki People, another photographer of Arizona Indians, engaged in a dance, probably in the 1940s—Barry Goldwater. Initiated in 1941, "Goldwater accepted and received the four tattoo marks each member bears on the side of his left hand." He often participated in dances and in 1964, the year of his presidential campaign, was "named an honorary chief, 'Flying Eagle.'"[71] A large Hopi protest in 1990 finally led to the end of the dances.[72] The museum the Smoki founded in 1933, with Cory's help, still exists today, housed in a beautiful building modeled after Hopi architecture and run by knowledgeable curators.

Like much of Cory's work, her involvement with the Smoki dances reveals the

49. Kate T. Cory,
Hopi schoolgirls in
cauldron, ca. 1905–
1912.

Courtesy Museum of
Northern Arizona, Flag-
staff. MS-208 #89.395.
Kate Cory Photography
Collection.

contradictions at play in the Euro-American fascination with Indians. Although she published in a Chamber of Commerce vehicle, Cory was no promoter after money. She envisioned other kinds of exchange. In "The Snake Dance and It's [sic] Origin," she wrote, "I like to think of the Smoki people as the 'white brother' who got separated in those old days coming out from the underworld at the beginning of things, and for whom the Hopi has ever since been on the lookout."[73] (Hopi oral history does contain stories about the arrival of whites, but not as "brothers.")[74] She certainly saw her role in the dances as educational, as promoting not tourism but more complex cultural understanding about Hopi traditions. And in the historical context of the times, with drastic prohibitions by various commissioners of Indian Affairs on the practice of dances and other religious rites, Cory and no doubt some of the Smoki genuinely believed they were practicing salvage ethnography, preserving what ethnologist Edgar Hewett called the "'rapidly disappearing splendor' of 'our redman.'"[75] But in the Smoki's reproductions of Hopi dances, as in Cory's photographs, the representation of the Hopis was in the hands of outsiders.

Throughout her fifty years of engagement with the Hopis, Cory believed her work advanced white knowledge of and respect for a particular nation and its unique cultural traditions. Late in her life she tried to publish two books, *People of the Yellow Dawn,* based on stories she wrote while living on the mesas, and *Children of Hopiland,* based loosely on the year she taught school. For the cover of the second book, she intended fig. 49, labeled "The school—Walpi. Just happened to catch them in this cauldron; used for boiling clothes. Center girl is daughter of

Nampeyo, the famous potter, [name deleted], by name. [Name deleted] at right
—[name deleted]—left." As her album demonstrates, some of Cory's best shots
are of children, with whom she seems to have had warm relationships. Perhaps
in these images the childless Cory practiced her own kind of reproduction. Her
album contains a shot captioned in Cory's distinctive voice "Mother and twins.
Hardly the vanishing race." Her book would have demonstrated that the Hopis
were hardly a vanishing race and that their cultural traditions were still practiced,
but no presses were interested.

Why should we be interested in Cory and her photographs more than sixty years
later? Figs. 50 and 51 provide one answer. They are two in a series Cory took of
a woman; in her photo album Cory captioned these pictures "Unfriendly, Hotevilla with the traditional corn pollen on her face." Although the woman's resi-
dence in Hotevilla suggests that she was determined to resist white intrusions

50. Kate T. Cory, *Young married woman with corn pollen and braid*, ca. 1905–1912.
Courtesy Museum of Northern Arizona, Flagstaff. MS-208 #75.889N. Kate Cory Photography Collection.

51. Kate T. Cory, Young married woman with corn pollen and braid, ca. 1905–1912.
Courtesy Museum of Northern Arizona, Flagstaff. MS-208 #75.891N. Kate Cory Photography Collection.

into traditional Hopi life, she does not resist Cory's camera or gaze. As with other series in Cory's archive, the subject eventually "cracks up." Was her laughter the result of feeling silly? Something Cory said? In either case, the full series suggests that she was responsive to Cory's curiosity, was enjoying the encounter, and was certainly not "unfriendly" to all whites, only to their government. In *The Hopi Photographs,* Marc Gaede reproduces a more formal portrait, at much closer range, probably cropped, of the same woman smiling gently, her head tilted to one side. The two far more casual images I've chosen reflect more fully the subject's engagement with the photographer.

In *Looking for the Other,* E. Ann Kaplan makes a distinction that relates to these two photographs: "I will reserve the term 'look' to connote a process, a relation, while using the word 'gaze' for a one-way subjective vision," she writes. "Looking will connote curiosity about the Other, a wanting to know (which can of course still be oppressive but does not have to be), while the gaze I take to involve extreme anxiety—an attempt in a sense *not* to know, to deny, in fact."[76] Certainly we discern Cory's gaze in some of her photographs, a gaze characterized less by the anxiety and denial Kaplan explores than by Cory's aesthetic and personal desires. Some images—I think particularly of the image of a man carrying his dead child—seem "predatory," as defined by Susan Sontag: "There is something predatory in taking a picture. To photograph people is to violate them by seeing them as they never see themselves, by having knowledge of them they can never have; it turns people into objects that can be symbolically possessed."[77] But these two images reveal Cory's ability to "look"; they connote a process, defined as much by the woman with corn pollen as by Cory. Cory does not "capture" a view of this woman unfamiliar to the woman herself; instead she reveals the woman's self-knowledge and self-possession.

Of course I cannot prove that point; my conclusion is based on a purely subjective reaction to the woman's expression. Yet as discussed in the Introduction, Lippard had a similar reaction to Schäffer's portrait of the Beaver family, which exposed, she felt, "their undeniable personal presence."[78] "Meaning," say John Berger and Jean Mohr, "is discovered in what connects, and cannot exist without development. Without a story, without an unfolding, there is no meaning. . . . An instant photographed can only acquire meaning insofar as the viewer can read into it a duration extending beyond itself. When we find a photograph meaningful, we are lending it a past and a future."[79] That is exactly what Lippard does with the Beaver portrait, which she says "commemorates a reciprocal moment (rather than a cannibalistic one), where the emphasis is on interaction and communication; a moment in which subject and object are caught in exchange within shared time."[80]

This chapter chronicles my engagement with Kate Cory and her photographs, images I find meaningful. Although I certainly have told a story, I have purposefully tried not to make an argument about what other viewers should "read into" Cory's archive, what meaning they should develop. But I will say this: unlike some recent critics who have narrowed their lens to focus entirely on the all-too-visible shortcomings of Euro-American photographers and writers who attempted to "encounter" and celebrate "others," constrained by the assumptions of their historical time and place, I would use a wider lens to allow us to see what Masayesva sees in photographs, that "the negative contains the positive." I would follow the lead of another Hopi, Ramona Sakiestewa, who, in an essay on Mora, the photographer whose work most resembles Cory's, points out significant differences among Euro-American photographers of the Hopis, suggesting that, along with his extended time at the mesas, Mora's "artistic sensibilities and his own personal philosophy somehow allowed him to see the community with different eyes."[81]

Cory's eyes were certainly "different" from those of her Hopi neighbors, and yet one wonders how seven years of living on the mesas changed her vision. In *The Object Stares Back: On the Nature of Seeing,* James Elkins argues that vision inevitably "entangles us in a skein of changing relations with objects and people. . . . Vision helps us to know what we are like: we watch versions of ourselves in people and objects, and by attending to them we adjust our sense of what we are. Because we cannot see what we do not understand or use or identify with, we see very little of the world—only the small pieces that are useful and harmless. Each act of vision mingles seeing with not seeing, so that vision can become less a way of gathering information than avoiding it."[82] Cory used her life with the Hopis

52. Victor Masayesva, Jr., untitled, ca. 1980s.

Courtesy of Victor Masayesva, Jr.

to "adjust" her sense of self and change her values, but the attention she paid to them in her photographs also expanded what she was able to see and begin to understand of the world. Mingling seeing with not seeing, her photographs show us what we cannot understand and lead us to ponder what we, products of our own time and place, are unable to see.

Images and activities Cory recorded continue to be favorite subjects of contemporary Hopi photographers. One of the best known, Masayesva, has published photographs of Hopi men weaving, food production, groups of children, and women with corn pollen on their faces (fig. 52). His image of a dignified and serious contemporary woman provides a suggestive counterpoint to Cory's laughing "unfriendly" one. Although Faris would argue that such similarities in subject demonstrate that even the visual vocabularies of contemporary Indians have been infiltrated and dominated by Anglo ways of seeing, I suspect Masayesva would not agree. Nor do I. "For me," Masayesva says, "photography is a way of imagining life's complexity. . . . It is something I do personally because it leads me to some satisfactory understanding of that complexity."[83] I'll leave you to ponder—not judge—whether Cory came to some satisfactory understanding of life's complexity and whether she represented it in her photographs.

MELODY GRAULICH

CHAPTER THREE

MARY SCHÄFFER'S "COMPREHENDING EQUAL EYES"

On a crisp late summer day in the Canadian Rockies in 1907, two travelers crossed paths on the road into Banff. One was the British writer Rudyard Kipling, whose "white man's burden" defined both an attitude and a policy toward people of color in the age of empire. The other was Mary T. S. Schäffer, a well-off Philadelphia widow and amateur photographer, whose hand-colored lantern slides of alpine flora had won her some smaller renown. That two Anglo travelers would have encountered one another along a rugged road in the Canadian Rockies was not as unusual as it sounds. After all, the completion of the Canadian Pacific Railroad in 1885 made journeys through the mountain passes possible, and the network of railroad-owned hotels along the way could even make them pleasant.[1] But while Kipling rode decorously in a carriage on his way to the hotel, Schäffer and her party plodded in on horseback, four months' worth of camping gear strapped to the backs of ragged pack ponies: the two could not have had more different experiences of the Canadian wilderness.

Kipling viewed the ostensibly primitive landscape from the safe confines of rail car and carriage. His was a carefully choreographed journey to collect picturesque specimens for literary preservation and to promote his own reputation. He remained safely in the company of tour organizers and literary supporters, delivering genteel lectures to local admirers and in the process disseminating and reinforcing the assumptions that validated the expansionist policies of Britain— and of the United States—in the West.[2] In contrast, Schäffer moved within what Mary Louise Pratt calls "'contact zones,' social spaces where disparate cultures

53. Mary Schäffer, *The Headwaters of the Athabaska*, 1908.

meet, clash, and grapple with each other."[3] In the relatively unsettled and isolated wilderness area that was later to become Banff and Jasper national parks, she rode and camped and washed her socks out by hand in mountain lakes. Her "summer homes" ranged from desolate, mosquito-infested wetlands to sunny valleys at the foot of spectacular waterfalls (fig. 53).[4] Her social life included dinners with homesteaders, tea with prospectors, and shopping expeditions with Indian craftswomen. She cherished, she tells her readers, the name Yahe-Weha, or Mountain Woman, given her by two Stoney families she had befriended in 1906; this self-fashioning reveals how deeply she aspired to see herself as explorer and how much she valued what she knew of Indian life.

But however her experience differed from Kipling's, their encounter was nonetheless one of social equals, co-conspirators in the construction and dissemination of the Canadian Rocky Mountain West and of Euro-American views of its Native peoples; and like him, she chronicled her adventures in print, publishing a popular travel narrative, *Old Indian Trails of the Canadian Rockies* (1911), and preparing, over the course of several decades, scripts for hand-colored lantern slides of the region. This chapter explores where and how Schäffer's vision coincided with and diverged from that of the Kiplings of the nineteenth century by looking both at her published travelogues and photographs and at the unpublished materials she chose to exclude. How are we to read her engagement with Indians, and especially Indian women, and why does it matter?

Indeed, these travelers recognized their cultural kinship and viewed both themselves and the other with self-conscious irony. Kipling recorded the incident: "As we drove along the narrow hill road a piebald pack-pony with a china blue eye came round a bend, followed by two women, black-haired, bare-headed, wearing beadwork squaw jackets and riding straddle. A string of pack-ponies trotted through the pines behind them. 'Indians on the move?' said I. 'How characteristic!' As the women jolted by, one of them very slightly turned her eyes, and they were, past any doubt, the comprehending equal eyes of the civilized white woman which moved in that berry-brown face."[5]

Schäffer, too, registered a double take along that literal and figurative road that divided Kipling's "civilized" world from the ostensibly "savage" life of Yahe-Weha:

> Three days' easy travel brought us out on the Emerald Lake road near Field. Special toilets had been arranged on the previous afternoon: sundry grease-spots had been removed from our skirts, a scarlet neckerchief had been washed, some wool shirts ditto, two or three pairs of shoes, with toes and heels intact, came up from the depths of the duffle bags, and shaving soap had been liberally laid on. A smile of sincere admiration went round when we collected to behold our united elegance of appearance on the morning we started for our last ride.
>
> And then we struck the highway and on it a carriage with people in it! Oh! The tragedy of the comparison! The woman's gown was blue. I think her hat contained

a white wing. I only saw it all in one awful flash from the corner of my right eye, and I remember distinctly that she had *gloves on*. Then I suddenly realized that our own recently brushed-up garments were frayed and worn and our buckskin coats had a savage cast, that my three companions looked like Indians, and that the lady gazing at us belonged to another world. It was then that I wanted my wild free life back again, yet step by step I was leaving it behind.

We entered the little mountain town of Field. . . . Then we grasped the hands of waiting friends (who told us it was Mr. and Mrs. Rudyard Kipling we had passed on the road,) and fled from the eyes of the curious tourist to that civilised but perfect luxury—the bath-tub.[6]

The scenes echo with shocks of recognition. Kipling mocks his own conventions for seeing the other, recognizing his instant capacity for assigning the travelers to his imperialist taxonomy of the West. But he also confirms his own visual expertise: although he admits he first sees an "Indian on the move," it takes only a slight turn of the eyes for him to recognize Schäffer as white and "civilized," "comprehending" and "equal." Schäffer too mocks her own ostensibly reluctant complicity in the canons of civilization. Although she initially shares a "smile of sincere admiration [at her party's] united elegance of appearance," her sudden awareness of a lady's gloves reminds her that indeed they "looked like Indians": the comparison is a "tragedy." Although she longs for her "wild free life," "waiting friends" lead her to the bathtub that reinstates her in the civilized world. So transformative is the bath that later Kipling is surprised again, as he walks through the hotel lobby and sees her: "the same evening, in a hotel full of all the luxuries, a slight woman in a very pretty evening frock was turning over photographs, and the eyes beneath the strictly arranged hair were the eyes of the woman who had quirted the piebald pack-pony past our buggy."[7]

Like many of his class and race, Kipling was deeply concerned with understanding how clearly to define and maintain the boundaries between "Indian" and "white." A complicated calculus linked whiteness with civilization, with superiority, with power.[8] Kipling's inability to recognize Schäffer as "equal" to himself, however briefly, threatened the hierarchies on which lay the cultural authority of whiteness. For Kipling, her eyes continually contradicted the outward trappings of her attire and her setting; they hinted at some alternative identity, suggested some alternative way of seeing that discomforted him. But if she challenged Kipling's assumptions, he also challenged her: she was no Indian, regardless of external signifiers (buckskin jacket, bare head, riding astraddle a pack pony). Her "wild free life" was the temporary indulgence of the leisure-class white woman.

Certainly, Kipling was right to see Schäffer in these terms, for she herself was also concerned about her temporary misidentification as Indian. She after all felt her difference from the lady in gloves to be a "tragedy," fled to the bathtub, and put on an evening gown. With intentional irony she played the invaded object of the tourist's picturesque fantasy before she sought refuge in the "civilised but perfect luxury" of the tub. Her writings and her photographs all tacitly acknowledge her own position as white and wealthy, a "lady" with a degree of mobility and opportunity denied to people of color. She mocked her own ignorance about the land she rode through, recalled her naiveté about the West. Schäffer did indeed long for her "wild free life," symbolized for her by "the Indian," and yet she was aware that she remained within the tourist's metaphorical hotel lobby. As Philip Deloria puts it, she was "playing Indian"; her fascination with Indians had more to do with her own biography and her shared Euro-American obsession with "primitive" cultures than it did with Indians themselves.[9] Schäffer used Indians, and especially Indian women, as a vehicle for living out her own aspirations and for reworking a lifelong fascination with the "primitive."

But there are important differences between Kipling and Schäffer too, differences that encourage her readers to see beyond the carefully codified imperial iconography that structured even domestic images in the West.[10] Kipling perceives Schäffer's eyes as "comprehending" and "equal," but Schäffer sees the Kiplings' "curious" gaze as "belonging to another world," disconnected, yet possessive. In spite of the "pretty evening frock" and "the strictly arranged hair," she asserts that Yahe-Weha is at least in some capacity an earned and internalized identity. Her longing for a "wild free life" tells us something important about how she differed from Kipling. She had a lifelong investment in learning to see across the lines that Kipling worked so hard to erect and police. In fact, buried within the photographs she was so carefully turning over in the hotel lobby were some of Canadian First Peoples that still startle the viewer, so different are they from the turn-of-the-century European and Euro-American renditions of Indians we are used to. Had Kipling paused to look over her shoulder, he might well have seen one of her most recent pictures, the well-known and stunning family portrait of Stoneys Sampson, Frances Louise, and Leah Beaver (fig. 12 in the Introduction), an image Lucy Lippard calls "a miscocosmic triumph for social equality as expressed through representation."[11] It would no doubt have been a view of the Canadian Rockies unlike any other in his thoroughly civilized tour.

Schäffer published this remarkable photograph in her 1911 *Old Indian Trails* with the caption *Sampson Beaver, His Squaw, and Little Frances Louise;* the reference to Sampson Beaver's wife as "squaw" grates on contemporary viewers, who recognize this term as a racial slur and one with sexual implications.[12] It was a word Schäffer made easy and frequent use of, even, as we shall see later, referring to herself as a "white squaw," in a move that asserts her persona as Yahe-Weha. Her use of the term reveals her own unacknowledged and culturally conditioned racism: even as she sought to connect with Indian women across racial lines, she nonetheless conceived of them in impersonal and derogatory language. But the image itself belies the troubling title: a man and a woman sit on the grass in translucent sunlight, smiling directly into the camera, with a small girl between them. Behind them, white birches stretch delicately to the sky; leaves fade into soft focus, while in contrast the figures in the foreground are sharply etched. Their expressions are friendly, confident; his arms are folded, echoing his crossed legs; her hands are clasped in her lap as she sits back on her legs. Between their still, relaxed figures, the child is radiant energy injected into the soothing and pastoral scene: her head tilted, she beams at the photographer, a spray of leaves in one hand. No doubt told to stand still, she almost bursts out of her skin with the effort of it, arms outstretched, preening with delight. The three are dressed with conventional signals of "Indian-ness": braids and moccasins, buckskins and necklaces, a studded belt for Leah, and beaded leggings and a headband for the child. The woman wears an apron over a flowered dress; both she and her daughter have neatly arranged scarves around their necks.

Even without the identifying caption, sentimental conventions of family portraiture suggest that this is indeed a nuclear family. They are clearly secure with one another and with the occasion, returning the camera's gaze with their own. It is an image powerfully at odds with those we are more accustomed to seeing: of Indian parents deliberately contrasted with their "civilized" children; of single individuals in studios or otherwise isolated from their homes and families; of resistant prisoners, numbed children in boarding schools, defeated Indian leaders. It references Schäffer's sentimental investment in Indian families and her fascination with the stereotypical and colorful trappings of "the Indian." But it also and simultaneously reveals her relationship with the Beavers and, more important, theirs with her. They escape the flattened surface of the image long enough to register not so much their resistance to, but their temporary dismissal of, the pictorial conventions they might otherwise be subject to. In this, they are joined by Schäffer, who also, in this image, resists. I don't know whether Kipling ever saw this picture. But if he had, it is tempting to wonder whether he might have looked at Sampson Beaver and seen there, also, "civilized" and "comprehending equal" eyes. After all, for all that their attire suggests an alien culture, Sampson Beaver and his family seem remarkably familiar, even now.

Why begin this chapter, about a Euro-American widow expatriated to the Canadian Rockies, in a book about photographs of Native peoples, with the patrician observations of a British imperialist? Kipling's remarks encapsulate Euro-American attitudes toward Native peoples at the turn into the twentieth century. Scholars from a variety of disciplines remind us that those decades were a cultural moment in which "wilderness" places and indigenous peoples seemed to offer promise as objects of aesthetic, anthropological, and scientific study for Euro-American writers, artists, and anthropologists as diverse as Mabel Dodge Luhan, Frank Hamilton Cushing, Henry Adams, and Mary Austin. Kipling's focus on this incident, initially recorded in a letter to his son and later reworked and published as *Letters to the Family,* reveals not only his conventional perceptions of the North American West but also the degree to which he believed his fascination with the respectable Victorian lady he perceived to be cross-dressing as Indian would strike a chord with his British and American readers. He writes from within the colonial fantasy that the exotic primitive world is classifiable and containable: the Rockies are "wild"; Schäffer is a heroic—if racially suspect—explorer; he and his wife travel comfortably by rail across Canada sending home charming letters and sketches to their children, collecting material for future magazine articles, essays, and colonialist fiction. Kipling's reactions, in short, are a synecdoche of the context in and against which Schäffer lived and worked.

But for all his myopic colonialism Kipling saw with uncanny accuracy the two identities Schäffer struggled to reconcile: the straitlaced Victorian lady, at home in the tea parlor and concert hall, and the wild and free mountain woman, friend to Indians, homesteaders, trappers. Indeed, even the photographs we have of her speak to the same division that Kipling saw. A 1907 photograph taken by her traveling companion Mollie Adams shows Schäffer on her horse (fig. 54). The photograph appears as the frontispiece to *Old Indian Trails of the Canadian Rockies*, highlighting her role as author and explorer. The forty-six-year-old Schäffer is at some distance from the camera, set against a wide frame of snowy mountainside, standing timber, and knee-high wildflowers and grasses. Her features are barely discernable; but she faces the camera with her head up and her eyes alert. Significantly, she sits astraddle wearing a long riding skirt, not the trousers she normally wore on the trail; she has on a light shirt front, her favorite fringed jacket, a scarf knotted around her neck, and a battered, wide-brimmed hat. Nibs, her "Indian-bred pony," is a rugged and solid horse, well suited to hauling a sturdy rider over rough terrain; his tack has clearly been selected for comfort rather than looks; and his shaggy coat betrays his outdoor life. None of Schäffer's traveling companions, let alone the twenty or so pack horses, with their bundles of tents, camp utensils, camera equipment, and food, appears anywhere within the frame. She seems to be alone, empty-handed, in a mountain wilderness; the caption (*Nibs and His Mistress*), her own, signals both her ironic self-effacement and her genuine desire to shift the focus from herself to, in this case, the horse. The photograph highlights Schäffer as an exotic type in her own right, the lady adventurer in control of herself and her horse and comfortable with her place; it erases the considerable money, effort, equipment, and hired expertise that made such an identity possible.

The other Schäffer Kipling detected reveals herself in another photograph, this time in her Banff home and probably taken in the late 1910s; it was a Christmas gift to her Banff friend Mary Vaux (fig. 55). Although closer to the camera than in the picture with her horse, Schäffer here is neither centered in the frame nor facing the unknown photographer. Instead, she is profiled, to the right of the carefully bricked fireplace, her head and eyes tilted down and away from the photographer, as if caught in meditation. This is, significantly, a more common pose than facing the camera, as she does on Nibs; in most of her photographs she approaches viewers at this same oblique angle, like the one she presented to Kip-

54. Mollie Adams, *Nibs and His Mistress*, 1907.
Courtesy Whyte Museum of the Canadian Rockies, Archives and Library, Banff, V527/PS-1, Mary Schäffer Fonds.

ling. She is conventionally dressed in a short-sleeved and carefully trimmed gown with a light underskirt. She looks surprisingly uncomfortable: although the sleeping dog at her feet and her relaxed upper body would suggest repose, her lower body, with awkwardly crossed legs—an athletic pose—seems to indicate a kind of restless desire to be up and moving. The photograph, set in the living room at Tarry-a-While, again displays her surroundings more than it does her, and it also reveals Schäffer's dual allegiances: eighteenth-century English and American antique vases, fine porcelain, polished andirons, and an Eastlake mirror mix with smooth-grained Canadian fir planking on both floors and walls and an Indian

55. Photographer unknown, *Mary Schäffer at Home at Tarry-a-While*, ca. 1920.

Courtesy Whyte Museum of the Canadian Rockies, Archives and Library, Banff, NA 66–527, Mary Schäffer Fonds.

rug. Certainly the items all are personally significant. Inscribed on the back of the photograph is a note to Vaux: "A little corner of 'Tarry-a-while.' I wonder if thee will recognize any of the trimmings." The whole scene looks vaguely incongruous, as indeed does Schäffer herself; she seems more at home on Nibs than at her own fireside.[13]

Indeed, Schäffer's texts assert that she has come to know the Canadian wilderness and its people. A few of her images also, such as the portrait of the Beaver family, transcend the limitations imposed by convention and subject position. Unlike, for example, Frances Benjamin Johnston or Gertrude Käsebier, who photographed Indians in the domestic tranquility of their Washington and New York studios, Schäffer, like Jane Gay, Grace Nicholson, and Kate Cory, relocated to the West and photographed in the field, without the benefits of paid commissions or extensive professional training.[14] Her life was changed by what she saw and by those she encountered in the West. Her response to Kipling attempts a counter-narrative to his colonialist discourse, much as her photographs attempt a counter-archive to the flattened and depersonalized images of Indians taken by Edward S. Curtis, Adam Vroman, John N. Choate, and other would-be chroniclers of the "vanishing race" of Native North Americans. Schäffer's visual and written records thus reveal the contradiction at the heart of her meeting with Kipling, a contradiction that structured her work and her life. Inconsistent and unrealized, she presents us with a cautionary tale of good intentions rendered incomplete by acculturated perspectives and racialized visions. However sympathetic to and engaged by difference, Schäffer's views, like Kipling's, were formulated and articulated through the language of nineteenth-century imperial culture.

Certainly the complex history of Native peoples in the region is not visible in Kipling; nor is it present in *Old Indian Trails of the Canadian Rockies,* the 1911 travel narrative based on Schäffer's summer trips of 1907 and 1908. By the first decade of the twentieth century, the area around Banff was the shrinking homeland of the Stoney. Stoney are closely related linguistically and culturally to the Assiniboin and the Dakota and trace connections to the Sioux nations that live throughout the plains on both sides of the U.S.-Canadian border. They are the northwesternmost Siouan-speaking people and the only ones to live entirely within Canadian borders, mostly in Alberta and eastern British Columbia; their language is Nakodah, meaning "the People." The Stoney arrived in the Rockies in the eighteenth century, in an effort to escape smallpox epidemics; theirs is a familiar story of treaties breached by encroaching white settlement and "civilizing" efforts, of food supplies eradicated through mismanagement and inept government policies.

In 1877, Treaty Number 7 had deeded reservation land near Morleyville in Alberta to the Stoney, but by the time Schäffer traveled near Banff, those lands were coming under increasing pressure from mining and timber interests, farming, and tourism. The Indians she met in the mountains in 1907 and 1908 still held onto traditional lives, hunting and trading, many in small familial bands who followed seasonal changes at a series of longstanding home sites. Some were Christianized (Morleyville was named for the Methodist mission that had been established there in 1873), while others, such as Hector Crawler, insisted on maintaining the Sun Dance and other traditional sacred ceremonies and beliefs and even, in 1914, inaugurated a revival of the Ghost Dance religion at Morleyville. Many small bands organized by families—the Crawlers, the Wesleys, the Beavers—remained intact, but other Stoney intermarried with white homesteaders, trappers, and railroad workers. By 1900, bison herds were seriously depleted, and Stoney became well used to earning a living in the context of the tourist industry; Banff's "Indian Days" powwows had begun in 1889, the year Schäffer first visited the Rockies. The Stoney had to walk a fine line between maintaining cultural traditions and adapting to new industries, between keeping their cultural traditions alive and preserving the sanctity of sacred ceremonies, especially in an era when tourism, with Stoney as key and exoticized props, was becoming the dominant industry. By the time Schäffer died in 1939, regulations governing Canada's rapidly expanding national-park system, not only in Banff and Jasper but also in Yoho and Kootenay, restricted hunting in much of the land Treaty Number 7 had guaranteed the Stoney; and several decades of forced education at boarding schools threatened tribal affiliations, languages, and traditions.[15]

Schäffer likely knew relatively little of this history, and, in any event, it was not a part of her carefully crafted text, which was designed to appeal to nature enthusiasts, armchair tourists, and devotees of the "primitive." Instead, her narrative foregrounded hardy and competent campers in a glorious mountain wilderness; to illustrate the text, Schäffer chose one hundred photographs, mostly of mountain scenes, from among a larger archive of photographs she took during those summers. Widely circulated and well-received, *Old Indian Trails* and its unpublished leavings provide an entry into a network of intersecting stories, both about Schäffer and her contemporaries and about the ways in which we struggle to understand their legacy.

First, the story of the North American West is itself a complex web of many stories, told from many and competing points of view. Schäffer cannot be read simply as complicit with a colonial conquest of Native peoples and their land; although she is part of that history, she resisted the more blatant and exploitative activities of many of her generation. However, we should not see her as feminist heroine; her activities rested on a complex and powerful set of institutional and cultural privileges to which she had access by virtue of her gender, her race, and her class. Instead, her archive reminds us that white women and men interacted with Indians in many and contradictory ways, along a spectrum of engagement, and with contradictory motives, equivocal outcomes, and varied intentions.[16]

Second, Schäffer's photographs of Indians place in vivid relief both the possibilities and the failures of a gendered vision of the West; she provides an important glimpse into the central contradictions that structured white women's views of the colonized world. Schäffer's most transcendent images and her most empathetic writing come at moments when she sees herself in communion with other women and particularly with Indian mothers: a striking but not surprising pattern. Like many other women writers, she attempted to activate the sentimental notion that female empathy might resolve the differences between herself and the Native peoples of the land she was romantically attached to and that, by extension, empathy might reconcile contradiction. Her perceptions of Indian women allowed her to reconstruct white female identity as mobile, free from social convention, at home in both literal and metaphorical wilderness areas.[17] But although she claimed sisterhood with Indian women, across lines of color and class, she could not extend her empathy to those whose own stories did not yield to the sentimental stereotypes of Indian madonnas and sanctified children.[18]

Third, Schäffer's texts remind us that photographs, like all cultural texts, have different meanings and are put to different purposes over time. To reexamine them is to raise questions of subject, attribution, and context and to place those at the center of still turbulent pasts and ongoing political struggles. In her effort to achieve a cohesive reading of events, Schäffer carefully shaped her telling of these encounters for publication in her book, and she documented them in carefully chosen photographs, out of hundreds taken. Her encounters indeed suggest rich and complex stories, but they inevitably are framed by the partial and cropped lines of individual perspectives and unknown histories, and the careful control over events cracks as the contexts that surround them are reconstructed. Other versions of events appear in the diaries of Mollie Adams and in the unpublished manuscripts of the Schäffer archives; and unchosen photographs comment on the published versions. The record as a whole reveals the difficulties contemporary scholars have with reading photographs: How are we to recover the frames surrounding the images, and to what end? It highlights the problems inherent in recovering the history of Euro-Native interactions: What histories have been lost, and how might they be reconstructed? It insists, moreover, that scholars recognize their own investments in the material as well as those of the figures in the text: Is it possible for Euro-American writers—or Euro-American scholars—even temporarily to inhabit a conceptual and literal space governed by a Native viewpoint—what Patricia Penn Hilden calls "the Red Zone"?[19] Schäffer's work suggests some of the problems and the possibilities of working with photographs in the context of Native history.

Schäffer's photographs therefore reopen what is for some critics a closed question. Kipling's attitude toward Schäffer mirrors, albeit with more irony and in many cases more tolerance, the attitude of many scholars today toward women (and men) like her. We are skeptical, quick to recognize the very real imperialist implications of their presence in the West, their participation in the policies of expansion that led to the destruction of Native cultures and Native communities. As scholarly studies such as those by Leah Dilworth and by James Faris remind us, photographs intended to be sensitive to Indian cultures recall to us a history of exploitation, asymmetries of power, and domestic complicity with an imperial and genocidal policy toward Native peoples. Even an exceptionally subtle critic such as Laura Wexler or a sympathetic one such as Judith Fryer Davidov struggles to articulate how someone like Schäffer, so much the product of white privilege and class advantage, can achieve a moment of empathy with her photographic subjects. As Wexler puts it, borrowing a phrase from Davidov, "Turn of the century 'women's camera work' naturalized the domination it was designed to document."[20] Schäffer's images epitomize this dilemma: they do not contradict the widely held skepticism that contemporary scholars hold toward those who, at the turn of the century, photographed people of color. She does condescend toward, package, and objectify her photographic subjects, both in the pictures and in how she writes about the encounters.

But just as Schäffer was the "civilized white woman," with all the associations implied in the phrase, so too was she Yahe-Weha, struggling to enact some resistant stance to the notion of civilization articulated by Kipling. In this, she participates also in another discursive tradition extant during her decades of travel in the Canadian Rockies, the one identified by Sherry Smith as that which "reimagined Indians." Smith argues that writers like Schäffer "wished to shape Americans' views of the Indian culture in their midst." "Astoundingly simple messages such as Indians are human beings, Indians have families that love one another, and Indians carry on lives of religious beauty and deep spirituality served to counter deeply held notions that Indians were more bestial than human, had little sense of connection to family or home, and were pagans." Smith acknowledges that the move to reimagine Indians as full and equal subjects was a partial, equivocal, and incremental process, often articulated through unexamined racist assumptions. Nonetheless, she argues, the efforts of artists, writers, and other popularizers of the North American West to recognize Indians neither as exotic features of the landscape nor as unidimensional representatives of an alien culture but simply as neighbors and friends was a significant departure.[21] To the extent that Schäffer shared those views, she participated in a long, slow, and as yet incomplete movement toward a more nuanced historical and political understanding of Native cultures by the dominant culture. She straddles not just the line Kipling identified, between the primitive and the civilized, but also the crucial but subtle distinction between those who recapitulated racist conceptions of Native North Americans and those who struggled to see differently.

Mary Schäffer's childhood friends might have been as hard-pressed as Kipling was to recognize her along the road into Banff. The unorthodox middle-aged woman Kipling encountered on the road to Banff came from unimpeachable mid-Atlantic Euro-American stock. Mary Townsend Sharples Schäffer Warren was born in 1861, a wealthy Pennsylvania Quaker of Anglophile parents. As the pampered daughter of an upper-class household, she was educated at the Friends Select School in Philadelphia and schooled in handiwork and the fine arts by private tutors. Like many well-off girls, she studied what one newspaper profile called the "old fashioned accomplishments of knitting, embroidery, and every phase of needlework" and had "a perfect genius for millinery."[22] More mundane housekeeping skills were not her forte; she admitted that "I did not know how to make a bed at the tender age of 18."[23] She read extensively, learned the conventions of polite conversation, and developed her talent for drawing and painting through serious study. But she also excelled at mathematics and natural history, interests fostered by her father, Alfred, an amateur mineralogist whom Mary accompanied on local research trips. She was part of a cohesive Philadelphia social network of well-to-do business people, professionals, and naturalists, a network that would extend throughout her life and reach into the heart of the Canadian Rockies.

She met Dr. Charles Schäffer during her first trip to the Canadian Rockies, with friends, in 1889 and married him shortly thereafter. Charles was also a member of Mary's Philadelphia social circles, a prominent physician and passionate amateur naturalist. Indeed, the only remarkable element of their union was the age difference: he was more than twenty-five years older. Sharing an interest in recording and classifying the natural world, they returned to the area around Banff starting in 1891; there Charles indulged his passion for botany, and Mary assisted him, at first sketching and painting his specimens and later developing a system for photographing them and hand coloring the images. So successful were these photographs that in 1900 she was solicited for participation in Johnston's series for the *Ladies' Home Journal,* "Notable American Women Photographers."[24]

But in 1903 Mary Schäffer's life was transformed when her husband and parents died within a few months of each other. Alone and unchaperoned for the first time in her forty-two years, she took charge of her finances first and then her life: "all this taught me such a bitter lesson, to count my pennies, to lean on no one, and make the best of the crumbling fortunes."[25] A year later, financially secure, she decided to return to the Canadian Rockies, intending to complete her husband's proposed botanical guide. She persuaded Stewardson Brown, the curator of the Herbarium of the Academy of Natural Sciences in Philadelphia, to coauthor the work: he would provide the botanical expertise, she would supply the field notes and the specimens; he would get primary publication credit. In middle age, with comfortable means, good social connections, and unimpeachable motives, she went alone to the West to camp, in the first of a series of trips that transformed her life, in a period when the region she adopted as her home was changed in equally dramatic ways.

To complete the fieldwork, Schäffer needed to move beyond the areas closest to the railway. Although she had briefly horse-camped in 1893, she had not especially enjoyed the experience, so it was with some reluctance that in 1904 she approached her former guide, Tom Wilson, with a request for someone to acclimate her to trail life. Wilson introduced her to Billy Warren, an English veteran of the Boer War, who was nineteen years younger and whom she nicknamed Chief. Schäffer began a series of summer camping trips with Warren, which became longer and more rigorous as both her enthusiasm and her expertise increased. Schäffer was therefore led into the wilderness by someone who had been directly involved in the work of building the British empire—an Imperial Yeoman, no less. Although Schäffer funded the annual expeditions and decided on destinations, Warren took complete charge of the logistics of travel: he bought horses, hired help, planned and purchased supplies, taught Schäffer to ride and set up camp, determined the pace and route for their trips. Although Schäffer cast herself as heroic explorer, as in the photograph with Nibs, she nonetheless acknowledged her dependence on Warren.

Moreover, Warren's vision, his assumptions, and his values framed the context in which she came to know the wilderness. In many ways, her association with Warren literally as well as figuratively enlarged her vision. In 1900, Schäffer had thought of herself as a photographic "realist": she produced "not pictures but records, and preferred botanical studies to mountains, which are too massive."[26] By 1907, she was clearly comfortable not only with mountains but with glaciers, rivers, rugged trails, and campsites. Originally trained to see photographs as documentary evidence or as enhancements of scientific texts, she came to understand that photographs could also depict relationships, aesthetic tastes, and social values. Schäffer's camera eye expanded as she went into the mountains, just as her life's possibilities opened.

She camped for several months in 1905, 1906, 1907, and 1908, with Mary "Mollie" Adams, a geology teacher at Columbia College. In the winters, Adams returned to teaching; Schäffer retired to Philadelphia, where she developed a reputation for her sketches and lantern-slide lectures of the Canadian Rockies, which she delivered to both scientific groups and lay audiences. In 1907, she illustrated *Alpine Flora of the Canadian Rocky Mountains,* a compendium of her husband's work finished by his colleague Stewardson Brown.[27] That summer, she and Adams planned their most ambitious trip yet: four months on horseback, "with a vow not to return till driven back by the snows."[28] They were inspired, Schäffer claimed, by their envy of the men they watched set off from the railroad stops and by their increasing recognition that the wilderness experiences that fascinated them were at farther and farther removes from their usual destinations. Finally, she said, "We looked into each other's eyes and said: 'Why not? We can starve as well as they can; the muskeg will be no softer for us than for them; the ground will be no harder to sleep upon; the waters no deeper to swim, nor the bath colder if we fall in,'—so—we planned a trip."[29] The two women hired Warren as their guide; Warren in turn hired Sid Unwin and assembled a string of horses. For four months, the group camped throughout a relatively uncharted region near what are now Banff and Jasper national parks. Schäffer spent the winter writing up her experiences, publishing several well-received essays in newspapers and in the journals of the Geographical Society of Philadelphia and the Alpine Club of Canada. So successful was the 1907 trip that the group repeated it in 1908, this time inviting Brown and a cook.

Then, in the winter of 1908, Schäffer and Adams traveled to Asia, where, in Kobe, Japan, Adams suddenly died. Encouraged by her family and especially her favorite nephew, Eric Sharples, Schäffer set about writing a book about their last trips together: it appeared in 1911 as *Old Indian Trails of the Canadian Rockies,* her best-known work. Increasingly lonely in Philadelphia and homesick for the mountains, in 1912 she settled permanently in Banff. In 1915, she married Warren; in age, training, temperament, and occupation, it would have been hard to find a man more different from Charles Schäffer. But just as her first husband had been engaged in extending taxonomic control over the land, her second was as deeply invested in extending economic control over the region: Schäffer married not only her guide but also someone as committed as she was to promoting the

Rockies as a tourist destination. If to her family and friends her resettlement to Banff at the age of fifty-one and her marriage at age fifty-four to a thirty-five-year-old man may have seemed, to put it mildly, unusual, Schäffer never mentioned it. Although she was much older and much wealthier than her young husband, he was, she claimed, "my Chief," a title that conferred on him masculine authority and appropriated for him Native identity.

As she had helped her first husband with his work, so too did Schäffer help her second, funding his economic enterprises and participating in his political ambitions. By 1920, Warren was the owner of the Alberta Hotel and the Cascade Garage; he founded Rocky Mountain Tours and Transports, a motorized transportation company; and he was active in Conservative Party politics, becoming close friends with R. P. Bennett, the parliamentary representative from Calgary West who was later to become prime minister of Canada. Schäffer and Warren were by all accounts a well-suited if unconventional couple, independent in their social lives but united in their desire to develop in Banff a community that both celebrated the wilderness experiences they enjoyed and was fully integrated into Canadian national politics. Banff changed quickly from an exotic outpost to an important tourist destination. Schäffer records relatively few encounters with other white travelers in 1907, several more in 1908, but by 1911, when her book was published and Schäffer again camped for an extended summer, this time with her sister-in-law and her nephew, her publisher could sanguinely describe the area as "the vast mountain playground of the Canadian Rockies."[30] Schäffer maintained an active interest in wilderness activities even as she herself slowed down; she was a founding member of the Trail Riders of the Canadian Rockies and claimed she logged over eight thousand miles. She died in 1939, having willed her personal possessions and papers to a family friend, who in turn donated them to what is now the Whyte Museum of the Canadian Rockies in Banff.

As did Kipling, Schäffer's Banff neighbors recognized her as having affiliations with both sides of Banff culture. As an early newspaper article put it, "Astride her surefooted little Indian pony and in her khaki saddle suit, topped by a hunter's picturesque felt hat, Mrs. Schäffer has hardly a sister's likeness to the mistress of her Philadelphia drawing room, rich in its belongings of heirlooms."[31] Her legacy in Banff similarly consisted of an uneasy coexistence of different values: although she often lamented how "civilization" had encroached into her beloved wilderness, in her 1939 obituary she is "credited with starting the first real flow of tourist traffic to these parts."[32] She participated actively in western Canada's economic development, followed political and scientific movements in Canada and the United States, popularized tourism and travel, but she was also what T. J. Jackson Lears has called an "antimodernist": her affection for the West was predicated on her positing it as an antidote to the more destructive forces of the modern, commercial, and industrial world. She championed what David Shi has called "the simple life," one in which harmony with the natural world replaced urban alienation and fostered mental and physical health.[33] In the opening of *Old Indian Trails,* she explicitly addresses these concerns. "Why must so many cling to the life of our great cities, declaring there only may the heart-hunger, the artistic longings, the love of the beautiful be satisfied, and thus train themselves to believe there is nothing beyond the little horizon they have built for themselves? . . . Can it be possible to see in such a summer's outing, one sight as painful as the daily ones of poverty, degradation, and depravity of a great city?"[34] Even in Banff, Schäffer lived and worked in a space between an embrace of the modern world and a critique of it.

The contradictions of Schäffer's life, sometimes perverse and sometimes appealing, inhabit *Old Indian Trails of the Canadian Rockies.* The book was well reviewed, particularly in the eastern United States, where she was able to capitalize on the popularizing of the West and its indigenous peoples. If *Alpine Flora* had been a testimony to her husband, *Old Indian Trails* was dedicated "To Mary Who With Me Followed The Old Indian Trails But Who Has Now Gone On The Long Trail Alone." It records "Incidents of Camp and Trail Life, Covering Two Years' Exploration through the Rocky Mountains of Canada," punctuated with, the publisher tells us, "100 Illustrations from Photographs by the Author and by Mary W. Adams, and a Map." As the lengthy subtitle suggests, the book is a self-conscious and hybrid text, in turn a comic tourist travelogue, an amateur naturalist's journal, a parody of the explorer's record, a disapproving index of civilization's reach, a sincere celebration of sublime landscapes, a satirical look at the discomforts of camping. Performing "exploration" against the backdrop of the developing tourist economy, Schäffer is an appealing narrator who doesn't take herself too seriously: she anthropomorphizes the pack horses' idiosyncratic behaviors, chides herself for her prejudices against unkempt men, satirizes the "excellent book on camping" that provides a vile recipe for pinole, a form of ground, roast corn that even the horses scorn. Those "100 Illustrations" include unspectacular distant mountains (one even titled *It Certainly Was a Dreary Scene!*), untidy campsites, disorganized packhorses, scruffy fellow travelers, and lots of downed timber.[35]

Schäffer's text is remarkable for how its appeal obscures the contradictory impulses and desires that structure a Euro-American imperial view of the "wilderness," a view that still informs white, middle-class, urban fantasies about the Rockies and, as Deloria reminds us, about Indians. Schäffer drew on existing literary and photographic models: her photographs of the Canadian Rockies and the Native peoples who lived there borrowed from the well-known visual idioms of U.S. Geological Survey photographers such as Timothy O'Sullivan and John Hillers; and she bears comparison to other writers of Euro-American women's travel narratives, such as Isabella Bird and Mary Kingsley.[36] She defuses these comparisons with gentle self-mockery and irony. She is clearly disdainful of what she calls the "imperial tourist," whose attraction to the wilderness is to "capture" as many summits as possible before returning to "civilization." She mocks the desire to find an "innocent" or authentic wilderness, both in others and in herself.[37] *Old Indian Trails* thus provides a comic and ironic look at masculinist narratives of exploration: the men hunt, fish, explore the lakes and summits, build a raft so that the party can venture out onto Lake Maligne.

Yet, as Schäffer never forgets, the men are hardly engaged in the kind of exploring usually celebrated in those works. Instead of heading up government or scientific excursions, Chief and K (Unwin) are young men charged with taking care of two well-off, middle-aged women who want to camp. The adventure is the women's, and it is a significant one for them. Schäffer manages through comic self-effacement to express the women's adaptation to the very real rigors of the trip—their equanimity, their toughness, their willingness to handle discomfort and uncertainty on the trails—without succumbing to self-aggrandizement. Quite the opposite: she describes her and Mollie's contributions to the daily running of the camp as those of more conventionally domesticated women; they wash, darn, repair tents, sometimes cook inexpertly. Indeed, Schäffer relishes her wilderness housekeeping both in the book and in the archive. Among the discarded photographs, for example, is a comical image of an afternoon when the men went off to hunt for fresh meat for supper. She and Adams remained demurely in camp to mend equipment, bake bread, and, through their trusty spyglasses, search the mountain slopes for signs of wild goat (fig. 56). In the book, Schäffer even celebrates a vigorous day hand-washing some especially ripe blankets: "When I saw the last of those four men, I knew what was going to happen." She heads to the shores of icy Lake Maligne: "What a grand day that was in camp, not a soul to pry into our domestic efforts! . . . With a lake of clean water, with soap, energy, and sunshine, I saw a chance [to wash smelly blankets]; and washing as the wash-ladies of foreign lands, the blankets were soon sweet and dry in the hot sunshine."[38] Thus, built into the narrative voice is both Yahe-Weha's sense of adventure and Mrs. Schäffer's sense of Victorian propriety. Her written and visual work is therefore both complicit with and resistant to the interlocking ideologies of gender and race that mark colonial literary and visual practices— most specifically in her case, those of the female tourist and traveler.[39]

The photographs that illustrate the book extend and complement the written text. They are a kind of currency: they sell her book to nature enthusiasts, readers of travelogues, and would-be adventurers. Schäffer took hundreds of photographs during her travels in those years (in her archive, there are seventeen hundred images altogether, mostly hers, spanning more than twenty-five years) and chose carefully among them. She included relatively few of people, let alone Indians; the choice to remove many traces of human activity from the mountain scenes reinforces the market-tested conceit that she and her party were intrepid explorers in an isolated landscape. But Schäffer and her party were not alone in the Rockies even in those early decades, and on the trail her images also operated

56. Mary Schäffer, *Looking for Goat While Baking Bread: Camp at the Lower End of Lake Maligne*, 1908.

Courtesy Whyte Museum of the Canadian Rockies, Archives and Library, Banff, V527/PS-72, Mary Schäffer Fonds.

as items of exchange in a barter economy, this time quite literally. In her encounters with other travelers, and particularly with Indians and Anglo settlers, miners, and trappers, she traded photographs for information, beadwork, and more opportunities for picture-taking. Her photographs and her written text are structured around these ostensibly benign encounters, which mask her real activities: a tourist trek in the Rockies provides a pretext for mapping the wilderness; a social call doubles as an opportunity to purchase Indian crafts.

The text echoes with Schäffer's determined construction of the North American West as pristine natural space, a bent that grew out of her early experiences: her excursions with her father, her family's travels in the West, her work with her husband, her recollection of childhood stories. Reconstructing her life in unpublished memoirs, she was convinced at least in retrospect that she began early to form the interests that led her to the Rockies and to the photographs she made there of Canadian First Peoples. Especially significant was a visit from a family cousin, an officer in the U.S. Army, who regaled the family with his stories of the campaigns of Indian Removal; she recalled the evening in an unpublished third-person autobiographical sketch, "The Heart of a Child," in which she claims "she first took the fever." "Cousin Jim's" most harrowing story told of the wholesale destruction of an Indian village; he described how the entire community—men, women, and children—were all murdered except, he discovered, a baby hidden under the mother's dead body. The incident haunted Schäffer:

> This was Mary's fever, an all-consuming one, a newborn love for a race that even her young mind taught her had not had fair treatment from the interlopers of their land. The baby's face, the dead mother, the smoking tepees remained in the child's mind forever after and governed many an act as she grew older. She never spoke of what she heard that night, but the shadow of the story always hung on her horizon. She asked for "Indian Stories," she tramped the Pennsylvania hills after the heavy rains looking for the old Indian arrowheads, dreamed daydreams over the Indian stone battle-axes, basins, anything which referred to the people who had once owned the continent which she and hers called "ours.". . . There always remained an insistent longing to see the peoples of the plains.[40]

Significantly, Schäffer refers to herself in the third person here, as Mary, the impressionable child whose ears and eyes have not yet been racialized, who can hear in Cousin Jim's story not the governmental fiction that justified the eradication of hostile forces but the conventionally sentimental narrative that exposed how those policies eradicated mothers. The exercise of imperial power was intertwined with and naturalized by maternalist sentimentalism, as Wexler has shown, but Schäffer opposes both.[41] Her use of the third person serves as an analogue to the photographic self-portrait; it provides "Mary" with a way to distance herself from the government's activities and provides her temporarily, and fictionally, with a way to escape her positioning as a white woman. Chased up to bed by exasperated adults, Schäffer as Mary makes herself the object of a disapproving parental gaze and so problematizes the conventions of disciplinary looking and colonial narrative.

But Schäffer's sentimental narrative of her own conversion to political justice for Indians focuses on her own transformation, not the transformation of conditions for Indians. It is a private and personal call, as Harriet Beecher Stowe reminded an earlier generation of white women, to "feel right."[42] She never fully lost the sentimental idealization of Indian motherhood that attached itself to Cousin Jim's story, and her "all-consuming" fever found expression in some of her most beautiful images, those of Indian children. Later, repeated subjects in her photographs were mothers and babies, young children, and nuclear families, all out-of-doors, in the vicinity of their homes. In stark contrast with narratives of "vanishing Indians" or of adults defeated or defiant, Schäffer's pictures present narratives of what Gerald Vizenor calls "survivance," that mode of existence where survival and resistance are codeterminant.[43] But the survivance she records is a female-centered one, involving not warriors or chiefs but women and children.

Against a backdrop of economic, cultural, and environmental change for aboriginal people and against Schäffer's violent introduction to Indian policy, her discussion of her relationships with Indians in *Old Indian Trails* is significant, then, for its deliberate cultivation of an idyllic tone. Reading her, one would never recall that a few miles away the Canadian Pacific Railroad was planning a northern spur to its transcontinental line or that the mission school at Morleyville was busily educating Stoney children or that white geologists and miners were camped at Tete Jaune Cache. Chapter 11 of *Old Indian Trails,* "On the Golden Plains of the Saskatchewan," chronicles three encounters over about a five-day period in 1907. Schäffer's party comes across a small group. "Knowing they must be Silas Abraham's and Sampson Beaver's families, acquaintances of a year's standing, I could not resist a hurried call," and, according to Schäffer, the children "ran to cover like rabbits." "Above the din and excitement I called 'Frances Louise!'" Frances Louise had been, she tells us, "my little favorite when last we were among the Indians." Schäffer recalls how, the previous year, she had made a doll for the child out of "an old table-napkin stuffed with newspaper." The child appeared, "her little face . . . just as solemn, just as sweet, and just as dirty as ever.[44]

Frances Louise's picture appears in the book only with her family. But a photograph in Schäffer's archive provides a closer look at the round-faced, beaming child whose energy is palpable (fig. 57). It is one of the photographs that asks us to complicate Schäffer's role as complicit in what Wexler explains is "domestic sentimentalism at work as an imperial instrument."[45] Frances Louise's portrait is filled with iconographic signifiers of Indian-ness: she is dressed in "traditional" Indian clothing, with beaded leggings, richly decorated dress, necklaces, earrings, and hair neatly held back with a bandanna. In her right hand she holds some flowers. She is a child of nature, exotic and lovely, innocent and untainted by civilizing hands. Unlike the shyer children, who run "like rabbits," she is a small "nature's nobleman," facing the camera with assurance and even pleasure; she has been given a cherished doll and is not afraid of Schäffer or her companions. She is neither "civilized" nor trapped; the dominant sensibility of the image is neither disciplinary nor elegiac, nor even sentimental. Although certainly depicted within recognizable visual codes, she is also a vibrant and unrepressed presence.

Another unpublished image depicts a similar scene; it is the picture of an Indian baby, bare toes wiggling in the sun (fig. 58). Schäffer has clearly not posed the child; she is wrapped in a blanket and placed on the grass and looks off-camera, presumably at her mother. Again, the child's costume and location signal her racial identity: her hair is incongruously covered with an oversized and ornate headdress that slips down over her forehead, and in the background are

57. Mary Schäffer, *Frances Louise Beaver*, 1907.

Courtesy Whyte Museum of the Canadian Rockies, Archives and Library, Banff, V527/PS-4, Mary Schäffer Fonds.

the bottoms of tipis. But other markers reveal that even this smallest and least mobile of Schäffer's subjects is not completely enfolded within the canons of "looking Indian." The baby's dress is gingham and is blowing up in a breeze; her blanket is rough wool such as Schäffer herself might have used camping. And the baby is not portrayed in a papoose board, as she might be in a Curtis photograph. Again, Schäffer is close enough to the child that the camera calls attention to her and not to the objects that make up the scene's context. With both images, then, Schäffer employs certain conventions of looking at Indians and yet allows for the gaze to be returned or disrupted.

But as John Berger and Jean Mohr remind us, these images cannot be divorced from the historical frames that surround them.[46] Although Schäffer no doubt saw

58. Mary Schäffer, *Indian Baby*, 1907.
Courtesy Whyte Museum of the Canadian Rockies, Archives and Library, Banff, M79/F6, Mary Schäffer Fonds.

Indian children as images of optimism and innocence, contemporary viewers cannot help but see them in light of policies that removed them from their homes and sent them to boarding schools to be "civilized." We don't know what happened to Frances Louise or the baby; perhaps they did indeed live with their families in their homes in Alberta into adulthood. But, equally likely, they went to boarding schools like the ones Gerald McMaster reminds us existed throughout Canada to "assimilate" Indians into the normative institutions of white Euro-Canadian culture.[47] Decontextualized, separated from their families, alone in the woods, these babies represent also a narrative of Indian survival as necessarily a solitary endeavor, one in which traces of Indian culture coexist uneasily with Euro-Canadian culture, and they also imply that survival can be won only through accepting loss. Beaming, Frances Louise faces the camera; but in return for this and other pictures her father traded a map drawn from memory of Stoney tribal hunting grounds on the shores of Lake Maligne, or Beaver Lake.

Schäffer's other images similarly suggest the gaps, elisions, and contradictions that pervade the history of Euro-Native interaction. For example, a relatively straightforward photograph, taken at the same time as the previous two, is of a Stoney woman and child (fig. 59). Appearing in *Old Indian Trails* as Schäffer's, the photograph, entitled *The Indian Madonna*, was taken twenty-five years before

59. Mary Schäffer, *The Indian Madonna*, 1907.

Courtesy Whyte Museum of the Canadian Rockies, Archives and Library, Banff, V527/PS-51, Mary Schäffer Fonds. (This image is also archived in the collections of Byron Harmon and Elliot Barnes, and although no definitive negative survives, it was probably taken by Barnes and a copy given to Schäffer, who used it in her book and colored it for use in slide lectures.)

Laura Gilpin's more famous *Navajo Madonna*.[48] Like Gilpin's, Schäffer's photograph plainly grafts Western and Christian aesthetic conventions onto a Native woman and child. Wexler describes the maternalist ideology extant in turn-of-the-century women's photography as based fundamentally on premises of whiteness: Käsebier, she argues persuasively, can sensitively render a white friend's heartbreak at the loss of her child and the breakup of her family, but when an Indian child whom she has photographed dies, Käsebier barely acknowledges the event.[49] Schäffer also borrows heavily from the visual language of maternalism: the Indian Madonna cradles the child to her, nestles her chin against the child's shoulder. Sitting in the doorway of their tipi, in bright sun, the woman looks natural and relaxed as she smiles at the camera and stills the child, who looks sleepy, bored, and restless. Like Frances Louise and the Indian baby, the woman and child in this picture mix "Indian" signifiers with "civilized" ones: braids, necklaces, earrings, tipi, all confirm the exotic nature of the "primitive," while the child's checked dress and the mother's dark skirt reveal their living within an interracial contact zone. The very mixture suggests Schäffer's own effort to bridge the racial divide Wexler describes. Moreover, it references her genuine recognition of the degree to which Indians were involved with and responding to the transformation of their land and their lives caused by white settlement. But that effort to connect naturalizes what has been a destructive transformation. After all, what more domestic and domesticated scene could there be than that of this loving, smiling mother holding her sleepy child? What more idealized maternal figure to appeal to the romantic sentiments of white, liberal, middle-class viewers? This is not a mother under siege, like the mother in Cousin Jim's story; in a sense, Schäffer relives, even seeks to redeem, that story of destruction through this one of sanctified motherhood.

In that spirit she describes the ostensible occasion for the photograph:

> When I hear those "who know" speak of the sullen, stupid Indian, I wish they could have been on hand the afternoon the white squaws visited the red ones with their cameras. There were no men to disturb the peace, the women quickly caught our ideas, entered the spirit of the game, and with musical laughter and little giggles allowed themselves to be hauled about and pushed and posed in a fashion to turn an artist green with envy. The children forgot their rabbit-like shyness, and copied their elders in posing for us; then one of them would suddenly remember he was hungry, would rush to the teepee, seize a lump of meat or a bone from a pot swung over a small fire, and rush out again shiny with the grease thereof. Yahe-Weha might photograph to her heart's content. She had promised pictures the year before, she had kept the promise, and she might have as many photographs now as she wanted.[50]

Here again, Schäffer uses the third person when referring to herself; here, she too is a "squaw," albeit, oxymoronically, a white one. Moreover, her words are attributed to the Indian women: Schäffer ventriloquizes for them, claiming their voices while appropriating their identities and capturing their images, all paradoxically in an effort to be with them and like them, separate from "those 'who know.'" Again, her third-person narration creates distance between "I" and "she" in an effort to escape her positioning as the white woman intruding, uninvited, on the daily lives of a group of women. She attempts to manufacture for herself a doubled consciousness, both colonized and colonizer, both viewer and viewed. Schäffer claims to connect with these women as fellow "squaws"; without a disrupting male presence, picture-taking, for her, is a game and a reciprocal act—she gave the women the pictures the year before, and now she can take more. She resists the pejorative category of "artist": an artist might exploit her subject or presumably try to capture something that is not freely given. Schäffer is no artist on this occasion but a "white squaw" who receives a gift that the artist would envy. Schäffer intends to present this scene as a kind of "two-way looking"—everyone, white women and Indian women alike, is aware of her part in the tableau vivant of the photograph and in the drama of the afternoon's picture-taking.

Schäffer's insistence on the reciprocity of the exchange between the "white squaws" and "the red ones" is undercut by her unconscious racism: the Indian women "looked as though wash-days were not over numerous"; their "grimy paws" were nonetheless "shapely . . . so small and dainty." Their laughs were "musical " and the children, while no longer "rabbit-like" nonetheless ran freely through the camp, grabbing food without apparent assistance or attention to regular mealtimes.[51] Moreover, in spite of her assertion that she is no artist, Schäffer certainly exerts the artist's prerogative to control poses and her audience's interpretation of them. For her, this Indian woman poses no threat except that she might loosen her grip on her child before the exposure fades; she is picturesque proof that Western modes of looking and classifying can be rooted in Western empiricism, and that Western hierarchies can remain intact even—or especially—in what appears to be a wilderness. Indeed, the photograph and the discussion of its being taken reflect the same ideological certainty that some universal "womanliness" and what Mary Ryan calls "the empire of the mother" can subvert class and racial lines.[52] But Schäffer's efforts to bring this narrative to closure falter on significant slippages between ideology and history—as do my efforts to bring this episode to critical closure. What is really going on?

The photograph, and its place in the album Schäffer carefully constructs, is richly complicated, not the least by questions of attribution and archive. In *Old Indian Trails*, this photograph is attributed to Schäffer; I had blithely made a slide from the book and cheerfully accepted the fact. Then I went to Banff, where I found the photograph as a postcard attributed to Byron Harmon, a Banff neighbor and fellow outdoorsperson. Curious, I asked the staff at the Whyte Museum of the Canadian Rockies, where Schäffer's materials are collected, about the attribution. The image is indeed in Harmon's archives. But the archivist also directed me to a third Banff resident, Elliot Barnes, and a fourth, Reggie Holmes. Instead

60. Mary Schäffer, *Lake Louise Photographic Party Mounting*, 1899.
Courtesy Whyte Museum of the Canadian Rockies, Archives and Library, Banff, V527/PS-214, Mary Schäffer Fonds.

of the giggles of the Stoney women, I imagined Schäffer, Barnes, Harmon, and Holmes sharing a last laugh. Searching for a way to call this question in the absence of a surviving negative, I compared images from their three archives. I saw over and over again the same Indian women and children in pose after pose after pose—it seemed that the "wilderness" Schäffer was so invested in promoting could not be traversed without encountering dozens of Euro-Americans and Canadians on photographic safari. The extensive group of professional and amateur photographers in Banff at the turn into the twentieth century apparently shared slides, cameras, and photographic outings, often gathering at well-known landmarks for a day of picture-taking (fig. 60). Small wonder so many of the images look so similar; they were often taken within seconds of one another, from almost identical angles and of the same subjects. Schäffer was an accomplished colorist for lantern slides, often working with plates taken by others, such as the professional George Noble. Don Bourdon, the head archivist at the Whyte Museum, theorizes that Schäffer colored a copy of Barnes's slide and felt free to use the image in *Old Indian Trails*.

So, I know quite a bit about the four would-be photographers. I don't know anything about the Indian Madonna, except that she appears in several images taken on the Kootenay Plains between 1905 and 1908. She may or may not even have been the mother of a child. The Madonna—at least so far—has been veiled to me by her iconographic function both in the text and in the larger cultural narrative of sentimental, holy motherhood. In other words, assessing the intercultural relations that photographs depict requires context. Donna Haraway calls for "situated knowledge," a doctrine of "embodied objectivity" based on "elaborate specificity and difference and the loving care people might take to learn how to see faithfully from another's point of view."[53] But that historical specificity can be elusive, and, without it, colonization, as both a historical and a theoretical act, of both the subject *of* the photograph *and* the photograph itself, is hard to counter. In Schäffer's photographs, Indians may not be constructed as vanishing, but their history nonetheless is.

Schäffer's narrative is further strained by two other photographs from the same afternoon, both in her archive and both attributed to her. Neither was included in *Old Indian Trails,* and both of them are considerably less picturesque than the Indian Madonna. In one, an Indian woman stands next to a tent, hands folded in front of her (fig. 61). She is wearing a long, dark cloak over a paisley apron and

61. Mary Schäffer, *Indian Woman with Papoose,* 1907.
Courtesy Whyte Museum of the Canadian Rockies, Archives and Library, Banff, V527/PS-705, Mary Schäffer Fonds.

62. Mary Schäffer, *Stoney Indians at Kootenay Plains,* 1907.
Courtesy Whyte Museum of the Canadian Rockies, Archives and Library, Banff, V527/PS-50, Mary Schäffer Fonds.

light checked skirt; her hair is covered with a white kerchief, a child is strapped to her back by way of a dark cloth tied around her shoulders. The backdrop is dreary: among the trees in the surrounding hills, early snow is visible; the light is gray; the woman's clothes guard against the chill air. She appears calm and poised but not as welcoming as the Indian Madonna; in spite of her child, her image does not suggest transcendent motherhood and so does not fit Schäffer's sentimental desire to convey Indian motherhood as a psychological state equivalent to Euro-American maternalism. Nor, however, does the image exist within the conventions of ethnographic photography, also an idiom available to Schäffer: the woman is not dressed consistently in "Indian" style, and the photograph does not represent any "information" about how an Indian mother would carry a child. The image thus falls between the maternalist and the ethnographic discourses and does not fit within the narrative conventions of *Old Indian Trails.* Schäffer hand-colored this slide, which suggests that she used it as part of her winter lectures to white Canadian and American groups interested in hearing about the Rockies as a form of entertainment. But we have no information as to how Schäffer might have used this image in her public lectures.

Similarly, a group photo of three Indian women and six children referenced by the Whyte Museum as *Stoney Indians at Kootenay Plains* is neither maternally sentimental nor pedagogically ethnographic (fig. 62). The women stand; they, too, are dressed in a mixture of identifiably Indian clothing (braids, moccasins, a blanket) and European skirts. Two little girls stand with the two women on the right of the photograph, looking hesitantly at the camera. In the foreground, three small boys sit squinting into the sun; one has his hand shading his eyes, another a hand over his face. They stand around a set of sticks that form the outline of a tipi; it appears to surround a cooking pot and be hung with bits of cloth; behind them is a small rise of rock, trees fading to forest, some oval objects that look a bit like cans. The photograph appears disorganized, as if the principals had simply randomly come together for a momentary pause, their relationships with each other and with the photographer unclear or accidental.

The woman on the far left of the image provides the only context we have. She is the Indian Madonna: same woman, same clothing as in the more controversial photograph, same child in the same checked head scarf. Surely these images were taken on, or at least close to, the same day. Rereading Schäffer's description of the afternoon, we imagine we see the corner of the "pot swung over a small fire" from which the children grabbed food. But this photograph suggests nothing of an afternoon filled with "musical laughter and little giggles"; the women hardly seem to have "entered the spirit of the game." Here the Indian Madonna stands, her child on her back peeking out at Schäffer as she clings to her mother's shoulders. She conveys no connection with Schäffer: she is as expressionless as the other women and the children in the photo. If as the stylized Indian Madonna she redeems the horrifying genocide Cousin Jim recounts, here she refuses to offer any ameliorative gesture. Schäffer cannot make her into a sentimental sister or a redemptive mother. The photograph of the Indian Madonna in isolation satisfies Schäffer's desire to see herself in some female solidarity with another "mountain woman": but not only "men [who] disturb the peace" must be edited out in order for that fantasy to be possible. Set the Indian Madonna among the other Indian women, and Schäffer cannot control her inevitable attachment to Euro-American ways of seeing, the distance between herself and the Indian women, or her complicity in the history behind Cousin Jim's narrative.

The Indian Madonna is the only Indian mother to appear in a photograph in *Old Indian Trails*, but Schäffer's written text offers one more, this one married to a Euro-American trapper named Lewis Swift, from Ohio, who had begun homesteading in Jasper in 1892 (fig. 63). In contrast with the Madonna, we know a lot about Mrs. Swift. She was Suzette Chalifoux, a Métis, born in St. Albert, married in Edmonton in 1897 at the home of the Wylie family, by Alec Taylor, Edmonton's pioneer telephone operator. She was thus hardly a "primitive" gigglingly confronting American tourists but rather a socially well-connected woman in the context of Canada's developing western frontier. Suzette Chalifoux Swift was known across the country for her excellent leatherwork—silk embroidered buckskin gloves, coats made of quills, beadwork moccasins—until her death in 1946.[54]

Schäffer took several photographs of Swift and her children but did not include one in *Old Indian Trails;* like the Indian mothers on the Kootenay Plains, Swift is not as picturesque as the Madonna and so does not fit as nicely into the

63. Mary Schäffer, *Mrs. Lewis Swift with Her Children*, 1908.
Courtesy Whyte Museum of the Canadian Rockies, Archives and Library, Banff, V527/PS-96, Mary Schäffer Fonds.

book's overall depiction of the Rockies for Euro-American tourists. Schäffer does, however, include a description of a conventional social call paid by herself and her friend Adams. The two Americans admire the snug cabin:

> Then Mrs. Swift (oh, we women are all alike!) unearthed a box from beneath her
> bed and showed us a half dozen gowns made by herself, most of them her bridal
> finery, and, as we looked on the carefully treasured garments, I realised—be it man-

sion or shack—there is sure to be stowed away just such a precious horde around which a woman's heart must always cling. Then came her fancy-work which she did in the short winter days and the long evenings by candlelight, and we began to take a deep interest. She had quantities of silk embroidery on the softest buckskin I have yet seen. Her silks she dyed herself, and her patterns were her own designing. There was a most delicious odor to the skins which she said was through their being tanned by poplar smoke. Gloves, moccasins, and beautiful coats, we took everything and wished she had more; it was a grand afternoon's shopping for us all, for the lonely Athabaska woman and the two white women who had seen none of their kind for many a long day.[55]

Schäffer's encounter with Swift begins with another assertion of female essentialism that crosses racial and class lines—over bridal finery, no less, the "precious horde around which a woman's heart must always cling." But her "deep interest" is reserved for Swift's intricate "fancy-work." In the mountain cabin, it appears to be—incongruously yet essentially, Schäffer suggests—the leisure work of a middle-class matron decorating her home and clothing. Indeed, at the beginning of the passage, Schäffer gives no suggestion that this encounter will shift to one that is radically different in its economic implications. Not until the last sentence does she reveal how the real economic relations between the Indian woman and her white guests stand: "we took everything and wished she had more." The empathetic moment when Schäffer recognizes that all women share a devotion to things, to decorative personal effects, gives way to, indeed prepares her for, the more important, the "deeper" moment: the white "guests" are shopping. Schäffer's sympathetic invocation of the sentimental provides enough understanding across racial and class lines to make her a discerning and appreciative consumer. She is able to recognize the worth of the materials, the texture, the colors, even the smell, of the items displayed. Their elegance is both the product of and in contrast to the cramped quarters of the cabin. They are themselves symbols of the contact zone: "silk embroidery on the softest buckskin." And that "grand afternoon's shopping" is grand for all of them—both "the lonely Athabaska woman and the two white women who had seen none of their kind for many a long day." Schäffer represents Swift's enjoyment as well as her own as a social pleasure.

But here too Schäffer's omissions are significant. She does not emphasize the economic significance of Suzette Swift's opportunity to obtain the hard currency that must have been a rare commodity for a homesteader's family. She does not mention Swift's growing reputation as an artist, skilled at blending traditional quill and bead work with European silk embroidery, a participant in both the preservation and the transformation of an artistic and cultural legacy. And she does not emphasize her own desire to acquire, display, and promote cultural artifacts: "gloves, moccasins, and beautiful coats, we took everything and wished she had more." Although she includes a photograph of Lewis Swift's homestead,

her book does not show us her photograph of Suzette Swift as a cheerful, affectionate, hardworking mother surrounded by her children, all dressed conventionally in checked gingham, smocks, aprons, trousers—no "savages" in this
photograph, here no bloody contact zone or violent colonial encounter, just an
interracial family participating in whatever economies present themselves.

Here, too, however, contexts and narratives multiply. Just as the photograph
of the Indian Madonna looks more complex the more we know (or don't know,
as the case may be), so too does the story of a grand afternoon shopping appear
different when read through another's eyes. In this instance, it is Adams, Schäffer's close friend and travel companion, to whom *Old Indian Trails* was dedicated,
who in her diaries provides a different perspective. Schäffer's economic relationship with Swift is clearly suggested in these records. Adams records their meeting Swift on August 11, 1907: "After lunch, we returned Mrs. S's. call. She had
some very pretty work, silk embroidery on buckskin, in which of course we invested somewhat largely." On August 20, the entire expedition is invited to supper at the mining camp at Tete Jaune Cache: "M. was very much dressed up. She
had on a pair of new moccasins Mrs. Swift made, and was carrying a clean pocket
handkerchief." On August 31, the two women return to the Swift's farm, "as
Mrs. S. was finishing a buckskin coat embroidered with silk work for M., and it
had to be tried on a good many times."[56] Schäffer and Swift have begun a significant economic relationship. As with the afternoon of picture-taking, where Schäffer focuses on the harmony between "white squaws" and red mothers rather than
on her own aesthetic agenda, here Schäffer depicts "a grand afternoon's shopping"
where female communion is highlighted over touristic acquisition.

But the fascination with Swift's handwork also recalls more violent moments
in the history of Euro-Americans' acquisition of Indian possessions. Schäffer's
childhood recollection of the orphaned baby in the Cousin Jim story, which she
claimed inaugurated her lifelong empathy for Indians, is casually, almost inci-
dentally, embedded in another of Cousin Jim's stories, this one involving Indian
craftsmanship:

> In his quiet fashion he told in simple language of the morning which had been set
> apart for his branch of the army to destroy a village of hostile Indians. They had
> been driving off cattle and horses, harassing the nearby settlers, shooting white
> men, threatening the women and the usual plan for obliterating such a nuisance
> was to wipe out the village—it was the only way understood in those days. . . .
> Cousin Jim moved among the dead to see that the work had been finished as di-
> rected. He had just removed a beautiful beaded coat and breeches from a dead
> brave ("Picked that up for you, Jack") when turning his head he saw a sight which
> sickened him. By a burnt tepee lay a dead squaw and beneath her sheltering body,
> sheltering even in death, peeped a wee brown face,—a live baby. "I tell you Jack,
> that was too much even for such a hardened sinner as me. I dropped the buckskins

and picked up the baby, for I felt the child had a heavy lien on the United States Government. It was such a starved looking little thing and its face was smeared with its mother's blood." [57]

Schäffer's retelling of this story contains several disturbing features. First is the situation itself. Under the guise of supervising soldiers, couched impersonally and euphemistically as ensuring that "the work had been finished as directed," Jim is in fact looting the massacred bodies of Indian men, women, and children, stealing valuables from those his men had slaughtered. He had "removed" a coat and breeches from a corpse, presumably stripping the man's clothes from his body before it was buried in a mass grave. Only the sight of the orphaned infant could make Cousin Jim drop his stash and experience a twinge of conscience: "it was such a starved looking little thing and its face was smeared with its mother's blood." But he still apparently brought the clothing home as a war trophy, a grisly gift for a relative. The child becomes incidental to the clothing itself; its story becomes an exotic, not to say obscene, backdrop against which the clothing's value might be assessed.

Second, Jim claims a moment of sentimental awareness: "the child had a heavy lien on the United States Government." A civilized, well-domesticated man as well as a soldier and executioner, Jim indulges a moment of liberal guilt over the regrettable consequences of his actions. But this regret does not effect any radical reconsideration of his or the government's policies nor, significantly, does it evoke any strong expression from Schäffer. Her apology for Jim's actions is again rendered in the passive voice: "it was the only way understood in those days." Neither Jim nor the soldiers nor even the U.S. government bears any direct responsibility for its work in "obliterating such a nuisance" to the ongoing imperial work of economically controlling western resources and peoples. Instead of implicating Jim in genocidal policies, she implicitly approves Jim's being moved by the baby's tragedy, as if Jim were a disinterested and benevolent observer rather than an active and rapacious participant in the events that created the baby's condition.

Third, although Schäffer's commissioning a coat from Swift is far removed from Jim's theft of one, her accounts of both contain the same easy slide away from the politics of acquisition. Just as Schäffer uses the Indian Madonna to redeem the violence that murdered an earlier Indian mother, so too does her kinder, gentler encounter with Swift seek to redeem Cousin Jim's violent theft. In both instances, Schäffer distances herself from the earlier encounters, claiming that earlier genocidal responses to cultural and political conflict have given way to benign moments of cross-cultural understanding and economic exchange. But her prose cannot quite escape the earlier conventions or the attitudes implicit in them.

The traces of Jim's story in Schäffer's encounters, the shadows his history cast over hers, are analogous to the relationship between the two maps that Schäffer

64. Sampson Beaver, captioned by Schäffer *Sampson's Map*, 1907.

Courtesy Whyte Museum of the Canadian Rockies, Archives and Library, Banff, V527/PS-53, Mary Schäffer Fonds.

includes in *Old Indian Trails*. In 1907 and 1908, Schäffer had set for herself the goal of mapping a lake "which was supposed to lie north of Brazeau Lake"; she and her party had tried during the summer of 1907 to find it, but without success. In late summer of 1907, Sampson Beaver provided them with crucial information. "One of the greatest trophies we carried with us on leaving the next day for the North Fork of the Saskatchewan was a tiny grubby bit of paper on which Sampson had with much care traced the lake we had tried so hard to find. . . . He had been there but once, a child of fourteen, and now a man of thirty, he drew it from memory,—mountains, streams and passes all included." [58]

Schäffer has taken pains to describe the friendship she and her party struck up with the Beavers: she gave the child a doll, took photographs of the family, supplied meals, and sustained the relationship over several summers. In return, Sampson provided "one of the greatest trophies," the map that will allow them to structure yet another trip into the Rockies—and other texts (fig. 64). The next summer, following Sampson's map, Schäffer and her party indeed made it to the lake, now renamed Lake Maligne: they built a raft, crossed it, sketched its outlines, photographed it, described their route and the lake's location. In 1911, when *Old Indian Trails* was published, Sampson's map appeared as an artifact of primitive cartography, tucked away in the center of the narrative and almost incidental. It is not "the map" referred to in the book's subtitle. That map is in contrast an "official" map, folded onto the back pages, *Outline Map of Section of Canadian Rocky Mountains Visited during 1907 and 1908* (fig. 65). The official map is both a consequence of and an impetus to the increasing economic development of the region, to which both Schäffer and her "Chief," Warren, contributed heavily; it is cited, debated, referenced, used, critiqued. But nowhere on the map or in the ensuing uses of it is Sampson's contribution referenced, although other survey maps by white explorers are credited. His contribution, given freely and

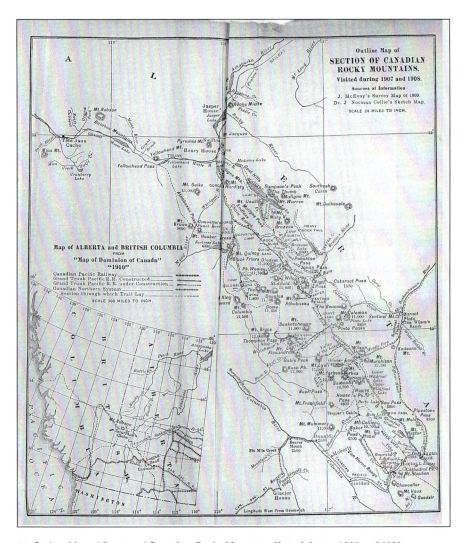

65. *Outline Map of Section of Canadian Rocky Mountains Visited during 1907 and 1908.*
Courtesy Whyte Museum of the Canadian Rockies, Archives and Library, Banff, V527/PS-116, Mary Schäffer Fonds.

in friendship, has vanished from the official narrative, erased from this official and two-dimensional rendering of the land and reduced to a colorful footnote in the autobiographical account. Schäffer's relationships with Indians were forged out of the violent history her cousin literally brought home, and yet she erases from her own text and from her consciousness the traces of that history. Schäffer's travel narrative is made possible by Beaver's map, and yet she erases that too from the official cartographic result. Both texts—*Old Indian Trails* and the outline map—bear the traces of previous Indian encounters: the suppressed history behind each map is central to understanding its relationship to the land and the people with whom Schäffer sought solidarity. Significantly, Schäffer receives the map on the "golden plains of the Saskatchewan," during her halcyon picture-taking afternoons; significant also is that she receives it only a few weeks before her encounter with Kipling. The map that Beaver gave to Schäffer stands as the symbol of the historical ironies central to relationships between Indians and Euro-Americans.

These may seem oblique connections, between innocent maps and autobiographical confessions, between incidental encounters and economic exploitation, between aesthetic pleasures and repressed histories. But as Louis Owens puts it, "Mapping is . . . an intensely political enterprise, an essential step toward appropriation and possession. Maps write the conquerors' stories over the stories of the conquered."[59] Just such "innocent" maps structured the division of land under the Dawes Act in the United States, an ostensibly rational act that Jane Gay's photographs and letters exposed as violently destructive of Nez Perce family relations and economic survival; and just such innocent exchanges of culture and commerce were the basis of Kate Cory's and Grace Nicholson's different relationships with Hopi and Karuk peoples.

Mary Schäffer unwittingly documented the results of her innocent acts in two photographs that are in the archive. First is an undated image, labeled simply *Indian on Banff Avenue* (fig. 66). The photograph is a forlorn one—the mountains, which may indeed be, in this case, "too massive" for Schäffer's eye, are in the left background. They have been crowded out of the frame by the buildings on Banff Avenue, where "Chief" Warren had his garage. The subject, at some remove from the viewer, and walking toward us, is a single Indian man, quite a different subject from most of Schäffer's others. No one else is on the street. The town resembles the stereotypical western ghost town, perhaps one haunted by ghosts of the Stoney who used to live there, ancestors of the lone Indian: by the time this image was taken, the Stoney had mostly moved to Morleyville, about thirty miles away.

The second photo is another one of the Beaver family, taken about the same time as the first (fig. 67). This time, Leah and Frances Louise are on horseback, and Sampson stands beside them. Here, they are not quite the relaxed, transcendent figures of the first image: Leah is guarded, Sampson serious and alert, even Frances Louise looks a bit suspicious when she's on horseback. With the horses,

66. Mary Schäffer,
*Indian on Banff
Avenue,* n.d.

Courtesy Whyte Museum of
the Canadian Rockies, Ar-
chives and Library, Banff,
V527/PS-256, Mary Schäf-
fer Fonds.

they are mobile, poised to leave. The setting is also close to that of the other image, but with more of the foreground exposed; the downed timber displayed, although no doubt the result of a rough winter, makes the landscape appear strewn
with debris. It is impossible to know what the differences were between the
specific circumstances of the two images of the Beaver family, whether accidental, coincidental, or triggered by some subtle difference in context or timing. But
when read in conjunction with the *Indian on Banff Avenue,* they both suggest the
eventual fate of the Stoney: their struggle to accommodate to encroaching governmental regulations and economic appropriation of their traditional hunting
grounds; their success in spite of that at keeping families and customs relatively
intact; and their effort to maintain cordial relationships with new residents and
transient tourists while recognizing that they have few options. If the first Beaver family photo provides us with a utopian possibility of cross-cultural understanding, this one suggests the more equivocal future that the Indian on Banff
Avenue inhabits.

Schäffer's and Kipling's encounter highlighted the context for this chapter, and
Kipling's startling phrase "the comprehending equal eyes of the civilized white
woman" provided the title. The questions raised by the phrase are central to any
discussion of the nature of photography, especially with this subject matter and in
this period, when photographs documented, validated, normalized, aestheticized,

67. Mary Schäffer, *Sampson Beaver Family*, 1907.

and finally mythologized expansionist policies that erased Indians from the land and from history. Take for example the images of the Indian on Banff Avenue and the Beaver family on horseback: What is it exactly that Schäffer's eyes are equal to or comprehend? What, for example, does it mean to call the eyes of a "civilized white woman" "comprehending" and "equal?" Is comprehension defined by analytic distance or by empathetic connection? To what or whom are the eyes equal? Can the comprehension of the eyes exceed the conscious knowledge of their owner? Can eyes transmit the comprehension and equality attributed to them? Or if the eyes are Schäffer's, is the comprehension that of her viewers, seeing her and her photographs in another place and time and setting? Considering the varied and tragic histories of Native peoples on the North American continent, Kipling's phrase is suggestively ambiguous in its relations.

As Kipling was writing that line, carefully packed away in Schäffer's gear were the photographs of First Peoples she had encountered on the trail—photographs that Kipling noticed but did not stop to inquire about. Just as a long hot soak in a scented tub transforms Schäffer from grubby trail rider into Victorian lady, so too does the genteel task of placing her photographs in albums domesticate her trip. But Hilden calls on critics to "consider the possibility of escape from the Eurocenter into a more nuanced border world for those not resident in the boundaries since birth."[60] Schäffer forces us to consider how to recruit the colonizer herself as a liminal figure who—consciously or not—issues a call to look beyond theoretical frames to alternative histories and subjectivities, to "encounter" them, in Davidov's term, and the history they invoke with a form of "two-way looking," where we resist easy oppositions between imperial eyes and reimagined subjects, between deterministic and liberatory readings, or even among viewers, subjects, and photographers. Lippard similarly asks that we "avoid the well-trod paths of theoretical tourism, while facing up to the impossibility of totally evading them."[61] As Berger and Mohr put it, "In itself the photograph cannot lie, but, by the same token, it cannot tell the truth; or rather, the truth it does tell, the truth it can by itself defend, is a limited one." Indeed, "all photographs are possible contributions to history, and any photograph, under certain circumstances, can be used in order to break the monopoly which history has today over time."[62]

Schäffer's texts, written and visual, suggest some possibilities for how this might be true. They demystify imperial practices of seeing and recording, yet at the same time those practices are central to how she records her experience. Thus her photographs insist that images are iconologic as well as iconographic—that is, that they theorize vision itself rather than simply visually represent a story.[63] Indeed, among Schäffer's often condescending narratives and my often discouraging readings, lurk texts, like that of the first image of the Beavers, that cannot be reduced to any single analysis and that trouble viewers long after a conclusion ought to have been reached. As Roland Barthes might put it, her images often contain a punctum, or point, that, in Barthes's words, contains "a power of expansion"

68. Mollie Adams, *She Who Colored Slides,* 1908.

Courtesy Whyte Museum of the Canadian Rockies, Archives and Library, Banff, V527/PS-1, Mary Schäffer Fonds.

that "wounds" because it cannot be reduced to a mere material representation of history; the punctum is "what I add to the photograph and what is already there." In other words, all photographs, and Schäffer's in particular, demand another kind of "two-way looking": between the image as an independent artifact and the image as dependent on multiple and intersecting frames of reference.[64]

As one last example, consider another view of an Indian mother and an Indian commodity, this archived in the Schäffer Fonds. Mary Schäffer appears in a lantern slide by Mollie Adams, hand colored by Schäffer. Schäffer is modeling an embroidered buckskin jacket (fig. 68). She is in front of her tent, facing away from the camera, at about a 145-degree angle; the photograph's purpose seems genuinely to be to display the coat. It is fringed, elaborately and skillfully decorated, apparently in bright blues, yellows, rusts, white, and brown; a collar appears to be fur, and the hide has been carefully tanned and sewed together so as to display the animal's markings. Unlike the coat and breeches Cousin Jim lifted from the massacred Indian brave, Mrs. Swift's coat is attributed to her by implication in Schäffer's text, and it is modeled as the work of art it is, not as a trophy designating western conquest. Beneath the coat, Schäffer wears lace cuffs and a brown riding skirt, not her work shirts and breeches. Her hair is tidily pinned on top of her head. The photograph is both a picture of her and not a picture of her; she is both the subject and a vehicle for the real subject, the jacket. Her back is to the camera: we look at the coat, both a synecdoche of Swift and a figure for Schäffer's implication in and resistance to her own voyeuristic and colonizing activities. It is significant that not only do we not see Swift, the coat's maker, but also we do not see very much of Schäffer, the coat's owner, either beaming or smug with the pride of possession. Here again, as with her discussion of herself in the third person, she resists making herself the focus. Turning her back, she is in profile, head down. The coat occupies the remaining portion of the photograph, but it is also partially concealed; presumably the concealed left side mirrors the right. Finally, the photograph is titled *She Who Colored Slides;* the title ostensibly mimics "Indian" speech patterns and, more important, allows Schäffer to claim kinship as an artist with Swift, to collaborate in disseminating her work to the public. Significantly, then, the photograph reveals partially both Schäffer and the coat, just as Schäffer's other texts show partially both her life and prejudices and the stories she struggled to represent and contain.

If we follow Schäffer's gaze, off camera, into the background, we might be led into what Gloria Anzaldúa called "the space in-between from which to think": the place where we might suspend final positions in favor of fluid and contingent readings that allow for those involved with the photograph to escape Berger and Mohr's "monopoly of time."[65] Schäffer's photographs and text indeed participate in the imperial iconography we associate with photographs of turn-of-the-century Native Americans. But they also are iconologic—that is, they call on us to uncover what Davidov calls "sub-versions," whole archives of texts and images that force us to linger over paradoxical and idiosyncratic details.[66] They compel us to rethink theoretical paradigms in more nuanced ways that acknowledge the multiple, shifting, site-specific histories of active historical agents. In this, the photograph is itself the perfect metaphor for both the historical recovery of an erased Native American past and the struggle for a theory commensurate with that task. As Jolene Rickard says, "A photograph is not going to give that first hand experience, but it may haunt your memory into seeking life."[67]

LISA MACFARLANE

CHAPTER FOUR

CAPTURING AND RECAPTURING CULTURE

Trailing Grace Nicholson's Legacy in Northwestern California

I n September 1930, Pasadena-based Grace Nicholson (fig. 69), a self-described "collector and disposer of art," received a letter from Hoopa Valley Reservation Superintendent O. M. Boggess, asking whether she were still interested in purchasing Hupa baskets. In her reply, she noted that she had hundreds of Hupa baskets in stock, but they were no longer marketable.[1] The market for Indian baskets and "curios," which Nicholson had helped to shape in the first two decades of the twentieth century, had mostly vanished by 1930, a sign of Euro-America's cyclical fascination and forgetfulness regarding Native Americans. Even after Nicholson's death in 1948, her assistants met with great difficulty in convincing old clients to take in her own collection of baskets. Yet when Nicholson first traveled to northern California in 1903, and three years later to the Klamath River region in the state's northwestern corner, she enmeshed herself in a nexus of business and personal relationships that enabled her to become southern California's premier dealer in Indian cultural materials. By forging selective long-term patronage relationships with individual Native artists and countless shorter-term relationships with both whites and Indians from whom she bought what she alternately termed "stuff," "old things," and "specimens," Nicholson left her imprint on the region, one still felt amid contemporary tribal efforts at repatriation. We have a record of these varied relationships, a record furnished not only by her diaries and correspondence but by the thousands of Karuk, Hupa, and Yurok items that, through her efforts, were subsequently housed far from their homelands at prestigious museums.

69. Carrol S. Hartman, *Miss Nicholson en Route to Orleans*, 1908.

Reproduced by permission of The Huntington Library, San Marino, Calif., Album A, page 77.

Most particularly, Nicholson left behind a photographic trail of her buying trips throughout northwestern California in the early twentieth century, a visual legacy comprising several hundred images of Karuk, Hupa, and Yurok people, images of those whom she simply encountered as well as of those who traded more than gazes. These photographs, and the woman who produced them and who at other times posed for them, present a complicated legacy for those interested in making sense of turn-of-the-century cross-cultural "contact zones" in northwestern California, particularly instances of interaction between white women and the Indian communities they visited in their capacities as teachers, collectors, missionaries, and tourists.[2] I consider here the contexts informing the production, function, and circulation of some of these photographs and chart their historically shifting status within cross-cultural and cross-regional circuits of exchange. In doing so, I argue that these photographs, together with written and oral accounts of Nicholson's interactions with northwestern California Indians and others, suggest the multiple and ultimately irresolvable conflicts that she sustained between the poles of ethnography and commerce, economics and art, exploitation and exchange. At the same time, these photographs direct us to an ongoing story of tribal resistance and repatriation that makes Nicholson's legacy a still unfolding story.

Grace Nicholson's route to becoming a major collector and dealer of California Indian cultural items in the early twentieth century was shaped by a confluence of broader cultural movements in the era, movements such as women's increasing professionalization, southern California boosterism, and the commodification of American Indians for varied modes of consumption by tourists, anthropologists, and collectors. Nicholson's trajectory from genteel easterner to western entrepreneur fits the contours of the New Woman displayed in varying ways by Gay, Cory, and Schäffer. In 1877, sixteen years after Schäffer, Nicholson was born into an upper-middle-class family in Philadelphia, the daughter of Franklin and Rose Nicholson. Her mother died when Nicholson was an infant; her father died when she was thirteen. Raised subsequently by her grandparents, Nicholson attended the exclusive Girls' High School, graduating in 1896 with a specialization in commercial courses. She then did secretarial work for Carrol Hartman, an erstwhile businessman who later became her employee and travel associate in California. After her grandparents' deaths in 1901, she moved alone to Pasadena, in part because of ill health. According to a biographical statement left in her papers, "When Miss Nicholson had a couple of winters being ill with colds and—etc. her doctor advised her to come to California and she met Mr. Hartman again. She had a short time of sectyial [sic] work but had more ambition, a great curiosity, borrowed $500, on her 'face' from a Pasadena banker and plunged into the collecting field."[3]

Nicholson's move was part of a great migration to southern California that in-

cluded affluent easterners and middle-class Midwesterners lured there by ag-
gressive real estate advertising and a legendarily therapeutic climate. Pasadena at
the turn of the century was both a mecca for wintering easterners and home to a
coterie of boosters of southern California's rejuvenating climate, its burgeoning
economic opportunities, and its cultural wealth of Indian baskets and "curios."
Nicholson's solo move across the country, while more conventional than Cory's
radical retreat to the Hopi mesas, was certainly uncharacteristic of eastern upper-
middle-class women of her era. In choosing Pasadena, she joined other ambitious,
unconventional women, such as Charlotte Perkins Gilman and Mary Austin, who
made their homes or sojourned in the area. She remained unmarried and un-
tethered to family save for an uncle, her sole remaining close relative. Like Schäffer and Cory, she remade herself as a "westerner," never returning to her native
Philadelphia.

Nicholson had had no previous contact with Native peoples, let alone with
Native basketry or art, and yet, within several months of her arrival in Pasadena,
she had opened a small gallery specializing in Indian "collectibles." Her career
choice was inspired by her fortuitous association with George Wharton James,
for whom she briefly worked as a secretary. James, one of the era's reigning promoters of Native basketry, was at the forefront of a group of Pasadena-based in-
tellectuals, writers, and artists that nourished the development of southwestern
history, art, landscape, and literature as a field of celebratory study. Along with
his rival, Charles Fletcher Lummis, James presided over the commodification
and mythologization of southern California's mission era, a process that had been
set into motion by the extraordinary popularity of Helen Hunt Jackson's *Ramona*
(1884). The region's tourist boom, which followed in the wake of the novel's publication, enhanced by railroad expansion and increased travel opportunities for
the middle class, spurred the market for baskets made by Native women in southern California. Moreover, in books such as *Through Ramona's Country* (1908) and
In and Out of the Old Missions (1886), James fueled "ethnostalgic" tourism in southern California through his culturally persuasive and eminently marketable vision
of what Carey McWilliams aptly termed the "fantasy heritage" of the California
mission era.[4] For his part, in 1888 Lummis helped to launch the Association for
the Preservation of the Missions, worked to establish the Southwest Museum in
1907 (to which Nicholson later transferred countless Native cultural items), and
created and edited the magazine *Land of Sunshine,* later titled *Out West.*

Nicholson's association with James and his cohort was serendipitous: in 1902,
she opened what she later advertised as "California's Treasure House of Oriental
and Western Art: A Notable and Fascinating Shop," which emerged over the years
as a cultural center for Pasadena (fig. 70). She quickly carved a lucrative niche for
herself within the region's already flourishing Indian curio market. Ever alert to
shifting trends in collectible "exotic" art, she moved toward showcasing Asian art
in her gallery by 1911, gradually replacing Native arts with items gathered by

70. Grace Nicholson, *Grace Nicholson's House*, ca. 1906.
Reproduced by permission of The Huntington Library, San Marino, Calif., Album B, page 71.

buyers in Japan and China. Although she continued a patronage relationship with a few individuals, she curtailed her travel to Native communities. By 1924, her avid collecting of Asian art had culminated in her commission of a gallery modeled after a Chinese imperial palace and her own turn toward Buddhism. At her death, Nicholson donated her gallery to the city of Pasadena. Since 1971, the building, still commonly referred to as the Grace Nicholson House, has been home to the Pacific Asia Museum.

Nicholson's decision to plunge into the Indian art trade was fueled by the era's vogue for Indian collecting, epitomized by artfully arranged "Indian dens" in bourgeois homes as well as by newly minted museums. Both domestic and institutional settings were thus poised to display and "preserve" the seemingly dying arts of vanishing cultures gathered up by anthropologists and dealers in Indian communities throughout the American West. According to Marvin Cohodas, the "epicenter" for basket collecting was Pasadena and, to a lesser extent, Los Angeles, where "much of the literature on baskets and collecting was either written or published . . . before 1908."[5] Two decades before Nicholson arrived on the scene, wealthy eastern transplants and sojourners in Pasadena such as Belle Jewett were not only collecting baskets but having them photographed for nationally circulating magazines (fig. 71). By the 1890s, the "basket craze" was a nationwide phenomenon, generated by magazine articles, by department-store displays, by exhibits at regional and national expositions, such as the 1893 Chicago World's Columbian Exposition and the St. Louis World's Fair of 1904, and by railroad corporations' promotion of "Indian country" as a tourist destination.[6]

As the era's most visible boosters of basketry, James and Lummis promoted competing theories of Native basketry's role and its relevance to a contemporary Euro-American feminine consumer-collector. Although they sharply disagreed in their interpretations of Native basketry's "symbolism," both drew on the American Arts and Crafts Movement's construction of the "natural," lauding basketry's artistry amid a broader discourse of domestic primitivism that entwined notions of the Native, nature, and femininity. In James's 1901 article, "Indian Basketry in House Decoration," for example, he encourages his female readers to collect baskets so that "every well-appointed house might appropriately arrange an Indian corner."[7] The consolidation of baskets from diverse regions and tribes within a single room or "corner" enacted, on a domestic scale, the national move toward

71. Grace Nicholson (?), *Karuk Baskets*, ca. 1905.

Reproduced by permission of The Huntington Library, San Marino, Calif., Album B, page 83.

consolidation of indigenous lands wrought by conquest, the reservation system, and western economic development. An example of what Amy Kaplan has labeled "manifest domesticity," "Indian corners" inside American homes indexed the "safe" containment of Native peoples inside reservations.[8]

Through the organization and display of Native baskets, collectors also participated in the era's obsessive embrace of the "salvage paradigm," which sought the preservation of "authentic" material productions of "vanishing" cultures. In her 1904 article, "Humboldt Indians: A Sketch," published in *Out West,* Winifred Fry contrasts the "fad for all things Indian" with the "the love of . . . . Indian treasures," concluding with a lament that "Indian art work is becoming defiled by the touch of that commercialism belonging to our own white world. The basketmaker, finding such an open market for all her products, now makes her baskets simply for the money she can get out of them."[9] Fry's invocation of Indian authenticity was shared by Nicholson, even as her marketing of such items contributed to what Fry called the "decadence" of Indian baskets specifically designated for a consumer economy. Indeed, in her quest for the "pure" products of California Indian cultures, Nicholson turned toward particular regions in the state considered by other collectors and anthropologists to be the least "tainted" by dominant cultural commercialism.

Yet, despite Fry's nostalgic embrace of a static image of Native cultural productions, the basket trade was well established in northwestern California by the late nineteenth century. A common form of barter between Indians and whites, stretching back at least to eighteenth- and nineteenth-century New England, baskets were sold alongside roads or door-to-door, exchanged for goods at local stores, and given as gifts.[10] In northwestern California, tourists and locals purchased baskets and other items at Brizard's, a regional chain of general-merchandise stores, as well as at photography studios and other businesses in Eureka and Arcata. At the same time, the completion in 1889 of a railroad line from San Francisco to Ukiah (one hundred miles south of Eureka, one hundred miles north of San Francisco), aided by prominent area brokers and dealers, such as John Hudson, expanded the market for local Indian baskets.[11] Coveted by tourists and by institutional and private collectors since the late nineteenth century, Native baskets from northern California have rarely been understood by non-Natives as vital, continuing expressions of spiritual and cultural identity. In this way, Fry, despite her misperception of Native basketry as frozen in time, perhaps was inadvertently correct in her chagrin at the commodification of baskets. Although the basket trade enabled many Native families to survive within the interstices of new economies, the baskets themselves were and are most importantly spiritually alive, rooted in and giving ongoing form to indigenous world-views.[12]

Though her entrée into the Indian curio trade was baskets, Nicholson nourished the era's transformation of all kinds of Native arts into artifacts. A shrewd marketer, she was also a self-taught ethnologist, displaying some of her collection at the 1905 Lewis and Clark Centennial Exposition in Portland, Oregon, and even winning a silver medal for her solicited collection at the Alaska-Yukon-Pacific Exposition in Seattle in 1909. A member of the Sequoya League, an advocacy group for Indians cofounded by Lummis, she made use of articles, correspondence, and personal interactions to educate herself about the cultures she marketed. Her dual engagement with anthropology and commerce enabled her to cater skillfully both to eastern museum personnel and to a wealthy western clientele.

That a woman with neither professional training nor institutional affiliation was able to engage in both academic anthropology and commerce stemmed from the relative fluidity of the emergent field of anthropology in the early twentieth century. Although the founder of California Indian anthropology, Alfred Kroeber, was steering the field toward professional academic status, anthropology still offered rare access to women who worked either alone or under institutional supervision. From the Southwest to the upper Midwest, contemporaries and near contemporaries such as Matilda Coxe Stevenson, Elsie Clews Parsons, Natalie Curtis, and Frances Densmore pursued varying field projects, from collecting and recording songs to photographing daily life to conducting ethnographic research. Although Nicholson did travel to the Southwest and did purchase items from intermediaries in Arizona and New Mexico—the locus for many early women anthropologists—she focused most of her research efforts in California. Most strikingly, Nicholson was one of the first white women to make a career out of purchasing Native "artifacts" in northern California. As the lone woman among a mostly male cohort, she occasionally encountered anthropologists such as Kroeber, even providing him with items for University of California at Berkeley archives, while competing at other times with academic collectors such as Stewart Culin, curator of the University of Pennsylvania Museum and later of the Brooklyn Museum.

Nicholson benefited not only from the fluidity of gender restrictions in the field but also from the porous boundaries between academic and museum anthropology and nonacademic ethnological collecting. Those not formally educated in the field, such as Nicholson, Lummis, Charles P. Wilcomb, and John Hudson, served as curators, brokers, and collectors for regional, state, and national museums. Although lines were drawn between academic and nonacademic anthropologists in the first decade of the century, there was still significant overlap between the two groups as they enabled institutions, such as the Smithsonian and the University of California, to acquire capacious collections of California Indian materials, especially between 1900 and 1910, the peak decade of collecting in the state.[13] Samuel A. Barrett, for example, earned Berkeley's first doctorate in anthropology in 1908, following an early career as a merchant selling Pomo baskets in Ukiah, while anthropologist Pliny E. Goddard first conducted research on Hupa baskets while employed as a missionary at Hoopa Valley Reservation in the 1890s. Self-taught collector Charles P. Wilcomb loaned his personal collection of northern California Indian materials to the Golden Gate Museum in San Francisco, where he became curator of its California Indian exhibits in 1894.[14]

Similarly, many of Nicholson's activities in the field resembled those undertaken by academics such as Kroeber: gathering stories and information, taking photographs, and buying ceremonial and material items for museum study and display. In a field rendered competitive by the perception of California Indian peoples and their material cultures as equally vanishing "resources," she moved between anthropology and commerce as she forwarded the seemingly opposed yet complementary goals of preservation and consumption. By initiating ties with curators at Chicago's Field Museum, the University of Pennsylvania, and the Peabody Museum at Harvard University as early as 1902, Nicholson quickly positioned herself as a diligent and credible ethnologist; she then formalized that reputation by joining the American Anthropological Association in 1904.

At the same time, she developed a repertoire of marketing strategies that enhanced her authority and influence in the trade of Native cultural materials. For example, according to Cohodas, Nicholson adopted the patronage strategy used to lucrative ends by sometime rivals Amy and Abe Cohn, Reno-based dealers known for their exclusive contract with Louisa Keyser, a Washo weaver. Marketing Keyser's work under her Washo name, Dat-So-La-Lee, the Cohns inflated market demand for her baskets by advertising them as authentic and rare.[15] After Nicholson first met Mary Benson, an accomplished weaver, and her husband, William, in 1903, she established a patronage relationship with this Pomo couple that lasted for more than thirty years. In doing so, she gained exclusive access to the baskets Mary Benson wove and to the replicas of ceremonial items and other pieces that William Benson made as well as to their services as interpreters, informants, and brokers in surrounding Pomo communities. The Bensons, for their part, were already well-versed in such transactional exchanges with Euro-American dealers: they had worked for well-known local collector John Hudson and for curator Stewart Culin. With the help of Hudson, they had also spent several months at the St. Louis World's Fair demonstrating weaving techniques and selling their baskets, even winning the "highest award given at the fair, a gold medal," for a "sun basket."[16] In exchange for their work, the Bensons received payment, gifts, and funding for Mary Benson's eye surgery. In the winter of 1906–1907 Nicholson seemingly borrowed another Cohn business tactic by bringing the Bensons to stay with her in Pasadena, paying them to weave a large granary basket in front of her gallery.[17]

Nicholson proposed and established a similarly exclusive and sustained contract with Elizabeth Hickox, whose baskets she considered the "best of them all" when she first visited her along the Klamath River north of Orleans in 1908.[18]

72. Grace Nicholson, *Hickox Family*, ca. 1911.

Reproduced by permission of The Huntington Library, San Marino, Calif., Album A, page 83.

Over the ensuing decades of their business relationship, her baskets, and those made by her daughter, Louise, became collector's items through Nicholson's patronage, and in more recent years several exhibitions have been devoted to their artistry.[19] In a Nicholson photo from 1911, the Hickoxes—Luther, Elizabeth, Louie, Jessie, and Louise—stand in front of their home (fig. 72). In sporadic correspondence beginning with the words "Dear Friend Grace," the Hickox family related stories about people, events, and daily life in their region until Elizabeth Hickox's death in 1947.[20]

Nicholson's close ties with the Hickox family and her long-term contract with the Bensons were strengthened in part by her personal regard for Pomo and Karuk cultural and narrative productions. Such regard was also indexed by the contracts she made for specific Pomo creation stories and "ethnological" data from William Benson as well as for Karuk creation stories from Evaline (Dolly) Nelson, a Karuk woman with whom she stayed while on buying trips to the Klamath River area.[21] Her correspondence with both Nelson and Benson indicates that she had planned on publishing the narratives they shared with her, though such plans never came to fruition. Yet Nicholson's efforts to buy access to cultural information at times set her at odds with Benson, as her proprietary interests in these narratives overrode her ethnological stakes in them. For instance, in a letter from 1931, she expressed her anger and sense of betrayal on hearing that Benson had shared the Pomo creation-story cycle with Berkeley linguist Jaime De Angulo. Most strikingly, the letter asserts her sense of rightful title and ownership of his translations, which she had purchased.[22]

Thus drawn to northern California by the entwined imperatives of ethnographic salvage and consumer demand, Nicholson embarked in 1903 on her first collecting trip to the area with the aim of forging direct contacts with Indian agents, field matrons, merchants, and Indians who could then furnish her gallery. Many of her buying trips—trips to Alaska and British Columbia in 1905, summer trips to the lower Klamath River region beginning in 1906 and continuing in 1908 and 1911, several trips to the Southwest and other regions of California— were captured in photographs by both Nicholson and Carrol Hartman. Not a professional photographer but a prolific and sometimes gifted one, she took several thousand photographs, mostly of California Indians, which she captioned and pasted into about a dozen personal albums.

A crucial, and unusual, feature of her work was the inclusion of many of these images in her shipments of Native cultural materials to museum clientele.[23] Nicholson also notably included several pictures taken of her "in the field" by travel companion and associate Hartman, whose images reinforce her narrative self-representation, as suggested in a letter to the Peabody Museum's curator in which she describes their first trip to Karuk communities in 1908. "The trails were something fearful, in many places not safe for even mules to travel. It seemed all up and down but mostly *up*. I do not wonder that most collectors stay out of this region. Then too material is scarce and what few things they have they do not care to part with except at a good price."[24] Nicholson's letter partakes not only in the narrative of solitary exploration typical of the era's ethnographic travelogues— made more dramatic by her gender and class status—but also in the narrative of wilderness travel that, by implication, accentuates the authenticity of the items she wrests only at "a good price." In similar fashion, Hartman's photographs forward her self-representation as "lone ethnographer" by recording the physical challenges of traveling in the isolated Klamath River region, whose rugged coastal mountain ranges, whitewater rivers, and lack of roads required travel by pack trains over precipitously cliff-hugging trails and by canoe until 1912.[25] Hartman emphasizes this isolation and ruggedness in his photographs of Nicholson, confirming for viewers by implication the cultural purity of the region's tribes.

At the same time, Hartman's absent presence as documentarian of her buying trips directs us to the physical apparatus and human labors that made Nicholson's travels possible. In *Resting on the Klamath* (fig. 73), for example, Nicholson is seated alongside the river between two redwood dugout canoes. In the background, a community is visible, occupying the distant hillside; in the foreground, driftwood and stones demarcate the rest stop as a meeting ground between "wilderness" and human habitations. Near her are two Yurok ferrymen who enable her to travel through a region devoid of roads. In *Grace on Awful Swing Bridge over Salmon* (fig. 74), she inches her way across the Salmon near its confluence with the Klamath. In the far background two men wait for her to cross. In her travel diary from July 26, 1908, Nicholson, who had to use this bridge to visit communities at Katimin and Oak Bottom, writes, "Ready to leave and I surely would not cross that swing bridge again for any sum."[26] Whether poised on a dizzyingly high swing bridge, against a boulder, on a horse, or in a canoe, Nicholson in Hartman's snapshots thus always appears en route or in motion. This visual narrative of feminine mobility, however, is counterbalanced by the hidden presence of the photographer himself, accompanying Nicholson, and the more distant yet indispensable presence of local Hupa, Karuk, and Yurok men who ferried her across rivers, shouldered the items she bought, and advised her where to visit. An exception to this narrative is a photo captioned *Waiting for the Photographer* (fig. 75), which shows Nicholson, visibly sweating in the region's notorious summer heat, stoically waiting in a dugout canoe; Frank Ruben, her Yurok guide, is in front posing for the camera, and another ferryman is in back. Behind her is a stuffed canvas sack, overflowing with the items she has purchased along the river, including baskets.

While highlighting the physically dramatic rigors of Nicholson's buying trips to northwestern California, Hartman's visually engaging photographs also situate her as a lone white female in heroic pursuit of "authentic" Native cultures. Yet, although she was most likely the only white woman in this region actively engaged in buying "artifacts," Nicholson was in fact one of several unmarried white women who lived or worked in this region in the early twentieth century. A lengthy travel-diary entry from July 17, 1908, however, suggests what she thought of at least some of the other Euro-American women who also gained their living from Indian communities and whose local presence was similarly shaped by national policies of cultural assimilation and colonial regimentation. Notable both for its length and biting sarcasm in the midst of otherwise brief descriptions of the locales and people she visited and the types of transactions she made, her entry mocks Mabel Reed and Mary Arnold, two women who were part of a small regional network of field matrons, white women hired by the government to be "civilizing" influences in Native communities across the American West between 1891 and 1938.[27] Reed and Arnold spent two years in the Klamath River area and later published their experiences in a memoir still popular in the region, *In the Land of the Grasshopper Song* (1957). For their part, Reed and Arnold refer to Nicholson and Hartman in their book only in passing as "two buyers of Indian baskets," despite several extended encounters with them.[28] Field matrons such as Marie Johnson in nearby Requa wrote Nicholson in hopes of "find[ing] a suitable market for

baskets—to see if you would buy from us. I can secure you large or small baskets. I charge no commission as I am anxious to provide cash sales for the Indians."[29] Nicholson undoubtedly encountered other white women in the region, especially at Hoopa Valley Reservation, located downriver from the Karuk, where she made several buying trips and where white schoolteachers and missionaries

73. Carrol S. Hartman, *Resting on the Klamath*, 1908.

Reproduced by permission of The Huntington Library, San Marino, Calif., Album A, page 9.

worked in the early twentieth century. Nicholson's derisive observations about Arnold and Reed's "mission" and demeanor bespeak an ambivalence toward other white women professionals in this region, perhaps even a reluctance to "share" cross-cultural encounters, as she worked to make sense of her own conflicted role in the region and her attitudes toward the Native peoples living there.[30]

74. Carrol S. Hartman, *Grace on Awful Swing Bridge* over *Salmon*, 1911.

Reproduced by permission of The Huntington Library, San Marino, Calif., Album C, page 17.

75. Carrol S. Hartman, *Waiting for the Photographer*, 1908.

Reproduced by permission of The Huntington Library, San Marino, Calif., Album A, page 84.

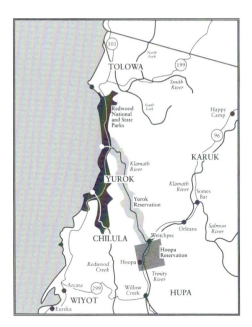

76. *Map of Northwestern California Tribes,* 1994.

Courtesy *News from Native Calif.* and the Calif. Park Service.

Nicholson's presence in the lower Klamath River region, like that of her female peers, was occasioned most immediately by reservation-era assimilation policies intended to strip Native Americans of their cultural, economic, and spiritual moorings. More broadly, her trips to the area were part of an ongoing, though shifting, migration of Euro-Americans beginning in 1850. By 1900, the lower Klamath River region, home to Karuk, Yurok, Hupa, and other Native peoples, white miners and settlers, and mixed-blood families, had undergone a half century of genocidal violence and ruinous land-use practices, such as hydraulic and placer mining, deforestation, and resource depletion (fig. 76). Like much of indigenous northern California, the Klamath River region was forever transformed by the Gold Rush, which spread from the Sacramento and Sierra regions northward to the area surrounding Mt. Shasta and Yreka, and westward through the Trinity and Marble mountains. By 1850, miners had started searching for gold along the lower Klamath and Salmon rivers. In September 1851, Redick McKee, an agent deputized to conduct "peace treaties" with tribes throughout northwestern California, ostensibly produced such an agreement for the Karuk and neighboring nations. The resulting document was at best a fiction, ignorant of the radically different social and political systems along the Klamath, and at worst a false implication that the government would protect the Indians from the depredations of miners. The following year, in the face of vehement opposition from white constituents and congressional representatives alike, none of the eighteen treaties were ratified because they would have conceded "extensive tracts of the most desirable mineral and agricultural Lands in California," according to the committee formed to investigate McKee's treaty making.[31]

Throughout the first decades of "contact," many Karuk and surrounding peoples were dispossessed of their homes and livelihoods as some miners and settlers burned homes and communities, kidnapped and raped girls and women, killed off game, and polluted the rivers. One of the major Karuk ceremonial centers, Panámniik, was burned and overlaid with the booming mining town of Orleans. Orleans became the county seat of what was then Klamath County; it had a population of two thousand in 1870. This figure includes a number of Chinese miners, who were driven out of the region in 1885. During the Red Cap War of 1855 the *Humboldt Times* reported that "citizens of Orleans Bar," "after a meeting to discuss the Indian problem, voted to kill on sight all indians [*sic*] having guns."[32] Newspapers on the coast in Eureka and Union (Arcata) echoed their peers throughout northern California by claiming that Indians needed to be exterminated or forcibly removed to distant reservations. In doing so, they were also echoing the stance of the newly minted state government, which as one of its first acts passed the 1850 Government and Protection of Indians Act allowing for indenture of "loitering, intoxicated, or orphaned" Indians, amended in 1860 to include adults.[33] According to Lee Davis, "In the coastal regions of Spanish occupancy from 1769 to 1848, the local Native American population was reduced by 90 percent. . . . Between 1845 and 1870, the Indian population in California declined by 80 percent, from 150,000 to 30,000 people. As many as 40 percent of these deaths were the result of extermination killings."[34] State-funded militias were paid for their services in securing scalps of Indian adults and children. The murder of adults and the kidnapping and subsequent enslavement of their orphaned children were common practices throughout northern California in the first few decades of statehood.

Because of their relative geographical isolation and inaccessibility, the Karuk, Hupa, and Yurok were better able to survive the onslaught of settlers and miners than their neighbors living on coastal and riverine lands attractive to farmers and ranchers. Each of these neighboring peoples—the Shasta, Chilula, Mattole, Wiyot, Nongatl, Lassik, and Tolowa—were either decimated or completely annihilated as distinct nations by the close of the nineteenth century. Northwestern California was the site of some of the nation's most infamous mass murders of indigenous peoples, murders that were overtly and covertly sanctioned by local leaders. One particularly notorious massacre, publicized by the outraged editorial of Bret Harte in the local paper and by editorials in San Francisco, was carried out at Indian Island (later called Gunther Island) in Humboldt Bay across from Eureka on February 25, 1860.[35] Over the course of a single night, a series of carefully coordinated massacres by local whites in the settlements of Indian Island, Eel River, and Bucksport wiped out hundreds of Wiyots.[36] The white men who led and participated in the massacres were well known in the area but were never charged or brought to trial. Other massacres in the region were also carried out with the participation or complicity of local leaders—at Hayfork in 1852, at Yontoket in 1853, and at Needle Rock in 1862. Surviving Indians were moved to the few area reservations or folded into communities such as Round Valley and Hoopa Valley. In the wake of the coercive loss of land and livelihood throughout the region, many of the area's indigenous people subsisted on the margins of the new economy of mining and logging. By the early twentieth century, forced removal of children to boarding schools, allotment, and the creation of the Forest Service land continued the assaults on the people's survival. Anthropologists, government and Forest Service employees, and missionaries converged on this region for the varied purposes of managing and eradicating the seemingly last vestiges of "authentic" tribal cultures and tribal land.

Into this volatile intercultural climate Nicholson also arrived, equipped with money, notebooks, and, most notably, a camera. Although she neither sold her photographs nor circulated them for broad public consumption, Nicholson created a visual archive of Hupa, Karuk, and Yurok peoples that cannot be understood apart from the images made by those who had already aimed their cameras at Native peoples in the region as well as at the dramatic landscape of redwoods, rugged coastline, and whitewater rivers. Peter Palmquist's research has uncovered at least "6,000 individuals involved in California photography before 1900," with "more than ten-percent of them women."[37] In northwestern California alone, many women harnessed photography as a means of documenting their cross-cultural encounters. At the turn of the century, for example, schoolteacher Nellie McGraw and missionary M. E. Chase used their automatic cameras to record their experiences at Hoopa Valley Reservation. In the same era, professional photographers Emma Freeman and Abbie Cardozo operated commercial galleries on the coast. From 1915 through the 1920s, Ruth Roberts took countless pictures of Yurok as part of her independent ethnographic research, while to the south Grace Hudson, whose husband was a major collector, took photographs around Ukiah to serve as models for her well-known oil paintings of Pomos, particularly women and children.[38]

Nicholson's collection of clipped articles and photographs suggests her familiarity with the work of some of the photographers in northern California, particularly the collectors and anthropologists who used photography to complement their research in the region. Henry W. Henshaw photographed Pomo for the Bureau of American Ethnology in 1892; Harvard graduate student Roland Dixon photographed the Maidu in 1899; Goddard photographed Hupa at the turn of the century. Kroeber took several hundred photographs of Karuk, Hupa, and Yurok people and posed for Nicholson's camera (several pictures of him are in one of her photo albums). Many of Kroeber's images were frontal and profile views made in the anatomical mode of physical anthropology, some of which were used to illustrate his compendium *Handbook of the Indians of California,* published in 1917.[39]

Ira Jacknis notes that "conspicuously absent" from Kroeber's archive are ceremonial images such as those taken by popular regional photographer A. W. Ericson; Ericson's pictures of Yurok, Karuk, and Hupa circulated locally and nationally, codifying a visual vocabulary of these nations.[40] Like his contemporary J. A. Meiser, another local commercial photographer, Ericson made several trips inland from the coast to Hoopa and the lower Klamath River in the 1890s in order to photograph ceremonies. Local newspapers, such as the *Arcata Union,* reported bitter resistance to his efforts: "The Indians have a holy terror of being photoed [*sic*] and when they sit at all for pictures, the privilege is based altogether on a cash consideration. Photographers are regarded as their natural enemy, and the approach of a 'picture man' to one of their camps, particularly if a dance happens to be in progress, is generally an occasion for threatened hostilities against the pale face."[41] Three years earlier, the newspaper applauded Ericson's success in prevailing despite such rebuffs: "He procured a number of excellent views of the Red-headed Woodpecker and White Deer-Skin dance. Mr. Ericson had to pay them $5 before he could get a picture, and then had to catch them on a jump."[42] Ericson's photographs of ceremonies were collected by curators such as Culin and by California-based magazines such as *Out West* and *Overland Monthly.*

The marketability of such images in this era underscores the ways in which the production and circulation of Indian photographs played vital roles in northwestern California's developing visual self-representation. After being chosen to represent Humboldt County at the California Building of the 1893 World's Columbian Exposition with selected images of the county's natural resources and "Indian relics," Ericson became the region's leading photographic emissary; his prints were used to "sell" the county's timber, agricultural, and other industries to prospective markets.[43] Given the history of violent conflict between settlers and indigenous people in the area, the turn toward images of local Indians as favored promotional tools could be imaginable only after the settlers viewed the Indians as unthreatening, safely contained by law and by the passage of time. By 1904, for example, an advertisement in the Arcata paper described Ericson's postcards as having "views of the redwoods of this county and of the Klamath and Hoopa [*sic*] Indians on them. They are for sale at the store of C. E. Gillis and the photograph gallery."[44] In its conjoining of nature and Natives, this advertisement participates in a form of cultural mythology stretching back to the Puritans' own imagined "errand" into the wilderness. The linked topoi of the vanishing Indian and vanishing forest, suggestive of the dual workings of "imperialist nostalgia" and a triumphal narrative of progress, similarly appear in an advertisement for Ericson's photographs printed six years later in the same paper: "California/Redwood and/Indian Views/Landscape photographs, photos of large redwood trees, also Hoopa [*sic*] and Klamath Indian pictures 7 × 9 inches."[45] Marking a dramatic representational shift in the dominant culture's view of northern California Indians, from scorned "Digger" to elegiac Native, such local advertisements paved the way for Edward Curtis to memorialize area Indians in 1923.

Well-versed in the region's iconography of Indian images, Nicholson herself collected the photographs of Ericson, Meiser, and many others, pasting them into albums.[46] She was also familiar with anthropological and touristic pursuits of Indian photographic subjects because Pasadena "was a mecca for photographers"—Adam Clark Vroman, Lummis, James, Frederick Monsen—who, singly or as members of the Pasadena Camera Club, took pictures of ceremonies in the Southwest such as the Hopi Snake Dance.[47]

Although she rarely took pictures of ceremonies, Nicholson did take countless pictures of the Native people she encountered on her buying trips and those who sold her items. Most distinctively, she made copies of many of these prints, sending them to tribal members as well as to museum curators. Although little is known of the types of cameras she used, and although she never signed and only occasionally dated her photos, she provided titles for many of the photographs taken in the Klamath River region, which can be verified by both her travel diaries and by contemporary tribal members.

Nicholson's own use of the camera, an already long-fraught medium in cross-cultural dealings in northwestern California, spotlights the tangle of personal, economic, and scholarly pursuits accompanying her transactions in the area. Rather than the stylized studio portraits of mixed-bloods favored by another popular regional photographer, Emma Freeman, Nicholson's pictures feature little that can be said to be "exotic" or romantic in the lexicon of Indian image making in the era. By including herself in certain pictures, she makes visible complicated moments of intercultural transactions; by situating in domestic settings subjects who display varying degrees of acculturation, she refuses fully to participate in the era's photographic discourse of Indian authenticity, best exemplified by the iconic images produced by famed contemporary Edward Curtis. Nicholson's images were produced not as ends in themselves but toward the multiple and at times conflicting ends of recording her economic transactions, building personal relationships with tribal members, and authenticating her merchandise for the eastern institutions that acquired many of these items.

I read a selection of these photographs, primarily of Karuks in 1908 and 1911, through the frames provided by her journals, correspondence, archival materials, and the perspectives of contemporary tribal members. In doing so, I pursue the ways in which Nicholson's photographs, like those made by Gay, Cory, and Schäffer, might lead us to what Judith Davidov terms "the missing story: one that would introduce and shift the focus to the term *encounter*."[48] Her presence in Hartman's photos, in the corner, on the edge, or center stage, highlights the broader histories of colonization that made these encounters, and hence these images, possible. However, Hartman's and Nicholson's photographs make available only part of the story informing these recorded moments of cross-cultural interaction. Karuk perspectives on these photographs point to the stories on the edge of or absent from the frame: the stories of these subjects, their lives and their communities, that were inaccessible to Nicholson and Hartman and that remain so for most contemporary viewers.

Nicholson's travel journals from 1908 and 1911 in the Klamath River region repeatedly reference photography as an indispensable part of her pursuit of cultural wealth, measured in part by ceremonial regalia, dentalia necklaces, and obsidian blades. Often linked within a single sentence—"made Oak Bottom Jack's picture and did business with him"[49]—her acquisition of cultural items and of photographs became twin signifiers of her success (fig. 77). A typical entry from July 13, 1908, conjoins the economic and visual sides of her transactions: about her meeting with a Hupa elder she called old Sanaxson, she writes, "Although we did not get all yet we secured the oldest and rarest finds—he did not want his picture taken but I hope the snap will come out all right."[50] Some of these intercultural transactions, however, are less easily dismissed as coercive and unwelcome, such as with a Karuk elder named Snappy, or Emma, who enabled Nicholson to "secure her picture without any trouble."[51] In the close-up snapshot of Nicholson and Snappy (fig. 1 in the Introduction), we see the two women, sitting together on the ground, engaged in conversation, seemingly oblivious to the camera's eye. Several other photographs in Nicholson's collection feature her in similar conversations with Karuk women.

Given the refusal of many Karuks in this era to pose for outsiders' cameras, Nicholson's ability to gain their permission on so many occasions is striking. As newspaper accounts about Ericson and articles in San Francisco's journal *Camera Craft* show, Native peoples in this region resisted, refused, or demanded payment from intrusive and persistent Euro-American photographers. In his 1903 article, "'Digger Indians' and the Camera," Horatio Stoll recounts Native reactions to his photography excursion along the coast north of Eureka: "They showed such a pronounced aversion to being snapped, I was prevailed upon by friends to lay aside my camera when traveling about among them." Stoll then gleefully details his refusal to do so, noting that when he did "snap" Native people without their permission, "the average Indian scowls fiercely and slouches away, muttering inarticulate things to himself, covers his head with his hands or coat, or tries to make the best possible bargain with you for a few poses."[52] Over twenty years later, in 1924, Mildred Ring observed during a trip along the Klamath River that although younger Indians often owned Kodaks, "their consent to be kodaked is oftentimes as difficult to obtain as that of the older Indians." Her attempts to "kodak the Indians" succeeded only with "repeated visits, repeated gifts, repeated friendly overtures and, with those mercenarily inclined, a dollar or two, to overcome this superstition."[53] Rather than being based in "superstition," such responses signified resistance to yet another invasion of cultural and personal privacy.[54]

While Stoll and Ring refer to photography "in the field" of northwestern California, Nicholson's contemporary Emma Freeman, a self-taught photographer and painter based in Arcata, specialized in artistic portraiture of Hupa and Yurok in the Klamath region.[55] Her photographs of Indians, including the Karuk, partake in the stylized romanticism of noble savagery. Her studio photographs tend to be posed against painted backdrops, with signature props of Indian authen-

77. Grace Nicholson, *Oak Bottom Jack*, ca. 1911.

Reproduced by permission of The Huntington Library, San Marino, Calif., Album C, page 19.

ticity, belied by the mixing of tribal accessories and the mixed-blood friends she used as her subjects. Much like Curtis, who clothed his Hupa fishermen subjects in breechcloth and wigs, Freeman posed her subjects in an invented pastiche of "Indian" costumery. Her beautifully hand-colored pieces, with such titles as *Klamath Tango, Call of the Wild,* and *Enchantress,* won her regional acclaim

78. Emma Freeman,
Weaver of Dreams,
ca. 1914–1915.

Courtesy Edward E. Ayer Collection, The Newberry Library, Chicago, Ill.

and accolades at the Panama-Pacific Exposition in San Francisco in 1915. One of Freeman's artfully designed studio portraits features a contemplative young Yurok "maiden" posed amid a variety of Native baskets, gazing demurely at the display (fig. 78).

In contrast, Nicholson's photographs of Klamath-area women—Dolly Sanderson, Mary Ike, Elizabeth Hickox, and Hickox's mother, Polly (Conrad) Steve—present basket weavers with their own work at or near their homes. According to Sally McLendon, "Collectors and dealers frequently photographed Native American basketmakers together with their products and basket collections/ors, and once they had assembled a sizeable collection, usually had it photographed."[56] Similarly, Nicholson meticulously documented many of her purchases, including the baskets displayed in the portraits of Sanderson and Steve (figs. 79 and 80). Both basket weavers are seated outside, Sanderson on the rocky shore along the Klamath River, Steve on an unidentified rocky hillside. Motivated by her interest in the authenticity of the items rather than by authentic "Indians," Nicholson doesn't conceal her subjects' syncretic mix of clothing nor related indices of acculturation in her other photographs of Karuk. Unusual in Nicholson's collection for their setting—most of her snapshots are less formal and taken in front of people's homes—these two pictures denote her investment in these women's baskets. Her particular care here in pairing these specific baskets with their weavers, and her subordination of background, even the person, to the baskets being photographed, underscores the high value she placed on them and their subsequent marketability to museums and other collectors.

At the same time, Nicholson found purposes for these photographs other than as documentation, by using them as a means of improving her own image in Klamath country. Steve's daughter, Elizabeth Hickox, for example, received and passed along photographs of her friends and neighbors. She writes, "Many thanks for the photograph of Old Hippey and Bob's, I think they look so natural. If you have a photo of Bernard's family, I would like to get it. And will make it all right with you." She also received a copy of the photograph of her mother: "The photos you sent me and my mother many thanks for them. My mother is very proud of them, she thinks her basket took such a clear picture. Louise Joe said she received the pictures you sent her and her Grandma. They think they are very nice."[57] Blurring the borders between economic and personal exchange, Nicholson sent prints as gifts back to Karuk, Hupa, and Yurok, as well as to local whites,

79. Grace Nicholson, *Mrs. Dolly Sanderson Selling Me Her Baskets* on *Klamath River below Red Camp Karok,* 1911.

Reproduced by permission of The Huntington Library, San Marino, Calif., Album C, page 29.

80. Grace Nicholson,
Mrs. Polly Conrad,
1911.

Reproduced by permission
of The Huntington Library,
San Marino, Calif., Album C,
page 20.

thereby (re)casting her work in the region as one built on friendship and reciprocity rather than on financial gain and ethnological study. After she returned from her first Karuk trip, she made copies of her photographs and sent them to the people whose pictures she had taken. On scraps of paper kept in her files, she carefully wrote down names and addresses of the people to whom she owed copies of prints. Nicholson seems to have gained permission to take people's pictures in part by promising to send them a copy of the picture. Thus conceived, her photographs circulated as a form of exchange between rare items: the ownership of pictures by area residents and the ownership of Karuk cultural items by outsiders.

Nicholson's care in sending these photographs back as she had promised complicates, though doesn't exonerate, her troubling presence in the region as a dealer in Native cultural patrimony. She seems to have borrowed a favored technique of ethnographers such as George Mooney who frequently used photographs as an entrée into different Native communities in the late nineteenth century. Jacknis relates Mooney's story of how he obtained the first photograph of Jack Wilson

("Wovoka"), the Paiute founder of the Ghost Dance. Mooney showed Wovoka's uncle photos he had taken "of some of my Indian friends across the mountains and brought over the photos of several Arapahoe and Cheyenne who I knew had recently come as delegates to the Messiah [Wovoka]. This convinced him that I was all right, and he became communicative."[58] After meeting with Wilson, Mooney gained access to a Cheyenne-Arapahoe community by producing the very photograph he had just taken of Wilson. As part of a repertoire of photographic strategies incorporated into his fieldwork, exhibition work, and research, Mooney wielded photographs as forms of exchange and entrée rather than simply as aesthetic or ethnographic documents.[59]

Nicholson similarly sent photographs as souvenirs along with baby or Christmas gifts to certain families in the Klamath River region. In turn, some Natives and whites placed great value on these photographs; one was Julia Jones, who had sold Nicholson some of her baskets and who wrote her in 1912, thanking her for the gifts she had received for her children. Nicholson paid high prices for Klamath-area baskets and cultural items, upward of $100 and more in some cases, and thus received letters from whites and Indians offering to sell or to mediate the sale of particular items sought by Nicholson. Sam Frame, Brizard's store manager in Somes Bar and later at Weitchpec, thanked her in a letter for the photographs she sent him, noting that "I think everybody who you sent pictures to got them" and in turn enclosing postcards he had made of Karuks and Somes Bar. He also described his own negotiations to obtain ceremonial items for her, claiming in one 1908 letter, "They tried to back out . . . but I wouldn't let them."[60] His successor, W. H. Hotelling, asked her, "Now in regard to Indian caps and baskets. What kind would you like and about what would you like to pay for them?"[61] Other white residents wrote to Nicholson letters dictated by Indians, offering to send items for her inspection, while many others detailed negotiations for particular ceremonial items, such as woodpecker headbands and obsidian blades. For example, in a letter from 1912, Nellie Wright, wife of a Brizard's store manager, wrote, "An Indian wanted me to sell a woodpecker roll for him as he needs some money so we sent it to you on approval, if it suits you let us know how much you are willing to pay for it."[62]

That so many Klamath residents initiated contact with Nicholson and willingly transacted with her reminds us that these encounters not only spanned the continuum of participation, agency, and control but often involved multiple cross-cultural interactions among whites, mixed-bloods, and full-bloods. In his article "Tricks of the Trade," Douglas Cole cautions that scholarly charges of appropriation and theft by Euro-American collectors, dealers, and anthropologists in the early twentieth century are often overly reductive, making victims out of those who frequently initiated and sought out such trades. He argues that "Natives entered the art and artifact market themselves, often exploited it for their own needs and often welcomed the opportunities which it offered."[63] In his own research on

81. Grace Nicholson, *Mrs. Ike*, 1911.

Reproduced by permission of The Huntington Library, San Marino, Calif., Album C, page 27.

Northwest Indian traders, Cole found that "they had their own interests, their own values, and their own needs," which informed, for example, their willingness to sell off household items no longer in use.[64]

The Ikes, pictured in front of their house in fig. 81, knew some of the tricks of trading with outsiders for information and for items. Mary and Little Ike, well-known residents who lived across from Ameekyáaraam, on the Klamath River, were the subject of many photographs by Nicholson and by anthropologists Kroeber and E. W. Gifford. Little Ike was a primary informant for Kroeber in 1902, while Mary Ike shared Karuk cultural information with Gifford between 1939 and 1942. Their experience in dealing with outsiders irritated Nicholson, who complained about Little Ike's shrewdness in her diary. "He wanted four bits before he would show us anything but finally brought his old stuff out and at last parted with some of it."[65] With his steady and confident gaze Little Ike is literally and figuratively at home with the camera, while Mary seems to be in mid-sentence as she glances over at him. They have arranged around them some of the possessions that they have probably just sold to Nicholson—work baskets, an elk-horn spoon, and some bundles. Nicholson's travel diaries in the Klamath region confirm that other Native people shared the Ikes' ability to dictate the terms of the trade or, more subtly, refuse her by setting prices higher than she would pay. She considered a headband she wanted priced too high ($100), and, in Weitchpec, she "found some fine things but in most cases the prices were very high." Nicholson thus met with a range of individuals who resisted or negotiated on their own terms.[66]

Yet still other travel entries make clear that she could be equally persistent, particularly with elders strapped for cash in a new market economy. In notes accompanying an inventory list sent to C. C. Willoughby, curator at the Peabody Museum, Nicholson describes a Hupa elder who needed a few hundred dollars to put on his final Jump Dance, and "as he had very little ready cash, I succeeded in prevailing upon him to show me all of his old possessions, and purchased everything possible."[67] The irony of this individual's divesting his wealth in order to be able to put on a ceremony is all the more wrenching in light of Nicholson's willingness to seize the opportunity raised by his predicament.

Such letters, as well as the photographs of baskets, then, underscore the personal privation driving many of these cross-cultural transactions. Financial necessity, for example, clearly underlined Margaret Harrie's decision to sell her baskets to Nicholson: "I have a hard living because I have childrens [*sic*] to take care all by myself."[68] The solemn, hard-edged lines of her face, the half-quizzical glance of the boy, and the tight fist of the daughter signal their tenseness and stiffness in the face of Nicholson's camera (fig. 82). (Nicholson spelled the family

82. Grace Nicholson, *Margaret Harry and Two Children*, 1911.

Reproduced by permission of The Huntington Library, San Marino, Calif., Album C, page 18.

83. Grace Nicholson, *Willie Rubens*, ca. 1908–1911.
Reproduced by permission of The Huntington Library, San Marino, Calif., Addenda.

name "Harry.") Yet, the mother's fingers, gently resting on her daughter's shoulders, and the twinned dresses of mother and daughter bespeak a familial closeness that they make largely inaccessible to Nicholson. Moreover, their facial and
bodily resistance to the camera directs us to the stories that are not yielded by
this image alone. A photograph of Margaret Harrie as a much older woman,
printed in Karuk scholar Julian Lang's book *Ararapíkva*, is entirely different: it
portrays an elder in a basket cap holding a half-made cradle basket; her relaxed
and softened features bear scant resemblance to Nicholson's image. As one of the
Karuk storytellers honored in Lang's book, an elder rooted in her culture and language, Harrie cannot be contained by the political and economic inequalities that
structured the 1911 photograph.[69]

Many of Nicholson's photographs do expose, however, the subject's watchful
reverse gaze at Euro-American outsiders. Although some of her subjects are playing the game of the market they are forced into, their expressions say, "You won't
get to know us";[70] this attitude is evidenced in the slightly derisive and direct
expression of Willie Ruben in fig. 83. Meanwhile, in *Nellie Rubens and Child*
(fig. 84), the little girl is half turned to her mother or grandmother, with her eyes
looking back at the photographer with curiosity and wariness. (Nicholson mis-

spelled the family name.) Nellie Ruben, an acclaimed basket weaver, stands solid and inexpressive, framed by the doorway to their home. Although her soiled dress might suggest poverty, her wealth is openly displayed in the dentalia necklaces around her neck. Her body language symbolically blocks the viewer's access to both her home and her own thoughts on the recording of this cross-cultural encounter.

In *Fugitive Poses,* Gerald Vizenor writes that "the crucial stories of natives in photographs are in the eyes and hands. . . . The eyes and hands of wounded fugitives in photographs are the sources of stories, the traces of native survivance; all the rest is ascribed evidence, surveillance, and the interimage simulations of dominance."[71] A photograph of a young Yurok girl (fig. 85), with brows furrowed, lips compressed, arms stretched across the frame of her family's door, tells just such a story of "native survivance." Policing the border between outside and inside, Genevieve Brooks stands firmly, directing a steely and uninviting look at the photographer. This image of a young girl's assertion of her autonomy and inaccessibility even as her privacy is being violated is remarkable as much for what

84. Grace Nicholson,
*Nellie Rubens and
Child,* ca. 1908–1911.
Reproduced by permission of
The Huntington Library, San
Marino, Calif., Addenda.

85. Grace Nicholson, *Genevieve Brooks at Requa*, ca. 1908–1911.

Reproduced by permission of The Huntington Library, San Marino, Calif., Album D, page 82.

it doesn't reveal as for what it does. By standing guard against Nicholson's photographic intrusion into her world, Brooks refuses Nicholson entry into the stories, experiences, and histories of her community. At the same time, the occupant of this image serves cautionary notice to those contemporary viewers who share Nicholson's position outside the door, one best summed up by Native photog-

rapher Jolene Rickard. Referring to an early-twentieth-century photograph of a
Crow ceremony, she argues that "the Crow people . . . are inside the camera's
frame but conceptually beyond the grasp of most observers."[72]

A final example here, of Phoebe Maddux and her daughters (fig. 86), perhaps
best illustrates the way in which these photographs motion toward other ways of
seeing Nicholson's legacy among the Karuk. In this image, Maddux, a medicine
woman who also shared Karuk culture with anthropologist John Harrington in
1928, sits for a more formal pose while her two daughters stand shyly behind
her. In this portrait, both mother and daughters wear their wealth of dentalia
necklaces, while the mother is draped in what appears to be an otter skin. Inadvertently cut off from the frame but still visible on the ground is a half-finished
basket, perhaps intended for Nicholson. Attention to the edges of this photograph yields other details, such as the open doorway that frames an open win-
dow offering a glimpse behind the house. The frequent appearance of doorways
as visual frames for Nicholson's photographs serves as an apt metaphor for the
lack of closure signified by these images. Although some of her photographed
subjects close off entryways into their lives, the open entryway in the Maddux
photograph suggests the multiple directions in point of view and perspective in-
stigated by these images and the occasion of their production.

86. Grace Nicholson, *Phoebe Maddux and Daughters*, 1911.

One such direction in which these photographs have traveled is as artifacts intended for view by museum personnel. Nicholson sent copies of prints not only to tribal members but to museums like the Peabody, which amassed a huge collection of Karuk and Hupa cultural items through her collecting efforts. She sold these items to Lewis Farlow, a wealthy Pasadena resident who in turn donated them to the Peabody. Nicholson was responsible for transferring as many as twenty thousand "specimens" from tribes across the American West to museums such as the Peabody, the Southwest Museum, the Field Museum in Chicago, and the Smithsonian.[73] Even as Nicholson personalized her transactions with Klamath River residents by sending them photos and gifts for their children, she sent the Peabody's curator gifts, photographs, and detailed inventory lists that identify the item, its owner or maker, and sometimes the story of how she obtained the item. In this context, her photographs not only circulated as indices of ethnographic authenticity but were also meant to forge relationships between the often faceless, anonymous "artifacts" collected by museums and the people who had previously used them. The multiple functions and recipients of these photographs encapsulate Nicholson's dual efforts as both entrepreneur and ethnologist, efforts that left a complicated legacy for northwestern Californian Indians.

The most obvious legacy of Nicholson's work is recorded by other photographs, those of numbered Karuk inventory in museums across the country. Nicholson's success in securing what she once called "the trophies" can be measured by her claim in 1908 to the Peabody's curator that "you will notice that the Karok material is quite complete; and I am sure equals that owned by any Museum in the country especially in old objects."[74] In turn, the curator congratulated her in a letter dated October 13, 1910. "I think you and Mr. Hartman deserve much credit for your method of handling the Indian. You have been very successful in every way and I congratulate you both."[75] The long-term impact of Nicholson's expeditions appears in a telling letter from Elizabeth Hickox written in 1923, inviting her to a multitribal celebration: "I only wish you and Mr. Hartman could come up and bring us some Indian dresses and beads. So we could dress up with the rest of them. If you come be sure to bring your camera."[76] Her letter echoes a comment made by Mary Arnold in the wake of Nicholson's 1908 trip: "the Indians at Kotemeen and Pichpichi had sold all their ceremonial things."[77] A powerful visual counterpart to Arnold's claim is a picture Hartman took of Nicholson following behind Tin Tin, a Karuk *fatewanan* (medicine man), who carries a large sack of purchased items on his back (fig. 87). With their backs to the viewer, the two figures move away from Katimin and Íshipish, the first crucial steps away from Karuk lands and toward metropolitan centers.[78]

Although this photograph is out of focus, Nicholson's transactions, and their long-term consequences, are not: like hydraulic mining in this same era, Nicholson's extraction of Karuk culture for the economic and cultural enrichment of others wrought devastation. By removing such a wealth of materials from the

87. Carrol S. Hartman, *Tin Tin Packing Stuff from Katimin and Ishipichi,* 1911.

Reproduced by permission of The Huntington Library, San Marino, Calif., Album C, page 21.

Karuk and neighboring tribes, Nicholson and the many other collectors, dealers, and anthropologists who engaged in similar pursuits throughout Indian country performed a cultural strip-mine. And yet, in ways that she probably never could imagine, Nicholson's photographs not only circulate now as a valued part of Karuk tribal history but also play an ongoing part in cultural repatriation and tribal nation building. Aided by the Native American Graves Protection and Repatriation Act (NAGPRA) of 1990, the Karuk and other Indian nations are trying to wrest control of some of the cultural heritage removed during the era of ethnographic salvage by pursuing legal claims for some of the items purchased by Nicholson and stored at museums across the country.

NAGPRA allows for the repatriation of items that meet the federal government's definition of "cultural patrimony": "any object having ongoing historical, traditional, or cultural importance central to Native American groups, rather than property owned by an individual Native American, and which, therefore cannot be alienated, appropriated, or conveyed by any individual and such object shall have been considered inalienable by such Native American group at the time the object was separated from such group."[79] Since its passage, NAGPRA has become one of the focal points of contemporary tribal activism, inseparable from Indian nations' broader struggles for cultural, political, and economic sovereignty. In the words of Thomas Biolsi and Larry Zimmerman, "The alienation of cultural property and its repatriation to Indian peoples has emerged as one of the most important themes in the analysis of knowledge production in the context of late imperialism in Indian/non-Indian relations."[80] NAGPRA calls for museums to inventory their holdings of Native American human remains, funerary objects, and ceremonial items and to make their findings readily available to tribes.

In the wake of NAGPRA, museums and Indian nations must negotiate over sometimes contesting notions of ownership and property, of art and artifact. In a historical irony, some of the very photographs used to document the removal of tribal items are now being wielded as documentary evidence in support of repatriation claims. In several successful repatriation cases involving Alaskan Natives, for example, historical photographs have been indispensable in proving legal claim to particular ceremonial items.[81] Yet photographs can go only so far. Although Nicholson's meticulous documentation, both written and photographic, facilitates the identification of specific items, very few of these items are eligible for repatriation under NAGPRA's provisions. The economic and psychological duress under which many individuals parted with their cultural patrimony is not admissible evidence nor is the problem of Nicholson's unethical acquisitions, such as her purchase of an item inadvertently sold to her. In a 1908 note accompanying an inventory list to the Peabody, Nicholson writes, "Medicine charm, Karok. This was in a case filled with some feathers and root, obtained from an old woman at Camp Creek. . . . I kept this charm trusting for some information regarding same but it seems impossible to secure any. In fact the Indians are rather anxious to have it returned to them, they did not seem to know it was in the case at the time."[82]

However, Nicholson's photographic trail at least has provided a means to trace the movements of thousands of Karuk and Hupa items far from their homelands. For example, the Karuk are pursuing repatriation claims at several museums, and the Hupa received seventeen items claimed under NAGPRA—some of them originally acquired by Nicholson—from the Peabody in the fall of 1998. These items were placed at the Hoopa Museum, a "living" museum that both displays items on loan and lends items for ceremonial use. In the words of then-Hupa tribal chairman Merv George, "It's a victory for not only the regalia itself—because we believe it is living and has a life and spirit of its own—but for the people who created it."[83] However, an article in *News from Native California* reveals the "hidden cost" of successful repatriation: the regalia reclaimed by the Hupa has been found to be so contaminated with pesticides from decades in museum storage that it cannot be used.[84]

The story of Grace Nicholson's impact on tribes in northwestern California is still unfolding, over ninety years after she first arrived in the region. The shifting roles played by historical photographs, such as those by Nicholson and Hartman, are evident in the reclamation, reappropriation, and nation building being undertaken by California Indian tribes. Various statewide projects, such as the California Indian Library Project, have made copies of early field notes, photographs, and sound recordings available in county libraries throughout the state.[85] In a reversal of the trope of the "vanishing Indian," which dictated much early photographic production in California, "the early photographs (of ceremonies), along with the material collections of museums, have been used by some indigenous groups to help revive the old dance costumes and other material aspects of community."[86] Similarly, the grassroots Native American History Project, based in Ukiah, is aimed at re/connecting Pomo families with old photographs of their relatives, some of whom are being "seen" for the first time. Catalyzed by a donation of photographs to a historical society, this project has sponsored community gatherings in which people come together to share and identify photographs.[87] Similarly, a collection of Nicholson's photographs, purchased back by the Karuk nation, has been on view in one of the tribal complexes. In a move suggestive of what Hulleah Tsinhnahjinnie calls "photographic sovereignty"—the right to claim and take control of Indian photographs—the poster board featuring these photographs is fittingly framed by a Karuk tribal design.[88] The Karuks' planned creation of its People Center will forward these initial efforts to recover the archive of Karuk photographs taken by outsiders. In the words of Director of Natural Resources Leaf Hilman, the People Center "will be a reflection of a living culture as opposed to showing something from a lost past.[89] In this and other ways, Indian nations such as the Karuk are taking what Vizenor has termed "the simulation of a tribe in photographs" as one tool for affirming and reaffirming their ongoing presence and vitality as a people.[90]

In her article "A Curator's Perspective: Native Photographers Creating a Visual Native American History," Theresa Harlan writes, "My question is, how much can we really learn from photographs taken of Native Americans by Euro-Americans? My answer is very little."[91] What "we" can learn is this: that the federal laws and cultural policies that made many of these images possible have utterly failed, turned back by Native peoples who not only have refused to vanish under the camera's lens but have recaptured these images as part of their continuing story of survival.

SUSAN BERNARDIN

THEIR SHADOWS BEFORE THEM

Photographing Indians

I have a photograph in front of me that I brought back from Cuzco in the Peruvian Andes almost three decades ago (fig. 88). Shot from above, the photo shows a dozen Quechua men and women on a pale, hard-packed dirt street between railroad tracks and whitewashed, tin-roofed sheds. Three women sit beside thick piles of what appears to be straw for thatching. One woman carries a large bundle on her back, slung in the traditional shawl pouch. A man and woman walk through the middle of the scene, the trim young man dressed in a snug black sweater, black jeans, and black knit hat, looking rather chic and jaunty in mid-stride, while the woman walks stolidly with her full skirt casting a wide shadow and her face hidden beneath the broad brim of her hat. The man's hands are in his pockets, and he looks into the distance with a detached air, as if perhaps he's listening to something the woman is saying. All but one of the women wear the high-crowned and broad-brimmed white hat common among the Quechua. The exceptional woman wears a black hat and stands talking with two other women while a child who looks to be at least two years old hangs limply in a sling on her back. It is past midday, and everyone casts a long and heavy shadow against the nearly white dust of the street.

The air, Roland Barthes writes in his famous discussion of photography, *Camera Lucida,* "is the luminous shadow which accompanies the body; and if the photograph fails to show this air, then the body moves without a shadow, and once this shadow is severed, . . . there remains no more than a sterile body."[1] In the crystal-bright Andean air, the Quechua objects in my photograph are frozen with

88. Louis Owens, Snapshot of Cuzco, ca. 1975.

Courtesy of Louis Owens.

their shadows before and behind them—their shadows deceptive illusions of temporal existence—but the air has been sucked out of the moment by a great colonial vacuum leaving not the sterile body but no body at all, no substance beyond the paper in my photograph album. I could read the photograph as inscribing the Quechuas' economic oppression in late twentieth-century Peru, but nothing in the scene conveys such information; the people appear contented, even happy as far as body language and facial expressions convey such feelings. The history of genocide and ethnocide and brutal political and economic oppression of these native Andeans is a history I bring to the tableau in the photo, not something I read therein. This is a text that can be written only over the inert shapes in the photograph, not one the Andeans themselves inscribe or decode.

No tourists are to be seen in this photo taken in a popular tourist destination scant miles from world-famous Machu Picchu, though it is unmistakably a tourist picture, a representation of the "other" from outside, like a view down into not an aquarium but a tide pool, where the denizens go about their business as nature intended and the unseen observer inhabits a different sphere, breathes a different medium. There is no indication whatsoever that the people in the photograph are aware that they are the subjects of my camera. Descended from Native North American Choctaw and Cherokee peoples, as well as dislocated Irish and French, I have not asked permission to take a photograph of these indigenous individuals and have, in fact, rudely invaded their intimate community from a bridge at a safe distance above them, a Choctaw-Cherokee conquistador rapacious for golden images to bring home. Today, as I try to read the photograph thousands of miles and many years away, I am stranded in ignorance. I was there, felt the knife-thin Andean air, and smelled the odors of llamas and crowded humanity and wood smoke, but I am lost within the lacunae of the photographic signs. I remain outside, confronting flat and resistant surfaces. I see, in fact, only myself in this photograph.

Barthes comments that "essentially the camera makes everyone a tourist in other people's reality, and eventually in one's own." He argues further that "a photograph is always invisible: it is not it that we see[;] . . . the referent adheres."[2] It seems to me that my photograph has not made me a tourist in the Quechua people's reality (though it has, without question, made me a tourist in my own for this moment) and that the referent, in fact, has not adhered at all. What has adhered is the opacity of the medium, the geometrical shapes before me that are plainly here but not there; in freezing a moment from outside, "shooting" the people on that Cuzco street, I have simply removed a particle of my own existence and identity from time and history. Cuzco for me, and the Quechua people, will always be here, in this moment removed from history, and thus never in the present, never imminent. There is no referent except the subjective splinter of memory that resolves itself into utter solipsism. These many years later, here in New Mexico, nothing depends on my static construction of the Quechua people who strode through the scene, sat or stood gossiping, cast shadows through time. Barthes admonishes, "The Photograph does not call up the past."[3] The photograph may possess great affect, but of effect there is none. Coming across the photograph these many years later, I recognize it for what it is finally: an *objet trouvé* of colonial commodification, like those countless thousands of pictures of Native Americans in drawers and boxes and museums and books all over the world.

I should have known better even more than twenty years ago, should have known that my act was worse than larceny, for I wasn't taking anything, not even a picture. We speak of "taking" and "shooting" a photograph, and truly shooting is the more accurate term. When one rubs charcoal over a piece of paper held to the face of a gravestone, one "takes" the graphic impression of the marker of death and bears it away. The interface between the living and dead is tactile, immediate, intimate; contact is made, and thus the iconography of death assumes a life the photograph cannot attain. The photograph, in contrast, prevents interfacial contact of any sort, demands distance as an essential part of the medium. The camera literally comes between subject and object.

Furthermore, rather than "taking" the photograph, it is more accurate to say that we bring the photograph with us, an internal negative always ready to be superimposed over the object of desire. It is true that we take the artifactual reality of the photograph away with us, but then isn't it even more true that we brought the imminent artifact with us in the first place? The photograph of this Cuzco street existed ages before I aimed a camera, before my plane rose out of Lima and then dipped its wing to edge past a mountain shoulder into the old Incan capital. I had brought the photograph with me from North America, from the United States, from my college classes, from magazines and every medium that had already produced and reproduced the exotic other for me and everyone—that had produced me *as* the exotic other in differing circumstances. All was predetermined. I did not take their picture; I brought that already extant negative and imposed it on those descendents of the Incas, *exposed* them to it, for it was the preexisting picture that told me these women and men were interesting, colorful, photogenic, vulnerable to intrusion and definition within the lens of my camera. To define, it should be remembered, is to limit, to set boundaries, to contain. The act of looking through the aperture and triggering the shutter defined the Native women and men as Not Me even as I subsumed their value into what I would become. And the images in the photograph ensure that the Quechua subjects are not themselves either, for they have been catapulted out of their own frame into another, not purely mine but rather my acquisitive culture's frame, in which their images have value utterly apart from any possible unique humanity.

I have another very different photograph from that South American journey, a picture taken in Buenos Aires during the terrifying time of the *desaparecidos*, when people were vanishing and bodies without heads or hands were regularly found floating in the river. Tensions were high. Streets were empty, doors locked, and shutters closed throughout the city. In this photo, an important-looking

gentleman is laying a wreath at a bronze statue of some national hero while surrounded by a dozen serious-looking men in black suits. Several of the men have
turned to face out of the picture, as if taken by surprise, and one has been caught
in mid-stride, his right hand reaching inside the jacket of his suit and his men-
acing dark glasses staring straight from the photograph. He is striding out of the
picture to confront the photographer, me. I had made the mistake of rushing up
to take a picture of this political affair, and one of the security men responded to
my sudden appearance and movement in the deserted square as a threat. The resulting photograph, which almost captured the instant of my demise, is an acci-
dent, unplanned and therefore unframed. Shooting the photo, I am almost shot.
The impromptu moment allowed for no pre-scripted narrative, no story prefigur-
ing the accidental confrontation. The borders of the photograph cannot contain
the convergence of the camera's aggression and the responsive aggression of the
bodyguard, and the result is photo-graphic dialogic in which the lens is suspended
between opposing forces. Whereas my picture of the Quechua people going about
their regular lives asserts a monologic authority, an authoritative utterance that
silences and subsumes them, this accidental picture forfeits authority; the object
assumes subject position and, in a very rare moment, talks back.

Most often when we photograph, we never merely "take" a picture. We "bring"
the picture with us and violently compel the object before us into the picture we've
brought. If we come with love, as when we photograph our children, spouses,
even pets, then perhaps it is love that we bring as an offering, a bribe, requiring
as we click the shutter that the object of our affection give itself over to us, trusting us. If we come as tourists, as cultural cartographers from a dominant else-
where—if we come, that is, to acquire the "other" as ornament for our private or
public lives as I had in Peru all those years ago—then we invariably violate.

It is a popular cliché that "primitives" often fear that the camera will steal their
souls. However, isn't it true that such a fear, in the quite rare instances when it
has been articulated, represents a sophisticated appraisal of the photographic
moment? Soul can exist only within cultural context because soul is obviously a
culturally conceived and constructed concept. The Hopi soul is not a Choctaw or
Parisian soul, the Parisian soul not the Ethiopian. Human beings have inexorably
arrived at culturally unique and independent heavens. Each community begets
and sustains stories that tell its people where they come from, where they are,
and where they are going. Soul is the vehicle bearing each of us, and all of us,
within a cultural narrative on this communally unique journey. Remove the cultural frame, the infinitely complex context, and you erase the soul. In my photograph of the Quechua women and men—a picture made ironically but without
ironic intent by a descendent of Native people of North America—their souls
have vanished to leave only appropriated material representations that constitute
my definition of them. The shadows remain, but only as false measures of time
and thus existence. I have subsumed the objects of the picture into my heaven.
Quechua women, I know from my photograph, are heavy and stoic objects, col-

orfully dressed. They don't gossip and laugh and miss the families who are else-where. Formal presences in a photograph, they serve to remind me of who I was and therefore am.

More than almost anyone else, "primitive" peoples can correctly complain, in the currency of countless movies, "We was framed." Indigenous peoples the world over have been photographed into the archives of the so-called First World. In the process, those people are subsumed into a dominant culture's definition of it-self, becoming relevant only as props in the story that culture tells about itself—that is, being contained within the frame of someone else's story. The four women who are the subjects of *Trading Gazes* could do nothing else but come to their ma-terials with their stories intact, and like other photographers they framed the ob-jects of their study within those preexisting stories. It is possible, however, to step around the frame and rub against the subject, to put down the camera and at least attempt to step into the other's story, however ephemerally and temporarily. It may be true that these women, being gendered into far different stories than their male counterparts behind the cameras, found it easier and more necessary to step around the lens and rub up against the objects of their desire. Being by gender profoundly (and probably unconsciously) accustomed to feeling themselves the objects of the universal male gaze, it may be that these women were more com-fortable in allowing themselves places within the photographic frames that also contain their indigenous subjects, including the narratives represented by such photographs. Thus Grace Nicholson sits in a photograph with a Karuk elder in California, apparently discussing the purchase of a headband. A telling moment, such a photograph lays bare a complex history of negotiation and appropria-tion; doubly so, for Nicholson, negotiating from a position of infinitely superior vantage, will take away the headband, the story of the headband, and the photo-graphic document of this moment of appropriation. In this sense, such a photo-graph is disingenuous in the extreme, for the Euro-American woman is in control of the medium and the message while posing in simulated equality.

Even more intriguing is the photographic gesture of Kate Cory, who, living amidst if not within the Hopi world, steps into the frame of her own graphic nar-rative to pose in a photograph with a loom and partially completed rug she is her-self weaving. The imaginative dislocation in such a document is wonderful—and wonderfully complex. On the one hand, the white photographer is implicating herself in the world of her Native subjects, deferring to that frame and in so do-ing confessing and inscribing her subjectivity. On the other hand, by penetrating the frame in that way, she is usurping, dispossessing the Native subject and claiming the territory on both sides of the aperture. In that sense, Cory's move is emblematic of the ultimate colonial desire, which is to define, empty, and reoc-cupy the indigenous space and thus achieve a relationship with the colonized place otherwise unattainable. The subtext to such a photograph is the admission that we always only photograph ourselves. The "other" remains a mirror that gives us back our self-reflection.

Photographs of Native people taken by non-Natives always participate in the construction of the colonized "other," always serve to facilitate dominance, for they can do nothing except subsume the Native subject into the colonizer's discourse. However, such images have nonetheless rich potential for appropriation and repossession by the Native subject. Several years ago, a friend, a member of the Yurok nation in northern California, played a nifty trick on me. She brought me a collection of Edward S. Curtis's photographs, the title of which, I believe, was *The Vanishing Race*. Opening the book, she showed me a photograph of her mother as a young girl dressed in traditional, beautiful Yurok clothing. An object of the salvage mission of photographers such as Curtis, her mother was there on the page, vanishing before our eyes. The picture was fragile-looking, lovely, and nostalgic beyond words. The next day, the same friend introduced me to her mother, a vibrant, energetic, and determined-looking woman in a smartly tailored business suit. I had been set up in an aboriginal bait-and-switch. The Native not only had survived the archival evidence of vanishment but had appropriated the text and turned the game around. Two of my friend's aunts were also photographed by Curtis; her grandfather and another aunt can be found in a Smithsonian book. Today, the family proudly peruses and displays these photographs.

This is perhaps the greatest paradox of colonial photography. The hand on the shutter and the eye behind the aperture may belong to the colonial acquisitor, and the purpose may well be to document a vanishing culture and in so doing participate deeply in that project of cultural erasure, but the artifact has the power ultimately to help ensure a cultural coherence, to play a crucial role in giving a people a picture of themselves. Admittedly, the picture Native people inherit in such instances is filtered through the lens of the dominant, invasive culture, and the frame that defines can obfuscate greatly, but nonetheless what adheres is the living air of a people and a culture, an air visible to those looking from within rather than without. My Yurok friend sees her Yurok family, not vanishing Americans.

Trading Gazes is a remarkable study of the photographs, and lives, of four women who lived and traveled among their Native subjects. The authors have illuminated and even come to terms remarkably with the contradictions, extraordinarily rich resonances, and infinite ramifications belonging to and arising from the photographic enterprise. "In America," Susan Sontag declares, "the photographer is not simply a person who records the past but the one who invents it."[4] Invention is always and inevitably a narrative of possibilities, and narratives by nature resist authority. The photographs of these women, and all photographs of Native peoples, tell more than one story, open themselves to different possibilities, different inventions.

LOUIS OWENS

NOTES

INTRODUCTION. EMPIRE OF THE LENS: WOMEN, INDIANS, AND CAMERAS

1. Grace Nicholson, travel diary, 23 July 1911, Box 16, Grace Nicholson Collection, Huntington Library, San Marino, Calif. We refer to this Karuk woman throughout as Snappy because Nicholson, seemingly annoyed, notes in her travel diary that this is the name she "insists" on, preferring it over Emma.

2. Throughout this book, we use the terms *Indian, American Indian, First Nations, First Peoples, Native, indigenous,* and *Native American* to mark shifting political and historical contexts. We recognize that each of these terms comes charged with particular connotations and emerges from debates about identity and resistance to the renaming that was integral to the colonial practices of the dominant cultures of the United States and Canada.

3. Cory quoted in Nancy Kirkpatrick Wright, "Kate Thompson Cory: Camera and Paintbrush," *Cactus and Pine* 9, no. 1 (1997): 8; Mary T. S. Schäffer, *Old Indian Trails of the Canadian Rockies* (New York: Putnam, 1911), 3, 2. "Turn toward the Native" is a phrase based on the title of Arnold Krupat's book *The Turn to the Native: Studies in Criticism and Culture* (Lincoln: University of Nebraska Press, 1996).

4. The noncommercial work of Gay, Cory, Schäffer, and Nicholson reminds us of other, as yet unexplored dimensions between their photographs' production and consumption. As Sandweiss says, "Much remains to be learned about the business of nineteenth-century western photography; the role of private, commercial, and government patronage; and the ways in which photographs were published, marketed, and exhibited." Martha A. Sandweiss, "Undecisive Moments: The Narrative Tradition in Western Photography," in *Photography in Nineteenth-Century America,* ed. Martha A. Sandweiss (New York: Abrams, 1991), 126.

5. The phrase here echoes the title of Paula Richardson Fleming and Judith Lynne Luskey's *Grand Endeavors of American Indian Photography* (Washington, D.C.: Smithsonian Institution Press, 1993).

6. Susan Sontag, *On Photography* (New York: Farrar, Straus & Giroux, 1977), 64.

7. Frederick Jackson Turner, "The Significance of the Frontier in American History," *Annual Report of the American Historical Association for the Year 1893* (Readex Microprint, 1966), 200, 208–211.

8. Wallace Stegner, *Beyond the Hundredth Meridian: John Wesley Powell and the Second Opening of the West* (1954; reprint, New York: Penguin Books, 1992), and Wallace Stegner, *Angle of Repose* (Garden City, N.Y.: Doubleday, 1971).

9. As Miller argues, the harmonious images characteristic of antebellum landscape painting consolidated a national narrative of divinely sanctioned expansion

and national unity. Angela Miller, *The Empire of the Eye: Landscape Representation and American Cultural Politics, 1825–1875* (Ithaca, N.Y.: Cornell University Press, 1993).

10. Elizabeth Edwards, "The Resonance of Anthropology," in *Native Nations: Journeys in American Photography,* ed. Jane Alison (London: Barbican Art Gallery, 1998), 196, 198. Clifford gives an example of how Edward Curtis's photographs and their captions are viewed by their subjects' descendants. He quotes a woman whose mother was one such subject: "I always see her picture. . . . Every time I look at the books, she's there. But they never use her name, just 'Hesquiaht woman.' But I know her name. It's Virginia Tom." James Clifford, *Routes: Travel and Translation in the Late Twentieth Century* (Cambridge, Mass.: Harvard University Press, 1997), 129.

11. Edwards, "The Resonance of Anthropology," 193.

12. *Indian Helper* 3, no. 52 (10 August 1888): n.p.

13. John Tagg, *The Burden of Representation: Essays on Photographies and Histories* (Amherst: University of Massachusetts Press, 1988), 12.

14. Ira Jacknis, "Franz Boas and Photography," *Studies in the Anthropology of Visual Communication* 10 (1984): 6.

15. Patricia Penn Hilden, "Readings from the Red Zone: Cultural Studies, History, Anthropology," *American Literary History* 10 (1998): 531.

16. Other scholars who have considered this image from the Geronimo archive include Mick Gidley, "A Hundred Years in the Life of American Indian Photographs," in *Native Nations: Journeys in American Photography,* ed. Jane Alison (London: Barbican Art Gallery, 1998), 153–167; and Linda Poolaw, "Spirit Capture: Observations of an Encounter," in *Spirit Capture: Photographs from the National Museum of the American Indian,* ed. Tim Johnson (Washington, D.C.: Smithsonian Institution Press, 1998), 166–178.

17. Theresa Harlan, "Indigenous Photographies: A Space for Indigenous Realities," in *Native Nations: Journeys in American Photography,* ed. Jane Alison (London: Barbican Art Gallery, 1998), 233.

18. Carolyn J. Marr, "Taken Pictures: On Interpreting Native American Photographs of the Southern Northwest Coast," *Pacific Northwest Quarterly* 80, no. 2 (1989): 61. Other scholars have argued that some photographs stayed with their Native subjects. For example, Albers and James describe the differences between photographic postcards intended for private use and those intended for public use. Before 1925, they suggest, "the postcard [often] functioned as a medium for reproducing private and local photographs." Such photographs, taken by itinerant photographers who lived near reservation communities, were characterized by their "ordinariness" and their attention to "life as it was being lived by Indian people" and were intended for "local sale" and for "local consumption"; in the view of Albers and James, they presented a rather realistic portrayal of both ongoing tribal practices and adaptation and change. In contrast, the postcards "that were sold primarily to national and regional-tourist audiences emphasized the exotic in Indian life rather than the ordinary," focused on a romanticized past, ignored or falsified tribal distinctions, and were marketed and directed to strangers. Patricia Albers and William James, "Illusion and Illumination: Visual Images of American Indian Women in the West," in *The Women's West,* ed. Susan Armitage and Elizabeth Jameson (Norman: University of Oklahoma Press, 1987), 45, 39, 41, 41. The not-for-sale work of Gay, Cory, Schäffer, and

Nicholson negotiates between these two poles, the ordinary and the romantic. Exploring the relationship between production and consumption, Albers and James remind us of Sandweiss's point that we have much to learn "about the *business* of nineteenth-century western photography" (Sandweiss, "Undecisive Moments," 126; italics added).

19. C. Jane Gover, *The Positive Image: Women Photographers in Turn of the Century America* (Albany: State University of New York Press, 1988), 5.

20. Laura Wexler cites Oliver Wendell Holmes's description of photographs as "social currency, the sentimental 'green-backs' of civilization" in "Seeing Sentiment: Photography, Race, and the Innocent Eye," in *Female Subjects in Black and White: Race, Psychoanalysis, Feminism,* ed. Elizabeth Abel, Barbara Christian, and Helen Moglen (Berkeley: University of California Press, 1997), 180.

21. Joan Mark, *A Stranger in Her Native Land: Alice Fletcher and the American Indians* (Lincoln: University of Nebraska Press, 1988), 111.

22. Melissa Banta and Curtis M. Hinsley, "Social and Cultural Anthropology: Responses and Responsibility in the Photographic Encounter," in *From Site to Sight: Anthropology, Photography, and the Power of Imagery* (Cambridge, Mass.: Peabody Museum Press, 1986), 103.

23. Renato Rosaldo, "Imperialist Nostalgia," *Culture and Truth: The Remaking of Social Analysis* (Boston: Beacon Press, 1993), 68–87.

24. Mary Austin, "The Walking Woman," in *Western Trails: A Collection of Short Stories by Mary Austin,* ed. Melody Graulich (Reno: University of Nevada Press, 1987), 97.

25. Nancy J. Parezo, "Matilda Coxe Stevenson: Pioneer Ethnologist," in *Hidden Scholars: Women Anthropologists and the Native American Southwest,* ed. Nancy J. Parezo (Albuquerque: University of New Mexico Press, 1993), 40.

26. Nancy Oestreich Lurie, "Women in Early American Anthropology," in *Pioneers of American Anthropology: The Uses of Biography,* ed. June Helm (Seattle: University of Washington Press, 1966), 33.

27. Helene Silverberg, "Introduction: Toward a Gendered Social Science History," in *Gender and American Social Science: The Formative Years,* ed. Helene Silverberg (Princeton, N.J.: Princeton University Press, 1998), 24.

28. Kamala Visweswaran, "'Wild West' Anthropology and the Disciplining of Gender," in *Gender and American Social Science: The Formative Years,* ed. Helene Silverberg (Princeton, N.J.: Princeton University Press, 1998), 89, 110.

29. Deborah Gordon, "Among Women: Gender and Ethnographic Authority of the Southwest, 1930–1980," in *Hidden Scholars: Women Anthropologists and the Native American Southwest,* ed. Nancy J. Parezo (Albuquerque: University of New Mexico Press, 1993), 132.

30. The "duties of field matron," intones the official Matron Report Form distributed in 1915, are "to visit Indian women in their homes and give them counsel, encouragement, and help in the general care of the house and surroundings; cleanliness, hygiene and sanitation; preparation and serving of food; sewing, mending, and laundering; keeping and care of domestic animals, including dairy work; care of children; care of sick; observance of the Sabbath; organization of societies building up character and intellectual and social improvement, and anything else that will promote the civilization of the Indians, especially the girls." "Report of the Field Matron,"

1915, Record of Employees, Box 155, Series 63, Record Group 75, Hoopa Valley Agency, San Bruno Federal Archives, San Bruno, Calif.

31. Gordon, "Among Women," 132.

32. Ibid., 129–130.

33. Lois Rudnick, "Re-naming the Land: Anglo Expatriate Women in the Southwest," in *The Desert Is No Lady: Southwestern Landscapes in Women's Writing and Art,* ed. Vera Norwood and Janice Monk (New Haven, Conn.: Yale University Press, 1987), 19.

34. Ibid., 10.

35. Lois Palken Rudnick, *Utopian Vistas: The Mabel Dodge Luhan House and the American Counterculture* (Albuquerque: University of New Mexico Press, 1996), 22, 29, 35.

36. Susan Brown McGreevy, "Daughters of Affluence: Wealth, Collecting, and Southwestern Institutions," in *Hidden Scholars: Women Anthropologists and the Native American Southwest,* ed. Nancy J. Parezo (Albuquerque: University of New Mexico Press, 1993), 99.

37. Schäffer, *Old Indian Trails,* 325.

38. McGreevy, "Daughters of Affluence," 99.

39. Mrs. Edward H. Kemp, "Photographing in the Hopi Land," in *Camera Fiends and Kodak Girls: 50 Selections by and about Women in Photography, 1840–1930,* ed. Peter E. Palmquist (New York: Midmarch Arts Press, 1989), 154.

40. Mary Ellicott Arnold and Mabel Reed, *In the Land of the Grasshopper Song: Two Women in the Klamath Indian River Country in 1908–1909* (1957; reprint, Lincoln: University of Nebraska Press, 1980), 88.

41. Mildred Ring, "Kodaking the Indians," in *Camera Fiends and Kodak Girls: Fifty Selections by and about Women in Photography, 1840–1930,* ed. Peter E. Palmquist (New York: Midmarch Arts Press, 1989), 229.

42. Aadland also writes that Tuell sometimes gave the photographs she had taken to the families of the people who had posed for them, as well as to reservation museums. Dan Aadland, *Women and Warriors of the Plains: The Pioneer Photography of Julia E. Tuell* (Missoula, Mont.: Mountain Press Publishing, 2000), 35–36.

43. This is not to claim that the profession of photography was completely open to women. Many women who came to its practice had served as apprentices to husbands and brothers; others worked as adjuncts to photographic enterprises as colorists, mounters, receptionists, and general assistants.

44. Naomi Rosenblum, "Women in Photography: An Historical Overview," *exposure* 24, no. 4 (1986): 13.

45. Frances Benjamin Johnston Papers, Manuscripts Division, Library of Congress, Washington, D.C.

46. Lucy R. Lippard, "Introduction," in *Partial Recall,* ed. Lucy R. Lippard (New York: New Press, 1992), 18. Palmquist's meticulous and exhaustive work in recovering the little-known archives of women photographers from the late nineteenth and early twentieth centuries is a welcome exception to the general paucity of material about such women. His research has yielded many bibliographical and biographical studies of women photographers, professional as well as amateur, who practiced their craft in the American West. See, for example, Peter E. Palmquist, *Shadowcatchers: A Directory of Women in California Photography, before 1901* (Eureka, Calif.: Eureka Printing Company, 1990); Peter E. Palmquist, *Shadowcatchers 2: A Directory of Women*

in California Photography, 1900–1920 (Eureka, Calif.: Eureka Printing Company, 1991); Peter E. Palmquist, "Women Photographers and the American Indian," in *Benedicte Wrensted: An Idaho Photographer in Focus,* ed. Joanna Cohan Scherer (Pocatello: Idaho State University Press, 1993), 121–133. For a complete list of his published work and projects, see his Women in Photography International Archive, www.sla.purdue/edu/WAAW/Palmquist/Bibliography.htm.

47. Bush and Mitchell list Amy Cohn and Lily White. See Alfred L. Bush and Lee Clark Mitchell, *The Photograph and the American Indian* (Princeton, N.J.: Princeton University Press, 1994), 297, 315. Fleming and Luskey list Mamie and Emma Gerhard, who worked at the St. Louis World's Fair. Fleming and Luskey, *Grand Endeavors,* 85–86, 90–97.

48. Leah Dilworth, *Imagining Indians in the Southwest: Persistent Visions of a Primitive Past* (Washington, D.C.: Smithsonian Institution Press, 1996), 7; Barbara Michaels, *Gertrude Käsebier: The Photographer and Her Photographs* (New York: Abrams, 1992); Laura Wexler, *Tender Violence: Domestic Visions in an Age of U.S. Imperialism* (Chapel Hill: University of North Carolina Press, 2000); Martha A. Sandweiss, *Laura Gilpin: An Enduring Grace* (Fort Worth, Tex.: Amon Carter Museum, 1986); Judith Fryer Davidov, *Women's Camera Work: Self/Body/Other in American Visual Culture* (Durham, N.C.: Duke University Press, 1998).

49. Lippard, "Introduction," 18.

50. Davidov, *Women's Camera Work;* Alan Trachtenberg, *Reading American Photographs: Images as History, Mathew Brady to Walker Evans* (New York: Hill & Wang, 1989).

51. Like Davidov, we recognize that "some women, because of the material circumstances of their own lives, are particularly responsive to 'felt experience'; others are quite capable of abusing positions of power." Davidov, *Women's Camera Work,* 7. Matilda Coxe Stevenson's self-described technique of gathering information in a pueblo is a perfect example to illustrate Davidov's contention. She wrote, "I spent the 22nd and 23rd at San Ildefonso observing the Eagle and Buffalo dances. The latter is the great spectacular feast of the year. I secured photographs of both ceremonies. I have never experienced such opposition to my camera—not by the elderly men who were pleased to have me make pictures but by the English-speaking 'educated' Indians. I had earth thrown at me with orders not to make pictures, and when the orders were not obeyed many threats were made, one fellow taking position beside me, with a club threatening to strike, but intelligence dominated brute force, and then the men threatened to break my camera. I extended it toward him but again intelligent force dominated, and I hope that my pictures secured under such trying conditions may prove satisfactory." Quoted in Parezo, "Matilda Coxe Stevenson," 51.

52. For more information about the distinction between iconology and iconography, see Larry J. Reynolds, "American Cultural Iconography: Vision, History, and the Real," *American Literary History* 9 (1997): 381–395.

53. John Berger and Jean Mohr, *Another Way of Telling* (1982; reprint, New York: Vintage Books, 1995), 92.

54. Laura Wexler, "Tender Violence, Literary Eavesdropping, Domestic Fiction, and Educational Reform," in *The Culture of Sentiment: Race, Gender, and Sentimentality in Nineteenth-Century America,* ed. Shirley Samuels (New York: Oxford University Press, 1992), 9–38.

55. James C. Faris, *Navajo and Photography: A Critical History of the Representation of an American People* (Albuquerque: University of New Mexico Press, 1996).

56. See, for instance, Roland Barthes, *Camera Lucida: Reflections on Photography,* trans. Richard Howard (New York: Hill & Wang, 1981); and Marianne Hirsch, *Family Frames: Photography, Narrative and Postmemory* (Cambridge, Mass.: Harvard University Press, 1997).

57. Lippard, "Introduction," 37, 13, 37, 43.

58. Davidov, *Women's Camera Work,* 18.

59. Horatio F. Stoll, "'Digger' Indians and the Camera: An Amateur Photographer's Experience," *Camera Craft* (February 1903): 161. Leslie Marmon Silko also imagines the threat of "the Indian with a camera" in an essay of the same name in *Yellow Woman and A Beauty of the Spirit: Essays on Native American Life Today* (New York: Simon & Schuster, 1996), 177.

60. Louis Owens, personal communication to Susan Bernardin, December 2000.

61. A subgenre within contemporary Native performance art and writing, the Indian looking back at mainstream U.S. culture can be seen in other photographs and pieces by Luna, such as "I've Always Wanted to be an American Indian"; in Zig Jackson's series "Indian Photographing Tourist Photographing Indian," both in *Strong Hearts: Native American Visions and Voices,* ed. Peggy Roalf (New York: Aperture, 1995), 38–41, 34–37; and in Jim Northrup's character Ben Looking Back, featured in *Walking the Rez Road* (Stillwater, Minn.: Voyageur Press, 1993).

62. Ralph Rugoff, *Scene of the Crime* (Cambridge, Mass.: MIT Press, 1997), 93–94.

63. Jolene Rickard, "The Occupation of Indigenous Space as 'Photograph,'" in *Native Nations: Journeys in American Photography,* ed. Jane Alison (London: Barbican Art Gallery, 1998), 68.

64. Gerald Vizenor, "Ishi Obscura," in *Manifest Manners: Postindian Warriors of Survivance* (Hanover, N.H.: University Press of New England, 1994); Jimmie Durham, "Geronimo!" in *Partial Recall,* ed. Lucy R. Lippard (New York: New Press, 1992), 58.

65. Gerald McMaster, "Colonial Alchemy: Reading the Boarding School Experience," in *Partial Recall,* ed. Lucy R. Lippard (New York: New Press, 1992), 78–79.

66. The concept of terminal creeds, one of Vizenor's catchphrases, plays a central role in his first novel, *Darkness in St. Louis Bearheart* (St. Paul, Minn.: Truck Press, 1978), reprinted as *Bearheart: The Heirship Chronicles* (Minneapolis: University of Minnesota Press, 1990), xi. See also Vizenor, *Manifest Manners.*

67. Lars Krutak and the National Museum of the American Indian Repatriation Office prepared the reports leading to the successful repatriation of Kwakiutl potlatch materials confiscated in 1924, of four Kootznoowoo Tlingit headdresses in July 2000; and of Cape Fox Village totem poles, house fronts, and funerary materials in July 2001. According to Krutak, historical photographs proved indispensable for "proving" tribal claims under NAGPRA. Lars Krutak, personal communication to Susan Bernardin, July 9, 2001.

68. Lippard, "Introduction," 20.

69. Rickard, "Occupation," 57.

70. Luci Tapahonso, "The Way It Is," in *Sign Language: Contemporary Southwest Native America,* photographs by Skeet McAuley (New York: Aperture, 1989), 17.

71. Louis Owens, *Mixedblood Messages: Literature, Film, Family, Place* (Norman: University of Oklahoma Press, 1998); Vizenor, *Darkness;* Vizenor, *Manifest Manners.*

CHAPTER 1. "LOST IN THE GENERAL WRECKAGE OF THE FAR WEST": THE PHOTOGRAPHS AND WRITINGS OF JANE GAY

1. E. Jane Gay, *Choup-nit-ki: With the Nez Percés* (Washington, D.C., and North Chelmsford, Mass.: Gay and Gay, n.d.), 3, handwritten manuscript,produced in London, 1909, Schlesinger Library on the History of Women in America, Radcliffe Institute, Harvard University (hereafter Schlesinger Library). A large portion of the text of this source is available in E. Jane Gay, *With the Nez Perces: Alice Fletcher in the Field, 1889–1892,* ed. Frederick E. Hoxie and Joan T. Mark (Lincoln: University of Nebraska Press, 1981). I quote from the original manuscript for the sake of accuracy and completeness.

2. Gay, *Choup-nit-ki,* 234. A few of Gay's photographs illustrate accounts of Nez Perce history such as Allen P. Slickpoo, Sr., and Deward E. Walker, Jr., *Noon-Nee-Me-Poo (We, the Nez Perces): Culture and History of the Nez Perces,* vol. 1 (n.p.: Nez Perce Tribe of Idaho, 1973), and Alvin M. Josephy, Jr., *500 Nations: An Illustrated History of North American Indians* (New York: Knopf, 1994). Caroline James's anthropological study, *Nez Perce Women in Transition, 1877–1990* (Moscow: University of Idaho Press, 1996), uses several less-well-known Gay images as well. To my knowledge, no scholar has devoted serious or sustained attention to the body of Gay's work. My forthcoming book, Nicole Tonkovich, *Archives and Nations: Alice Fletcher, Jane Gay, and the Nez Perce Allotment,* discusses a large selection of Gay's heretofore unpublished images.

3. Several private groups interested in reform measures designed to lead to Indian assimilation constituted the Friends of the Indian. These groups included the Boston Indian Citizenship Committee, the Women's National Indian Association, and the Indian Rights Association. The Friends also affiliated with the federally constituted Board of Indian Commissioners. These groups met annually at the Lake Mohonk resort; their deliberations were widely circulated in both private and federal venues. See Francis Paul Prucha, "Introduction," in *Americanizing the American Indians: Writings by the "Friends of the Indian," 1880–1900,* ed. Francis Paul Prucha (Cambridge, Mass.: Harvard University Press, 1973), 1–10.

4. Francis Paul Prucha, ed., "Introduction," *The Dawes Act and the Allotment of Indian Lands,* by D . S. Otis (Norman: University of Oklahoma Press, 1973), x.

5. Colin G. Calloway, *First Peoples: A Documentary Survey of American Indian History* (Boston: St. Martin's Press, 1999), 356.

6. Ward Churchill and Glenn T. Morris, "Table: Key Indian Laws and Cases," in *The State of Native America: Genocide, Colonization, and Resistance,* ed. M. Annette Jaimes (Boston: South End Press, 1992), 14.

7. Quoted in Francis Paul Prucha, *American Indian Policy in Crisis: Christian Reformers and the Indian, 1865–1900* (Norman: University of Oklahoma Press, 1976), 246.

8. Monroe E. Price and Robert N. Clinton, eds., *Law and the American Indian: Readings, Notes and Cases,* 2d ed. (Charlottesville, Va.: Michie, 1983), 628.

9. Judith V. Royster, "The Legacy of Allotment," *Arizona State Law Journal* 27 (1995): 1–78.

10. The Omahas and Winnebagoes had been recently allotted by Alice Fletcher. A minimal program of allotment had been considered, as well, when the Nez Perces accepted the provisions of the Treaty of 1863.

11. Prucha, "Introduction," *The Dawes Act,* x.

12. Alvin M. Josephy, Jr., *The Nez Perce Indians and the Opening of the Northwest* (New Haven, Conn.: Yale University Press, 1965), 430, 429, 430.

13. Joseph was only one of several Nez Perce leaders of this episode, and he was not a war chief. His widely publicized surrender speech solidified his image in white understanding as the sole leader of the antitreaty Nez Perces.

14. Josephy, *The Nez Perce,* 636. Other well-known portraits of Joseph include those made by Charles M. Bell (1879), John H. Fouch (1877), Wells M. Sawyer (1897), DeLancey Gill (1900), E. H. Latham (1903), and several by Edward S. Curtis (in the early 1900s).

15. This image is among the best known of Gay's *oeuvre,* although it is often misleadingly presented or printed (or both) without attribution. In Josephy's *500 Nations,* for example, it is cropped to eliminate Fletcher and Stuart (417); in Slickpoo and Walker, *Noon-Nee-Me-Poo,* its caption mistakenly identifies Fletcher as Kate McBeth, the Presbyterian missionary (197). In presenting Gay's photographs, I have tried to preserve her titles, following her captions in *Choup-nit-ki.* When the photographs I present here are not included in that manuscript or when they are included but not captioned, I have indicated that they are untitled. The Idaho State Historical Society (ISHS), which owns most of Gay's negatives, has titled all the images it owns, sometimes following Gay's own titles; sometimes following handwritten descriptions by Mary Crawford, a Presbyterian missionary who worked among the Nez Perces; and sometimes adding descriptive titles. I have indicated ISHS's titles after its cataloguing number.

16. Sources disagree about the spelling of James Stuart's name. I have chosen to follow the official Nez Perce tribal history.

17. According to Mark, "Fletcher explained to Mrs. Dawes that James Stuart had dropped to his knees simply to break the visual line, not out of reverence, as Jane Gay later liked to hint." Joan Mark, *A Stranger in Her Native Land: Alice Fletcher and the American Indians* (Lincoln: University of Nebraska Press, 1988), 180. Mark does not document the source of this information, which offers an unsupported interpretation of Gay's remark that "James has a peculiar habit of going down on one knee and putting his hat upon the other when under any stress of emotion" (*Choup-nit-ki,* 42).

18. Gay, *Choup-nit-ki,* 236.

19. Ibid., 41.

20. Identifications of the figures in this image are from Lillian W. Dawson, comp., *Jane Gay Photograph Collection Catalog* (Boise: Idaho State Historical Society, 1980), 7.

21. Ibid.

22. Gay, *Choup-nit-ki,* 295.

23. According to James, "Other agency employees . . . admitted to running cattle illegally on Nez Perce land with or without various agents' knowledge but claimed they were never ordered to stop. Several witnesses named Caldwell specifically as the most flagrant offender. Charles Fairfield, a reservation farmer, charged Monteith with having a financial interest in Caldwell's cattle business. Monteith and Caldwell denied the allegation, and it was never proven." Elizabeth James, "The Allotment Period on

the Nez Perce Reservation: Encroachments, Obstacles, and Reactions," *Idaho Yesterdays* 37 (1993): 14.

24. Dawson, *Catalog,* 7.

25. Jane Gay Dodge, "Sketch of My First Meeting with Alice C. Fletcher in 1888," ca. 1939, p. 2, unpublished manuscript, Schlesinger Library.

26. Jane Gay Dodge, "Brief Biography of E. Jane Gay," ca. 1939, p. 5, unpublished manuscript, Schlesinger Library. This informal reminiscence was prepared some fifty years after the meeting it describes between Gay and Fletcher as adults. Almost none of the details of Gay's life or of her relationship with Fletcher prior to 1887 have been verified.

27. Dodge, "Sketch," 2.

28. Gay lived in Washington during Johnson's administration, but no documents indicate that she was his grandchildren's governess. Mark claims that Gay was a nurse working with Dorothea Dix (*Stranger,* 166). Gay did write an affectionate letter to Dix and was in possession of some of Dix's correspondence; these facts suggest only that the two women had been close friends.

29. *The Red Man* 9, no. 11 (November 1889): 1.

30. Truman Trumbull, A.M. [pseud. E. Jane Gay], *The New Yankee Doodle: Being an Account of the Little Difficulty in the Family of Uncle Sam* (New York: Bourne, 1868).

31. Visweswaran has established the popularity of participant-observer ethnographic accounts in mass-circulation periodicals of the late nineteenth and early twentieth century. She cites Cushing's "My Adventures in Zuni," F. W. Putnam's "The Serpent Mound of Ohio," Sara Yorke Stevenson's memoirs of "the French intervention in Mexico," and Fletcher's "Personal Studies of Indian Life." Kamala Visweswaran, "'Wild West' Anthropology and the Disciplining of Gender," in *Gender and American Social Science: The Formative Years,* ed. Helene Silverberg (Princeton, N.J.: Princeton University Press, 1998), 91, 116–117, n. 28. Fletcher's "Personal Studies" is illustrated with unattributed engravings following photographs made by Gay.

32. To Putnam, Fletcher wrote, "I was ordered off on short notice, and I had to go, or lose any chance to boil my pot. It was a very, very hard thing to do. It was to give up what I cared most for. . . . Here I am down in the cañons of the Clearwater, and the rocky steeps that shut me in from all the world, seem like the walls of fate about me. Don't give me up. I will get the work done and before long, I trust,"; 2 August 1889, Peabody Museum Papers, Pusey Library, Courtesy of the Harvard University Archives.

33. Paradoxically, Fletcher's sense of exclusion from academic life was heightened in 1891, when she received the Thaw Fellowship, a lifetime stipend that would support her research. Before she could begin the academic work that it would support, she had to complete the Nez Perce allotment, a process that would take another two years.

34. Mark observes, "All her life Alice Fletcher looked to men for help, although the help she got [such as the generous Thaw Fellowship] often came from women" (*Stranger,* 14).

35. Dodge, "Brief Biography," 5.

36. See ISHS photograph 63–221.34, *Camp Gallinas* (described in Dawson, *Catalog,* 10).

37. Dodge, "Sketch," 1–2.

38. Gay, *Choup-nit-ki,* 58.

39. Dodge writes, "Years [after the expedition] . . . the two Misses Gay [Jane Gay and her niece Emma Jane Gay] . . . improvised background and costume for pictures of the two personalities described as 'The Cook' and 'The Photographer' in the *Letters.* There was no reason at the time of the experiences to take such photographs, even supposing there had been any person along who could have done so" ("Brief Biography," 6).

40. E. Jane Gay, "Camp Life Experiences: Miss Gay's Interesting Description of Miss Fletcher's Allotting Lands to the Nez Perces, Continued from the July and August Number," *The Red Man* 12, no. 2 (1891): 8.

41. Alice C. Fletcher to Commissioner of Indian Affairs, 5 June 1889, National Archives 15493; emphasis added.

42. Fletcher to Commissioner of Indian Affairs, 2 August 1889, National Archives 22323; emphasis added.

43. Laura Wexler, *Tender Violence: Domestic Visions in an Age of U.S. Imperialism* (Chapel Hill: University of North Carolina Press, 2000). Wexler's work traces the complicity of sentiment, domesticity, and imperialism in several enterprises—including the education of Indians and freed slaves—in the late nineteenth-century United States. Fletcher's activities of allotment serve as another instance of this nexus.

44. This image is filed as one of two photographs entitled *Nez Perce Women,* Idaho State Historical Society 63–221.88b (described in Dawson, *Catalog,* 28).

45. Gay, *Choup-nit-ki,* 129–130.

46. Ibid., 105.

47. Ibid., 351, 353.

48. Ibid., 122.

49. Fletcher to Commissioner of Indian Affairs, 5 June 1889.

50. Gay, *Choup-nit-ki,* 191.

51. According to Masteller, in landscape photography "an object in the foreground was essential, 'not too conspicuous, but standing in such relation to other objects as to add beauty to the perspective.'" Richard N. Masteller, "Western Views in Eastern Parlors: The Contribution of the Stereograph Photographer to the Conquest of the West," *Prospects* 6 (1981): 61. James Mullen advised stereoscope photographers to carry "a spade and a good axe; the latter particularly will often be found 'a friend in need,' when it is desirable to cut a small tree or remove a branch that would otherwise obscure some important point of your view"; quoted in Masteller, "Western Views in Eastern Parlors," 61.

52. Gay, *Choup-nit-ki,* 367.

53. *Camp Sunday,* the Idaho State Historical Society title for this image, is unexplained. In Gay, *Choup-nit-ki,* the image is neither captioned nor listed in the table of contents. It is included in a letter whose return address reads "Camp Prairie Chicken" (294). In Gay's small photo album, "Where We Camped" (Schlesinger Library), the image is captioned *Family Umbrella (Camp Blazes).*

54. Two photographs of groups of children decorating graves at Lapwai are included in Gay, *Choup-nit-ki,* 235.

55. Ibid., 235–236; emphasis added.

56. "Domestic dependents" echoes the phrasing of Supreme Court Justice John Marshall's opinion in *Cherokee Nation v. State of Georgia* (1831): "They may, more cor-

rectly, perhaps, be denominated domestic dependent nations" (quoted in Calloway, *First Peoples,* 254).

57. Quoted in Mark, *Stranger,* 106.

58. Missionaries had endeavored for years to regularize family structures among Indians, attempting especially to eliminate the practice of polygamy. Fletcher was able to buttress her interventions with the authority of the Dawes Act. Yet for all her care in documenting Nez Perce patriarchal relations, she did nor foresee the problems that would be caused by the Dawes Act's failure to provide land for subsequent generations of inheritors. See also note 62 below.

59. See *Nez Perce Reservation Allotment Book, Prepared by Alice Fletcher, 1889–1892,* photocopy held by the Idaho State Historical Society, original in the possession of Ralph Williams, Gifford, Idaho.

60. The best account of how photography was promoted as a technology of domestic surveillance is Shawn Michelle Smith, *American Archives: Gender, Race, and Class in Visual Culture* (Princeton, N.J.: Princeton University Press, 1999).

61. For a full account of the contretemps, see Allen Conrad Morrill and Eleanor Dunlap Morrill, *Out of the Blanket: The Story of Sue and Kate McBeth, Missionaries to the Nez Perces* (Moscow: University Press of Idaho, 1978), 237.

62. Fletcher to Commissioner of Indian Affairs, 24 December 1889, National Archives 173. See also Alice C. Fletcher to Commissioner of Indian Affairs, 24 December 1889, National Archives 174, in which Fletcher discusses the complexities of inheritance in the case of a Nez Perce man who, when he "became a Christian[,] . . . put away one" of his two wives, by whom he had a daughter, and was legally married to the other wife. This letter economically narrates a maze of subsequent claims and counterclaims on property made by the legal wife, the daughter, and the daughter's husband.

63. Gay, *Choup-nit-ki,* 227–228.

64. In the words of *Cherokee Nation v. State of Georgia* (1831), "They are in a state of pupilage. Their relation to the United States resembles that of a ward to his guardian" (quoted in Calloway, *First Peoples,* 254).

65. Gay, *Choup-nit-ki,* 127.

66. Ibid., 128, 128–129.

67. Ibid., 99–100.

68. Ibid., 324.

69. See, for example, *Camp Robusto,* ISHS 63–221.35, and *Camp Lily,* ISHS 63–221.38 (described in Dawson, *Catalog,* 10, 11).

70. Gay, *Choup-nit-ki,* 63.

71. Ibid., 217–218.

72. [E. Jane Gay], "Miss Fletcher and Miss Gay. Incidental Experiences in Allotting Indian Lands," *The Red Man* 3, no. 6 (1890): 3.

73. [E. Jane Gay], "A Woman Allotting Lands to Indians. A Rich and Racy View of a Trying Situation," *The Red Man* 9, no. 11 (November 1889): 5.

74. Ibid.

75. [E. Jane Gay], "A Brave Woman Allotting Lands to Indians in Idaho. Novel and Interesting Experiences, as told by the Companion of Miss Fletcher," *The Red Man* 10, no. 4 (April 1890): 2.

76. Gay, *Choup-nit-ki,* 193.

77. James, *Nez Perce Women,* 4.

78. Michael R. McLaughlin, "The Dawes Act, or Indian General Allotment Act of 1887: The Continuing Burden of Allotment. A Selective Annotated Bibliography," *American Indian Culture and Research Journal* 20, no. 2 (1996): 80.

CHAPTER 2. "I BECAME THE 'COLONY'": KATE CORY'S HOPI PHOTOGRAPHS

1. Kate T. Cory, "Life and Its Living in Hopiland—Good-Bye to Steam-Cars," *The Border: A Monthly Magazine of Politics, News, and Stories of the West* 1, no. 7 (1909): 1.

2. The conflict that broke out in 1906 had been simmering for years between two factions in Old Oraibi: a group led by Tewaquaptewa, the village chief, who was willing to compromise with representatives of the U.S. government, and a group of "hostiles," led by Youkeoma, who were, logically enough, opposed to the government's insistence that Hopi children attend boarding schools. Although white officials feared that a bloody war would take place, the two groups eventually drew a line in the sand and engaged in a pushing match. The losers, the "hostiles," were expelled from Old Oraibi and moved to a site near a spring, where they founded Hotevilla. Although the Hopis settled the conflict with no injuries, the split led to increased governmental interference in both villages. Cory took shots at both Oraibi and Hotevilla, and her captions sometimes address the conflict, as when she writes under one image "Unfriendly—but a fine man."

3. Margaret D. Jacobs, *Engendered Encounters: Feminism and Pueblo Cultures, 1879–1934* (Lincoln: University of Nebraska Press, 1999), 181.

4. My information on Cory's life comes from numerous sources, most of which repeat the same stories: Charles Franklin Parker, "Sojourn in Hopiland," *Arizona Highways,* May 1943, 10–13, 41; Marnie Gaede, "Kate Cory: Artist of Arizona," *Arizona Highways,* August 1987, 22–27; Nancy Kirkpatrick Wright, "Kate Thompson Cory: Camera and Paintbrush," *Cactus and Pine* 9, no. 1 (1997): 2–19. I am particularly indebted to Joanne Cline and Sylvia Duncan, curators at the Smoki Museum, who generously went through Cory's photograph album with me page by page, sharing their interpretations, and who helped me track down images and information. I also thank Joanne Cline for providing me access to Cory's diary; I have honored her request not to quote from the diary, which contains descriptions of many secret ceremonies.

5. Kate T. Cory, "Life and Its Living in Hopiland—The Hopi Women," *The Border: A Monthly Magazine of Politics, News, and Stories of the West* 1, no. 11 (1909): 1–2. I have found a total of eight short essays published by Cory, all focused on her understanding of Hopi traditions and culture.

6. None of Cory's photographs are titled. Throughout this chapter her photographs are identified by captions, which are not in italics. Captions identified as Cory's come from her photograph album. Because of the distinctive voice and richness of information, I assume that whoever wrote the captions in the album copied from the back of Cory's prints. I identify all captions taken from the MNA collection, which often differ markedly from Cory's. I was unable to ascertain from museum officials who provided those captions, which sometimes, perhaps inadvertently, lead the reader toward particular interpretations. Because Cory's captions are long and narrative, clearly not titles, and because I wanted more neutral captions than those at the MNA, I have provided my own brief captions for each photograph.

I thank the Smoki Museum in Prescott for permission to quote from Kate Cory's photograph album. At their request, I have replaced the names of Hopis identified by Cory with "[name deleted]." Joanna Cohan Scherer, "You Can't Believe Your Eyes: Inaccuracies in Photographs of North American Indians," *exposure* 16, no. 4 (1978): 6–19.

7. The images that accompany this chapter were made for me by the Museum of Northern Arizona from Cory's negatives. I thank the Museum of Northern Arizona for its help and for granting me permission to reproduce the images. I thank the Sharlot Hall Museum in Prescott for permission to reproduce *Kate Cory in Front of Her Loom* (fig. 9 in the Introduction), *Hopi Maiden,* and excerpts from Cory's papers.

In the 1940s, when Cory hoped to publish two books on the Hopis, *People of the Yellow Dawn* and *Children of Hopiland,* a local photographer, Leroy E. Eslow, made prints for both books, some of which are contained in the Kate Cory Collection in the Sharlot Hall Museum; presumably Cory lent Eslow the negatives, and they were either lost or never returned. Most of the negatives for Cory's shots of children—unposed, spontaneous, engaging—are among those missing.

8. Barton Wright, Marnie Gaede, and Marc Gaede, *The Hopi Photographs: Kate Cory, 1905–1912* (1986; reprint, Albuquerque: University of New Mexico Press, 1988). For a discussion of the controversy, see, for instance, David R. Roberts, "Sacred Sights," *American Photo* 6, no. 6 (1995): 44, 106, 109.

9. Quoted in Peter Whiteley, "The End of Anthropology (at Hopi)?" in *Indians and Anthropologists: Vine Deloria, Jr. and the Critique of Anthropology,* ed. Thomas Biolsi and Larry J. Zimmerman (Tucson: University of Arizona Press, 1997), 187.

10. James Clifford, "Introduction: Partial Truths," in *Writing Culture: The Poetics and Politics of Ethnography,* ed. James Clifford and George E. Marcus (Berkeley: University of California Press, 1986), 23–24.

11. Judith Fryer Davidov, *Women's Camera Work: Self/Body/Other in American Visual Culture* (Durham, N.C.: Duke University Press, 1998). The term *encounter* informs her whole argument.

12. Victor Masayesva, Jr., and Erin Younger, comps., *Hopi Photographers/Hopi Images* (Tucson: University of Arizona Press, 1983), 90.

13. Lucy R. Lippard, "Introduction," in *Partial Recall,* ed. Lucy R. Lippard (New York: New Press, 1992), 19.

14. Mary Louise Pratt, *Imperial Eyes: Travel Writing and Transculturation* (New York: Routledge, 1992), 4.

15. According to James, at one point, Tewaquaptewa, then chief of Old Oraibi, ordered Hopis who "had, or intended to, become Christians to leave Old Oraibi." They settled in New Oraibi. Harry C. James, *Pages from Hopi History* (1974; reprint, Tucson: University of Arizona Press, 1996), 13.

16. Wright, Gaede, and Gaede, *The Hopi Photographs,* n.p. Cory's captions for both images are lost—if she ever recorded them.

17. Quoted in Richard O. Clemmer, *Roads in the Sky: The Hopi Indians in a Century of Change* (Boulder, Colo.: Westview Press, 1995), 79.

18. James, *Pages,* 54.

19. The quoted passage appears on page 12 of Wright, Gaede, and Gaede, *The Hopi Photographs.* "Garces" should be spelled with an accent, Garcés. There is no page number for the images. In fact, Marc Gaede cropped several images, notably to produce

close-up portraits. The MNA now stipulates that scholars may not crop images reproduced from the Kate Cory Photography Collection.

20. John Wesley Powell, "The Ancient Province of Tusayan," *Scribner's Monthly* 11 (November 1875–April 1876): 193–213. James reports that the Hopis consider *Moki* or *Moqui,* widely used by Anglos, to be a "term of derision never used by the Hopi themselves" (*Pages,* xii).

21. Laura Graves, *Thomas Varker Keam, Indian Trader* (Norman: University of Oklahoma Press, 1998), 148, 167.

22. All passages in this paragraph are quoted in Anne Farrar Hyde, *An American Vision: Far Western Landscape and National Culture, 1820–1920* (New York: New York University Press, 1990), 213, 213, 214, 208.

23. Philip J. Deloria, *Playing Indian* (New Haven, Conn.: Yale University Press, 1998), 105–106, 91.

24. Rayna Green, "Repatriating Images: Indians and Photography," in *Benedicte Wrensted: An Idaho Photographer in Focus,* ed. Joanna Cohan Scherer (Pocatello: Idaho State University Press, 1993), 155.

25. Graves, *Thomas Varker Keam,* 148–149.

26. Quoted in Leah Dilworth, *Imagining Indians in the Southwest: Persistent Visions of a Primitive Past* (Washington, D.C.: Smithsonian Institution Press, 1996), 71.

27. Kate T. Cory, "A Realistic Story of the Great Hopi Indians," *The Yavapai Magazine* 13, no. 5 (1925): 9.

28. James and Monsen quoted in Erin Younger, "Changing Images: A Century of Photography on the Hopi Reservation (1880–1980)," in *Hopi Photographers/Hopi Images,* comp. Victor Masayesva, Jr., and Erin Younger (Tucson: University of Arizona Press, 1983), 19, 21. Jenkins quoted in Roberts, "Sacred Sights," 106.

29. Younger, "Changing Images," 20. In the 1990s the Hopis cosponsored a Curtis exhibit at Walpi, which, according to Leigh Jenkins, provoked "excitement" and "interest among the people of Walpi" (quoted in Roberts, "Sacred Sights," 109).

30. Graves, *Thomas Varker Keam,* 201.

31. Younger, "Changing Images," 24. Euro-American artists and writers also protested when "in 1921 Commissioner Charles Burke sent a series of recommendations to Indian superintendents that limited the times dances could take place and who could participate in them" (Dilworth, *Imagining Indians,* 67), while the missionaries continued their protests.

32. Younger, "Changing Images," 17.

33. The Fred Harvey Company developed restaurants—where the famed "Harvey Girls" waitressed—and shops at Santa Fe Railroad tourist stops. Later they developed a series of "trading posts" at national parks, where they marketed "authentic" Indian jewelry and art and where Indian artists were invited to "perform" their work. The company still exists today. When I visited Hopi House a few years ago, a Navajo weaver was at work in the shop.

34. James C. Faris, *Navajo and Photography: A Critical History of the Representation of an American People* (Albuquerque: University of New Mexico Press, 1996), 255.

35. Sarah Nestor, "Weaving: The Woven Spirit," in *Harmony by Hand: Art of the Southwest Indians, Basketry, Weaving, Pottery* by Patrick Hoolihan et al. (San Francisco: Chronicle Books, 1987), 51; Carolyn O'Bagy Davis, *Hopi Quilting: Stitched Traditions from an Ancient Community* (Tucson, Ariz.: Sanpete Publications, 1997), 26.

36. Kate Peck Kent, *Navajo Weaving: Three Centuries of Change* (Santa Fe, N.Mex.: School of American Research Press, 1985), 8, 9.

37. "Textile fragments exhibiting these Hispanic characteristics [were] found in a room built in the late 1690s—about the time of the Spaniards' return—in the Hopi Pueblo of Walpi." These designs were "blue-, black-, and white-striped." Kent, *Navajo Weaving,* 9.

38. Quoted in James, *Pages,* 124.

39. Harold Butcher, "Seven Years with the Hopis," *Desert Magazine* 14, no. 4 (1951): 18–19.

40. Kate T. Cory, "Life and Its Living in Hopiland—The Races," *The Border: A Monthly Magazine of Politics, News, and Stories of the West* 1, no. 9 (1909): 4. For more information on Akin, see Bruce E. Babbitt, *Color and Light: The Southwest Canvases of Louis Akin* (Flagstaff, Ariz.: Northland Press, 1973).

41. "Confessions of a Tomboy" and anonymous reviews of Cory's book are contained in the Kate Cory Collection at the Sharlot Hall Museum in Prescott, Ariz.

42. Lippard was allowed to reproduce this image in *Partial Recall.* Lucy R. Lippard, ed., *Partial Recall* (New York: New Press, 1992), 173.

43. Victor Masayesva, Jr., "Kwikwilyaqa: Hopi Photography," in *Hopi Photographers/Hopi Images, comp. Victor Masayesva, Jr., and Erin Younger* (Tucson: University of Arizona Press, 1983), 10.

44. Wright, "Kate Thompson Cory," 4.

45. Deloria, *Playing Indian,* 98–99, 96, 103.

46. Deborah Gordon, "Among Women: Gender and Ethnographic Authority of the Southwest, 1930–1980," in *Hidden Scholars: Women Anthropologists and the Native American Southwest,* ed. Nancy J. Parezo (Albuquerque: University of New Mexico Press, 1993), 129, 130.

47. Jacobs, *Engendered Encounters,* 59, 58.

48. Grace Gallatin Seton-Thompson, *A Woman Tenderfoot* (New York: Doubleday, 1900), 16, 22, 358–361.

49. Mary Austin, "The Walking Woman," in *Western Trails: A Collection of Stories by Mary Austin,* ed. Melody Graulich (Reno: University of Nevada Press, 1987), 97.

50. Mary Austin, *Earth Horizon: Autobiography* (1932; reprint, Albuquerque: University of New Mexico Press, 1991), 289.

51. Deloria, *Playing Indian,* 105.

52. Quoted in Wright, "Kate Thompson Cory," 6.

53. May 7, 1910, article in the *Prescott Journal Miner,* quoted in Claudette Simpson, "Kate Cory's Hopi House," undated news clipping from the 1980s, Sharlot Hall Museum, Prescott, Ariz. One can only hope Cory did not approve the text, which goes on, "While the building will be in charge of a white man during construction, the Moqui red man will have sway in laying the stone bricks. So will the Moqui squaw rule supreme in her tastes of ornamentation of the interior, in short it will be a counterpart of the Moqui environment as it is followed and lived out at the present time to the minutest detail."

54. Molly H. Mullin, *Culture in the Marketplace: Gender, Art, and Value in the American Southwest* (Durham, N.C.: Duke University Press, 2001), 39. The planting stick anecdote comes from Parker, "Sojourn in Hopiland," 13.

55. Renato Rosaldo, "Imperialist Nostalgia," in *Culture and Truth: The Remaking of Social Analysis* (Boston: Beacon Press, 1993), 68–87.

56. Cory, "Life and Its Living in Hopiland—The Hopi Women," 2.

57. Jacobs, *Engendered Encounters,* 2.

58. George Wharton James, *What the White Race May Learn from the Indian* (Chicago: Forbes & Company, 1908), 104.

59. Cory, "Life and Its Living in Hopiland—The Hopi Women," 2.

60. Quoted in Jacobs, *Engendered Encounters,* 96.

61. Lois Palken Rudnick, *Utopian Vistas: The Mabel Dodge Luhan House and the American Counterculture* (Albuquerque: University of New Mexico Press, 1996), 27, 33–34.

62. Mary Austin, "The Basket Maker," in *Western Trails: A Collection of Short Stories by Mary Austin,* ed. Melody Graulich (Reno: University of Nevada Press, 1987), 32.

63. Rudnick, *Utopian Vistas,* 22, 25, 34.

64. Jennifer De Witt, "'When They Are Gone . . . .': The Smoki People of Prescott and the Preservation of Indian Culture," *Journal of Arizona History* 37 (1996): 325, 327. Although critical of many of the Smoki's activities, De Witt presents a contextualized historical analysis, and much of my information comes from her. For a far more sarcastic critique of a dance as "racist parody," see Whiteley, "The End of Anthropology," 178.

65. De Witt, "'When They Are Gone,'" 327.

66. Cory, "A Realistic Story of the Great Hopi Indians," 7. The essay is preceded by Hall's poem, "Where the Smoki Dance."

67. Quoted in Peter Iverson, *Barry Goldwater: Native Arizonan* (Norman: University of Oklahoma Press, 1997), 164.

68. Quoted in De Witt, "'When They Are Gone,'" 331.

69. Quoted in Iverson, *Barry Goldwater,* 164.

70. Quoted in ibid., 165.

71. Ibid., 164.

72. Whiteley, "The End of Anthropology," 200.

73. Kate T. Cory, "The Snake Dance and It's [sic] Origin," *Arizona* 13, no. 7 (1923): 5.

74. "The day will come, when a white people will set foot on the eastern shores and claim this land as their own. They will build a white house near the shore from where they will govern their people. Upon establishing their government, they will raise a banner upon a flagstaff, on top of which they will place the spirit of the Hopi (Indian) people, this will be a sign to us that the Creator will keep his promises to us. This people, the 'Bahana,' will scatter our people, seek to destroy us down to the last child, and bring upon his diseases that we have never known before. (Oral History of the Hopi Prophecy) [as recounted by Will Numkena, Hopi]," quoted in Forrest S. Cuch, ed., *The Indians of Utah: A History of Utah's American Indians* (Logan: Utah State University Press, 2000), n.p.

75. Quoted in De Witt, "'When They Are Gone,'" 321.

76. E. Ann Kaplan, *Looking for the Other: Feminism, Film, and the Imperial Gaze* (New York: Routledge, 1997), xvi–xvii.

77. Susan Sontag, *On Photography* (New York: Farrar, Straus & Giroux, 1977), 14.

78. Lippard, "Introduction," 35.

79. John Berger and Jean Mohr, *Another Way of Telling* (1982; reprint, New York: Vintage Books, 1995), 89.

80. Lippard, "Introduction," 37.

81. Ramona Sakiestewa, "Weaving for Dance," in *Partial Recall,* ed. Lucy R. Lippard (New York: New Press, 1992), 75.

82. James Elkins, *The Object Stares Back: On the Nature of Seeing* (New York: Harcourt Brace, 1996), 201.

83. Masayesva and Younger, *Hopi Photographers,* 90.

CHAPTER 3. MARY SCHÄFFER'S "COMPREHENDING EQUAL EYES"

1. See James Blaine Hedges, *Building the Canadian West: The Land and Colonization Policies of the Canadian Pacific Railroad* (New York: Macmillan, 1939). Schäffer was an American expatriate who moved to Banff in her middle adulthood. Her cultural background was forged in a U.S. context; and some similarities exist between the United States and Canada in their relationships with, and policies and attitudes toward, Native populations. However, the Canadian West is quite different in its land policies, its governmental structures, and the development of farming and industry. Therefore, I have at times generalized from U.S. studies to place Schäffer: her childhood experiences and cultural reflexes were formed in postbellum Philadelphia. But I have also tried to be attentive to the specificities of Canadian history when discussing events in Canada and her life there.

2. For more on Kipling's Canadian tour, see David Gilmour, *The Long Recessional: The Imperial Life of Rudyard Kipling* (New York: Farrar, Straus & Giroux, 2002); Charles E. Carrington, *The Life of Rudyard Kipling* (New York: Doubleday, 1955); Lord Birkenhead, *Rudyard Kipling* (New York: Random House, 1978); and Angus Wilson, *The Strange Ride of Rudyard Kipling: His Life and Works* (New York: Viking, 1977).

3. Mary Louise Pratt, *Imperial Eyes: Travel Writing and Transculturation* (London: Routledge, 1992), 4.

4. Mary T. S. Schäffer, *Old Indian Trails of the Canadian Rockies* (New York: Putnam, 1911), 259. A twenty-six-square-kilometer area around the hot springs at Banff became Canada's first national park in November 1885. Over the next several decades, the national-park system in Alberta grew to encompass not only a significantly larger Banff but also Jasper, Yoho, Kootenay, and Waterton; next to them currently runs a series a provincial parks including Kananaskis Provincial Park in Alberta and Mount Assiniboine and Mount Robson in British Columbia.

5. Quoted in E. J. Hart, ed., *A Hunter of Peace: Mary T. S. Schäffer's Old Indian Trails of the Canadian Rockies* (Banff, Alberta: Whyte Museum of the Canadian Rockies, 1980), 2. Hart has abridged and heavily edited the original travelogue and has provided a biographical introduction and a previously unpublished manuscript account of Schäffer's 1911 trip to Lake Maligne. Kipling first mentioned the incident in a letter to his son dated October 12, 1907, and subsequently reworded the material for other occasions. Elliot L. Gilbert, ed., "O Beloved Kids": Rudyard Kipling's Letters to His Children (New York: Harcourt Brace Jovanovich, 1983), 50. Kipling either didn't see or avoided mentioning the other members of Schäffer's party; he had his own reasons for wanting to present a middle-aged Victorian lady as having "gone Native." Thus he participated in the fiction that Schäffer herself indulged, of herself as intrepid mountain explorer.

6. Schäffer, *Old Indian Trails,* 199–200.

7. Quoted in Hart, *A Hunter of Peace,* 2.

8. See Gail Bederman, *Manliness and Civilization: A Cultural History of Race and Gender in the United States, 1880 –1917* (Chicago: University of Chicago Press, 1996).

9. Philip J. Deloria, *Playing Indian* (New Haven, Conn.: Yale University Press, 1998); also Leah Dilworth, *Imagining Indians in the Southwest: Persistent Visions of a Primitive Past* (Washington, D.C.: Smithsonian Institution Press, 1996), and Lois Palken Rudnick, *Utopian Vistas: The Mabel Dodge Luhan House and the American Counterculture* (Albuquerque: University of New Mexico Press), 1996.

10. Wexler has made this case for reading photographs in the United States; a similar dynamic applies to Schäffer's photographs of the Canadian West. Laura Wexler, *Tender Violence: Domestic Visions in an Age of U.S. Imperialism* (Chapel Hill: University of North Carolina Press, 2000).

11. In her introduction to *Partial Recall*, Lippard retitles the photograph "Sampson, Frances Louise, and Leah Beaver," but I have kept Schäffer's caption to foreground the contradictions that structured her views of Indians and to emphasize the implications of her use of the term in other contexts. Lucy R. Lippard, "Introduction," in *Partial Recall*, ed. Lucy R. Lippard (New York: New Press, 1992), 37. Schäffer's images fall into two categories: those published in *Old Indian Trails*, to which she gave titles, and those that were unpublished, which the Whyte Museum has archived under its own, descriptive, titles. I note these distinctions in the discussion of each image. There are two exceptions to this general rule. One is the 1906 photograph of the Beaver family (fig. 12 in the Introduction), whose titling I discuss in detail here. The other is Molly Adams's 1908 photograph of Schäffer in the buckskin coat (fig. 68 and cover), which does not appear in *Old Indian Trails* but which was titled *She Who Colored Slides* by Schäffer.

12. "Other authorities have argued that the word 'squaw' is a corruption of the Iroquois word 'otsiskwa,' meaning 'female sexual parts.'" Louis Owens, *Mixedblood Messages: Literature, Film, Family, Place* (Norman: University of Oklahoma Press, 1998), 212.

13. I am indebted to Don Bourdon of the Whyte Museum of the Canadian Rockies for alerting me to the text on the original photograph and to Nicole Tonkovich for pointing out the similarity between Schäffer's pose and that in a portrait of Frances Benjamin Johnston, a woman Schäffer admired and whose work she followed.

14. Judith Fryer Davidov, *Women's Camera Work: Self/Body/Other in American Visual Culture* (Durham, N.C.: Duke University Press, 1998). Both Davidov and Wexler explicitly link the women photographers they study to their studio work and to their professional activities. Schäffer worked largely outside those networks, partly by virtue of Canada's different context and partly by her different practices: she did not do studio work; she was not a photojournalist or explicitly interested in "art"; and she began studying photography both as part of her touristic experiences and later to assist her husband in his botanical work.

15. See Raymond J. De Mallie, ed., *Plains*, vol. 13 of *Handbook of North American Indians*, ed. William C. Sturtevant (Washington, D.C.: Smithsonian Institution Press, 1996), especially Ian A. L. Getty and Erik D. Gooding, "Stoney," 596–603. Also, Jon Whyte, *Indians in the Rockies* (Banff, Alberta: Altitude Publishing, 1985); Frederick E. Hoxie, ed., *Encyclopedia of North American Indians* (Boston: Houghton Mifflin, 1996); Brock V. Silversides, *The Face Pullers: Photographing Native Canadians, 1871–1939* (Saskatoon, Saskatchewan: Fifth House, 1994).

16. See, among others, Patricia Nelson Limerick, *The Legacy of Conquest: The Un-broken Past of the American West* (New York: Norton, 1988); Clyde A. Milner, ed., *A New Significance: Re-envisioning the History of the American West* (New York: Oxford University Press, 1996); William Cronon, George Miles, and Jay Gitlin, eds., *Under an Open Sky: Rethinking America's Western Past* (New York: Norton, 1992).

17. On women travelers and their narratives, see Anne McClintock, *Imperial Leather: Race, Gender and Sexuality in the Colonial Conquest* (London: Rout-ledge, 1995).

18. See, for example, Glenda Riley, *Woman and Nature: Saving the "Wild" West* (Lincoln: University of Nebraska Press, 1999); Shirley Samuels, ed., *The Culture of Sentiment: Race, Gender, and Sentimentality in Nineteenth-Century America* (New York: Oxford University Press, 1992).

19. Patricia Penn Hilden, "Readings from the Red Zone: Cultural Studies, History, Anthropology," *American Literary History* 10 (1998): 524–543.

20. Wexler, *Tender Violence,* 7. Wexler later continues, "If photography could have provided an opportunity for a certain growth and transculturation, as [Gerald] Vizenor argues, it was also an effective platform for furthering interlocking domina-tions. The excitation and subsequent defeat of cross-racial empathy is the ultimate failure of these women's work" (208).

21. Sherry L. Smith, *Reimagining Indians: Native Americans through Anglo Eyes, 1880–1940* (New York: Oxford University Press, 2000), 14–15.

22. Unidentified newspaper clipping, Mary Schäffer Fonds, Whyte Museum of the Canadian Rockies, Archives and Library, Banff, Alberta (hereafter Schäffer Fonds).

23. Mary T. S. Schäffer, unpublished manuscript, Schäffer Fonds.

24. Frances Benjamin Johnston Papers, Manuscripts Division, Library of Con-gress, Washington, D.C.

25. Schäffer, unpublished manuscript, Schäffer Fonds.

26. Frances Benjamin Johnston Papers, Manuscripts Division, Library of Con-gress, Washington, D.C.

27. Stewardson Brown, *Alpine Flora of the Canadian Rocky Mountains* (New York: Putnam, 1907).

28. Schäffer, *Old Indian Trails,* 8.

29. Ibid., 5.

30. Quoted in Hart, *A Hunter of Peace,* 5.

31. Unidentified newspaper clipping, Schäffer Fonds.

32. *Crag and Canyon* (Banff National Park), 27 January 1939, 1–2.

33. Smith, *Reimagining Indians;* T. J. Jackson Lears, *No Place of Grace: Antimodern-ism and the Transformation of American Culture, 1880–1920* (Chicago: University of Chicago Press, 1984); David E. Shi, *The Simple Life: Plain Living and High Thinking in American Culture* (New York: Oxford University Press, 1985).

34. Schäffer, *Old Indian Trails,* 14.

35. Ibid., 205.

36. See, for example, Alan Trachtenberg, *Reading American Photographs: Images as History, Mathew Brady to Walker Evans* (New York: Hill & Wang, 1989); also, Pratt, *Imperial Eyes,* and McClintock, *Imperial Leather.*

37. Schäffer, unpublished manuscript, Schäffer Fonds.

38. Schäffer, *Old Indian Trails,* 278.

39. For more on the narrative strategies of white women travelers and for a discussion of the role of dirt in colonial discourse, see McClintock, *Imperial Leather.*

40. Schäffer, unpublished manuscript M79/7, Schäffer Fonds.

41. Wexler, *Tender Violence.*

42. Harriet Beecher Stowe, *Uncle Tom's Cabin; or, Life among the Lowly* (1852; reprint, Boston: Houghton Mifflin, 1892), 495.

43. Gerald Vizenor, *Manifest Manners: Postindian Warriors of Survivance* (Hanover, N.H.: University Press of New England, 1994).

44. Schäffer, *Old Indian Trails,* 175.

45. Wexler, *Tender Violence,* 35.

46. John Berger and Jean Mohr, *Another Way of Telling* (1982; reprint, New York: Vintage Books, 1995), 102–113.

47. Ibid.; Gerald McMaster, "Colonial Alchemy: Reading the Boarding School Experience," in *Partial Recall,* ed. Lucy R. Lippard (New York: New Press, 1992), 76–87.

48. Two decades earlier, Jane Gay made a similar image that she titled *Omaha Madonna.* The photograph appears on page 219 of E. Jane Gay, *Choup-nit-ki: With the Nez Percés* (Washington, D.C., and North Chelmsford, Mass.: Gay and Gay, n.d.), handwritten manuscript, produced in London, 1909, Schlesinger Library. Gay was apparently fascinated with this icon: she made numerous adaptations of the image both in other photographs and in hand-colored sketches drawn from the photograph. See, for example, negatives 63–221.28, *Indian Madonna;* 63–221.531, *Indian Mother;* and 63.221.14 a, b, and c, *Retrospect—Last of His Tribe* in Lillian W. Dawson, comp., *Jane Gay Photograph Collection Catalog* (Boise: Idaho State Historical Society, 1980), 4, 8, 16.

49. Wexler, *Tender Violence,* 204–205.

50. Schäffer, *Old Indian Trails,* 177–178.

51. Ibid., 175, 176, 178.

52. Mary Ryan, *The Empire of the Mother: American Writing about Domesticity* (New York: Haworth Press, 1982).

53. Donna J. Haraway, "Situated Knowledges: The Science Question in Feminism and the Privilege of Partial Perspective," in *Simians, Cyborgs, and Women: The Reinvention of Nature* (New York: Routledge, 1991), 188–190.

54. The Métis were a separate cultural and linguistic group, descended from both Native and European ancestry, primarily Plains Ojibwa, Plains Cree, French-Canadian, and Scottish. According to Payment, "Silk embroidery was introduced by the Gray Nuns in Saint Boniface" after the opening of their mission in 1844; "Metis women added to it the traditional method of using quills and beads on hide." Diane Paulette Payment, "Plains Metis," in *Plains,* ed. Raymond J. De Mallie, vol. 13 of *Handbook of North American Indians,* ed. William C. Sturtevant (Washington, D.C.: Smithsonian Institution Press, 1996), 671.

55. Schäffer, *Old Indian Trails,* 322–325.

56. Mollie Adams, unpublished manuscript M 79/11, Mollie Adams Fonds, Whyte Museum of the Canadian Rockies, Archives and Library, Banff, Alberta.

57. Schäffer, unpublished manuscript M 79/7, Schäffer Fonds.

58. Schäffer, *Old Indian Trails,* 183–184.

59. Owens, *Mixedblood Messages,* 211.

60. Hilden, "Readings from the Red Zone," 525.

61. Davidov, *Women's Camera Work,* 116–117. Lippard, "Introduction," 18. Davidov calls on readers to "untwist the strands of hybridization, acknowledge that there are other strands, and attempt to recover sub-versions without falling into the dialectical pattern of binary thinking." Citing Wlad Godzich, she asserts, "Encounter" implies "the irruption of the other . . . not [as] a threat to be reduced or an object I give myself to know . . . but that which constitutes me as an ethical being" (*Women's Camera Work,* 44). In analogous efforts, Pratt (*Imperial Eyes,* 11) invokes the "contact zone," and Trinh T. Minh-ha, in *When the Moon Waxes Red: Representation, Gender, and Cultural Politics* (New York: Routledge, 1991), searches for the "interval, the break without which meaning would be fixed and congealed" (30).

62. Berger and Mohr, *Another Way of Telling,* 97, 109.

63. See Chapter 1 for this crucial distinction, as well as Larry J. Reynolds, "American Cultural Iconography: Vision, History, and the Real," *American Literary History* 9 (1997): 381–395.

64. Roland Barthes, *Camera Lucida: Reflections on Photography,* trans. Richard Howard (New York: Hill & Wang, 1981), 45, 49, 55.

65. Gloria Anzaldúa, *Borderlands/La Frontera* (San Francisco: Aunt Lute Books, 1987), 172; Berger and Mohr, *Another Way of Telling,* 104.

66. Davidov, *Women's Camera Work,* 44.

67. Jolene Rickard, "Cew Ete Haw I Tih: The Bird That Carries Language Back to Another," in *Partial Recall,* ed. Lucy R. Lippard (New York: New Press, 1992), 110.

CHAPTER 4. CAPTURING AND RECAPTURING CULTURE: TRAILING GRACE NICHOLSON'S LEGACY IN NORTHWESTERN CALIFORNIA

1. O. M. Boggess to Grace Nicholson, 18 September 1930, Box 10, Grace Nicholson Collection, Huntington Library, San Marino, Calif. (hereafter Nicholson Collection). Nicholson's reply was handwritten on this note. Nicholson provided captions for virtually all her photographs, which were collected in personal photograph albums. She also identified the subjects of these images in the copies of prints that she sent to curators. "Hoopa" refers to the name of the valley and reservation in Humboldt County, California; "Hupa" refers to the people.

2. The term *contact zone* is borrowed from Pratt's formulation of the spaces of cross-cultural encounter created by colonization. Mary Louise Pratt, *Imperial Eyes: Travel Writing and Transculturation* (New York: Routledge, 1992), 4.

3. L. H. M., unpublished biography of Grace Nicholson, Nicholson Collection. Current biographical information about Nicholson is limited mostly to the Nicholson Collection, particularly Box 12. I also acknowledge the generous assistance of Pasadena resident and Nicholson biographer Jeanne Perkins.

4. See ch. 2 of Carey McWilliams, *North from Mexico: The Spanish-Speaking People of the United States* (1949; reprint, New York: Praeger, 1990). Also see Carey McWilliams, *Southern California: An Island on the Land* (1947; reprint, Salt Lake City, Utah: Peregrine Smith, 1973), and Mike Davis, *City of Quartz* (New York: Vintage Books, 1992).

5. Marvin Cohodas, *Basket Weavers for the California Curio Trade: Elizabeth and Louise Hickox* (Tucson: University of Arizona Press, 1997), 177–178. This exhaustive study of the socioeconomic, historical, and cross-cultural contexts underpinning the basket market in northern California, and specifically the Hickoxes' relationship with

Nicholson, has informed my own research on Nicholson, especially the ensuing discussion of the region's and era's vogue for basket collecting.

6. See, for example, Leah Dilworth, *Imagining Indians in the Southwest: Persistent Visions of a Primitive Past* (Washington, D.C.: Smithsonian Institution Press, 1996).

7. George Wharton James, "Indian Basketry in House Decoration," *Chautauquan* 33, no. 6 (September 1901): 620.

8. Amy Kaplan, "Manifest Domesticity," *American Literature* 70 (1998): 581–606.

9. Winifred S. Fry, "Humboldt Indians: A Sketch," *Out West* 21, no. 6 (1904): 511.

10. As scholars such as O'Connell point out, Native peoples in New England survived in the interstices of the colonizers' economy in the eighteenth and nineteenth centuries in part by selling baskets. Barry O'Connell, "Introduction," in *A Son of the Forest and Other Writings,* ed. Barry O'Connell (Amherst: University of Massachusetts Press, 1997), lxiii–lxvi. See references to basket making, for example, in Pequot William Apess's autobiography, *A Son of the Forest* (1829), reprinted in William Apess, *A Son of the Forest and Other Writings,* ed. Barry O'Connell (Amherst: University of Massachusetts Press, 1997).

11. Sally McLendon, "Collecting Pomoan Baskets, 1889–1939," *Museum Anthropology* 17 (1993): 49–60. This article details the development of a booming basket trade in Sonoma, Lake, and Mendocino counties, including a discussion of such key figures as John and Grace Hudson and Grace Nicholson.

12. For published articulations of Native perspectives on basketry, see, for example, Colleen Kelley Marks, "Preservation through Mutual Respect," *News from Native California* 9, no. 1 (1995): 17–21; Ron Johnson and Colleen Kelley Marks, *Her Mind Made Up: Weaving Caps the Indian Way* (Arcata, Calif.: Reese Bullen Gallery and Humboldt State University, 1998); Claudia Israel, ed., *Elizabeth Hickox; Baskets and Weavers* (Eureka, Calif.: Clarke Memorial Museum, 1996). The California Indian Basketweavers Association hosts programs, gatherings, and workshops, and distributes a newsletter.

13. This discussion has benefited enormously from the work of Ira Jacknis, especially his article "Alfred Kroeber as Museum Anthropologist," *Museum Anthropology* 17, no. 2 (1993): 27–32.

14. Bruce Bernstein, "A Native Heritage Returns: The Wilcomb-Sheedy Collection," in *Natives and Settlers: Indian and Yankee Culture in Early California: The Collections of Charles P. Wilcomb,* ed. Melinda Young Frye (Oakland, Calif.: Oakland Museum, 1979), 69–87.

15. See Marvin Cohodas, "Louisa Keyser and the Cohns: Mythmaking and Basket Making in the American West," in *The Early Years of Native American Art History: The Politics of Scholarship and Collecting,* ed. Janet Catherine Berlo (Seattle: University of Washington Press, 1992), 88–133. See also Cohodas, *Basket Weavers* for a detailed analysis of the Cohns' strategies for fueling demand for the work of this Washoe weaver. Nicholson complained about how high they set prices for Keyser's pieces. Nicholson did not share the Cohns' tactics of fabricating the uniqueness and authenticity of Keyser's work. According to Cohodas's archival research, the Cohns had ownership of all Keyser's baskets in exchange for room, board, food, and medical care.

16. Maria Del Carmen Gasser, ed., "Introduction," *"My Dear Miss Nicholson": Letters and Myths by William R. Benson, a Pomo Indian* (Pasadena, Calif.: Bickley Printing Company, 1996), iv.

17. Cohodas, *Basket Weavers,* 231.

18. Hickox grew up in and was part of Karuk communities, but her mother was Wiyot, a survivor of one of many massacres of Wiyot in the region. Travel diary, 18 July 1908, Box 15, Nicholson Collection.

19. For example, in 1990 the Southwest Museum had an exhibit of Hickox's baskets, and in 1991 some of her baskets were brought "home" in an exhibit, *Elizabeth Conrad Hickox: Baskets from the Center of the World,* at Humboldt State University in Arcata, California.

20. Box 4, Nicholson Collection.

21. Gasser's book, *"My Dear Miss Nicholson,"* collects three decades of correspondence between William Benson and Grace Nicholson. Evaline (Dolly) Nelson's correspondence with Nicholson (1915–1925) is in the Nicholson Collection, Box 6.

22. In a letter dated June 17, 1931, Nicholson writes, "I learned, yesterday, that you had finished the story of the 'creation' that we started many years ago, and which you have long promised to finish FOR ME. . . . Now other parties have had the benefit of your work. They will get all of the credit, including Mr. Boaz [*sic*], who will probably publish the matter you have given your Berkeley friend, and I will not even be mentioned for all my work in the matter even though I furnished the funds all these years to make it possible to preserve the legends, etc. In other words, they reap the reward of your work and information, and I have paid the bills. They have the completed story of the creation, and I have only part of it, when it was the agreement that I was the only one to have that story and the other legends." Gasser, *"My Dear Miss Nicholson,"* 131.

23. Nicholson to C. C. Willoughby, 4 June 1908, Collection Department Accession File 08–4, Peabody Museum of Archaeology and Ethnology, Harvard University.

24. According to Jacknis, many collectors did include photographs in their correspondence with museum personnel. However, unlike Nicholson, other collectors made this an occasional practice: photographs typically accompanied the shipment of only an especially rare item. Ira Jacknis to Susan Bernardin, personal communication, July 1, 2001.

25. The first road from Hoopa Valley to Happy Camp was built in 1912, with the first bridge over the Klamath at Orleans completed the same year. My thanks to Phil Sanders for this information.

26. Nicholson, travel diary, 26 July 1908, Box 15, Nicholson Collection.

27. An excerpt from this entry reads, "I walked back to the store in time to meet Miss Arnold and Miss Reed-Deliver me-! They are sort of English you know and Miss Arnold is such a talker." Nicholson, travel diary, 17 July 1908, Box 15, Nicholson Collection. For a detailed list of field-matron responsibilities, see the Introduction, note 30.

28. Mary Ellicott Arnold and Mabel Reed, *In the Land of the Grasshopper Song: Two Women in the Klamath River Indian Country in 1908–09* (1957; reprint, Lincoln: University of Nebraska Press, 1980), 134.

29. Marie Johnson to Nicholson, 23 March 1910, Box 10, Nicholson Collection.

30. Another reason for Nicholson's antipathy to Reed and Arnold has been suggested by Hillman, who notes that her association with certain families in the region might have biased her perception of Reed and Arnold. When she visited the region, Nicholson stayed with the Salstroms, who were engaged in a bitter legal dispute with

the area's largest mine owner, Frank Richards, with whom Reed and Arnold stayed when they visited Orleans. Nicholson also stayed with the Nelsons, a white mine owner and his Karuk wife (Dolly, who shared Karuk oral narratives with Nicholson). Mr. Nelson was intensely disliked by many Karuk because he took their land at Ameekayram and because he prevented Karuk neighbors from using water. Reed and Arnold describe their futile encounter with "Old Man Nelson" over this water dispute with Karuk neighbors. Personal communication with Leaf Hillman, director of natural resources, Karuk Nation, March 24, 1999; see also Arnold and Reed, *In the Land,* 123–126.

31. Ray Raphael, *Little White Father: Redick McKee on the California Frontier* (Eureka, Calif.: Humboldt County Historical Society, 1993), 110. For other studies of the history of treaties in California, see George E. Anderson, W. H. Ellison, and Robert F. Heizer, *Treaty Making and Treaty Rejection by the Federal Government in California, 1850–52* (Socorro, N.Mex.: Bellena Press, 1978).

32. Quoted in Jack Norton, *Genocide in Northwestern California: When Our Worlds Cried* (San Francisco: Indian Historian Press, 1979).

33. According to Rawls, "Under cover of the apprenticeship provisions of the laws of 1850 and 1860 the abduction and sale of Indians—especially young women and children—were carried on as a regular business enterprise in California." James J. Rawls, *Indians of California: The Changing Image* (Norman: University of Oklahoma Press, 1984), 95. For a detailed discussion of this Act and its ruinous implications for California Indians, see Rawls, 81–108.

34. Lee Davis, "California Tribes," in *Encyclopedia of North American Indians,* ed. Frederick E. Hoxie (Boston: Houghton Mifflin, 1996), 95. For additional studies of genocide in California following American settlement, see Rawls, *Indians of California.*

35. For detailed accounts of this massacre and the public's reaction, see Norton, *Genocide,* 84, and Raphael, *Little White Father,* 181–186.

36. Since 1994, an annual memorial service has commemorated the victims of this massacre as well as celebrating the Wiyot Nation's survival against all odds. See Auriana Koutnik, "Remembering Indian Island," *News from Native California* 9, no. 2 (1995–1996): 39. In the fall of 2000, the tiny Wiyot Nation bought 1.5 acres on Gunther Island, an extraordinary act of reclamation. Efforts are ongoing to raise funds for Wiyot land purchases.

37. Peter E. Palmquist, ed., *Camera Fiends and Kodak Girls: Fifty Selections by and about Women in Photography, 1840–1930* (New York: Midmarch Arts Press, 1989), ix.

38. Grace Hudson sent much of her work to Nicholson to be shown in her gallery. Correspondence between the two is located in the Nicholson Collection, Box 4. Hudson's paintings are showcased in a museum located in her home, the Sun House, in Ukiah, California.

39. Ira Jacknis, "Alfred Kroeber and the Photographic Representation of California Indians," *American Indian Culture and Research Journal* 20 (1996): 15–16.

40. Ibid., 28.

41. *Arcata Union,* 8 August 1896; quoted in Peter E. Palmquist (with Lincoln Kilian), *The Photographers of the Humboldt Bay Region: A. W. Ericson* (Arcata, Calif.: Peter E. Palmquist, 1989), 95.

42. *Arcata Union,* 16 September 1893; quoted in Palmquist, *Ericson,* 91.

43. Communities throughout northern California turned to photography in or-

der to capture the interest of potential investors and residents. See Peter E. Palmquist, "Capture the Shadow 'ere the Substance Fly," in *Silver Shadows: A Directory and History of Early Photography in Chico and Twelve Counties of Northern California,* ed. Ira H. Latour (Chico, Calif.: Chico Museum Association and Chico Art Center, 1993), 19–27.

44. *Arcata Union,* 14 September 1904; quoted in Palmquist, *Ericson,* 111.

45. Renato Rosaldo, "Imperialist Nostalgia," in *Culture and Truth: The Remaking of Social Analysis* (Boston: Beacon Press, 1993), 68–87; *Arcata Union,* 5 March 1910; quoted in Palmquist, *Ericson,* 121.

46. Nicholson's diary records her going to meet Ericson in Arcata on July 15, 1906. She dismissively writes that he "was full of booze" when she found him. Box 16, Nicholson Collection.

47. Paula Richardson Fleming and Judith Lynne Luskey, *Grand Endeavors of American Indian Photography* (Washington, D.C.: Smithsonian Institution Press, 1993), 37.

48. Judith Fryer Davidov, *Women's Camera Work: Self/Body/Other in American Visual Culture* (Durham, N.C.: Duke University Press, 1998), 116.

49. Nicholson, travel diary, 24 July 1911, Box 16, Nicholson Collection.

50. Nicholson, travel diary, 13 July 1908, Box 16, Nicholson Collection.

51. Nicholson, travel diary, 23 July 1911, Box 16, Nicholson Collection.

52. Horatio F. Stoll, "'Digger' Indians and the Camera: An Amateur Photographer's Experience," *Camera Craft* (February 1903): 155, 161.

53. Mildred Ring, "Kodaking the Indians," in *Camera Fiends and Kodak Girls: Fifty Selections by and about Women in Photography, 1840–1930,* ed. Peter E. Palmquist (New York: Midmarch Arts Press, 1989), 230, 229.

54. Voicing the objection of many traditional Indians to photographs in a way her Euro-American readers would understand, Yurok elder Lucy Thompson writes, "The old Indians do not like to look at a photograph or to have their photographs taken because they say it is a reflection or a shadowy image of the departed spirit." Lucy Thompson, *To the American Indian: Reminiscences of a Yurok Woman* (1916; reprint, Berkeley, Calif.: Heyday Books, 1976), 95.

55. See Peter E. Palmquist, *With Nature's Children: Emma B. Freeman (1880–1928)—Camera and Brush* (Eureka, Calif.: Interface California Corporation, 1976).

56. Sally McLendon, "Preparing Museum Collections for Use as Primary Data in Ethnographic Research," in *The Research Potential of Anthropological Museum Collections,* ed. Anne-Marie Cantwell, James B. Griffin, and Nan A. Rothschild (New York: New York Academy of Sciences, 1981), 203.

57. Elizabeth Hickox to Nicholson, 3 October 1911, Box 11, Nicholson Collection.

58. Ira Jacknis, "In Search of the Image-Maker: James Mooney as an Ethnographic Photographer," *Visual Anthropology* 3 (1990): 189.

59. Jacknis notes in another article that famed anthropologist Franz Boas did the same thing—promising that when he visited them the following year, he would bring to some Kwakiutl copies of pictures of them he was trying to take at the World's Columbian Exposition in 1893. Ira Jacknis, "Franz Boas and Photography," *Studies in the Anthropology of Visual Communication* 10 (1984): 6.

60. Julia Jones to Nicholson, 1912, Box 4, Nicholson Collection. Sam Frame to Nicholson, 17 November 1908, Box 3, Nicholson Collection. Sam Frame to Nicholson, [1908], Box 11, Nicholson Collection.

61. W. H. Hotelling to Nicholson, 20 February 1911, Box 3, Nicholson Collection.

62. Nellie Wright to Nicholson, 1 March 1912, Box 11, Nicholson Collection.

63. Douglas Cole, "Tricks of the Trade: Some Reflections on Anthropological Collecting," *Arctic Anthropology* 28 (1991): 48–52.

64. Ibid., 49.

65. Nicholson, travel diary, 16 July 1908, Box 16, Nicholson Collection.

66. Nicholson, travel diary, 13 July 1908, Box 16, Nicholson Collection.

67. Nicholson, list of articles sent to C. C. Willoughby, 8 August 1908, Collection Department Accession File 08–4, Peabody Museum of Archaeology and Ethnology, Harvard University.

68. Margaret Harrie to Nicholson, 29 April 1912, Box 3, Nicholson Collection.

69. Julian Lang, ed. and trans., *Ararapíkva: Creation Stories of the People, Traditional Karuk Indian Literature from Northwestern California* (Berkeley, Calif.: Heyday Books, 1994), 40.

70. My thanks to John Hitchcock for this observation of what he also calls the "Geronimo look."

71. Gerald Vizenor, *Fugitive Poses: Native American Indian Scenes of Absence and Presence* (Lincoln: University of Nebraska Press, 1998), 156, 158.

72. Jolene Rickard, "The Occupation of Indigenous Space as 'Photograph,'" in *Native Nations: Journeys in American Photography,* ed. Jane Alison (London: Barbican Art Gallery, 1998), 70.

73. Biographical notes, Box 12, Nicholson Collection.

74. "The trophies" are mentioned in Nicholson to C. C. Willoughby, 29 October 1908; "you will notice" is quoted from a letter from Nicholson to Willoughby, 13 August 1908. Both letters are in Collection Department Accession File 08–4, Peabody Museum of Archaeology and Ethnology, Harvard University. Until a few decades ago *Karok* (meaning up-river) was the term used in all published references to the tribe. Now, *Karuk* is the term in English used by Karuks and non-Karuks alike.

75. Willoughby to Nicholson, 13 October 1910, Box 11, Nicholson Collection.

76. Hickox to Nicholson, 10 October 1923, Box 4, Nicholson Collection.

77. Arnold and Reed, *In the Land,* 118.

78. This image is captioned *Tin Tin Packing Stuff from Katimin and Ishipichi.* According to Violet Super, *ishi pishi* means end of the trail, while Íshipish was the name of a community that formerly occupied the slopes above the Klamath River across from Katimin (personal communication to Susan Bernardin, 1997). As with most anglicized spellings of Indian words, the spelling of these sites and terms varies.

79. For extensive descriptions of NAGPRA, see, for example, Agnes Tabah, *Native American Collections and Repatriation* (Washington, D.C.: Technical Information Service, American Association of Museums, 1993). Also, the National Archive of Archaeology provides an on-line National NAGPRA Database of procedures, definitions, and active repatriation claims across the country: *http://www.cast.uark.edu/other/nps/nagpra/nagpra.html.*

80. Thomas Biolsi and Larry J. Zimmerman, "Introduction," in *Indians and Anthropologists: Vine Deloria Jr. and the Critique of Anthropology,* ed. Thomas Biolsi and Larry J. Zimmerman (Tucson: University of Arizona Press, 1997), 7.

81. In several major repatriation claims—Tlingit, Kwakiutl—historical photographs have provided crucial documentary evidence of the use and value of particu-

lar items removed from Indian nations on the Northwest Coast and in Alaska in the early twentieth century. According to Krutak, "Without historical photographs of certain objects in use by traditional leaders, lineal descendants, etc., these repatriations would never have been possible." Lars Krutak to Susan Bernardin, personal communication, July 9, 2001. My thanks to Lars Krutak and the National Museum of the American Indian Repatriation Office for providing me with his reports on these specific NAGPRA cases.

82. Nicholson to Willoughby, 29 October 1908, Collection Department Accession File 08–4, Peabody Museum of Archaeology and Ethnology, Harvard University.

83. Quoted in "Big Times/Little Times," *News from Native California* 12, no. 2 (1998–1999): 36.

84. Lee Davis and Niccolo Caldararo, "The Repatriation Dilemma: Museum Objects Are Contaminated with Pesticides," *News from Native California* 13, no. 4 (2000): 46–47.

85. See Lee Davis and Don Koué, *Going Home: The California Indian Library Collections Manual* (Berkeley: California Indian Project, 1989).

86. Lee Philip Brumbaugh, "Shadow Catchers or Shadow Snatchers? Ethical Issues for Photographers of Contemporary Native Americans," *American Indian Culture and Research Journal* 20 (1996): 37.

87. Dot Brovarney, "From the Inside Out: The Native American History Project," *News from Native California* 10, no. 1 (1996): 32–34.

88. Hulleah J. Tsinhnahjinnie, "When Is a Photograph Worth a Thousand Words?" in *Native Nations: Journeys in American Photography,* ed. Jane Alison (London: Barbican Art Gallery, 1998), 42.

89. *Prosperity Journal* (Bayside, Calif.) (Summer 2001): http://copia1.copia.net/prosperity/pjlibrary.nsf/

90. Gerald Vizenor, "Ishi Obscura," in *Manifest Manners: Postindian Warriors of Survivance* (Hanover, N.H.: University Press of New England, 1994), 129.

91. Theresa Harlan, "A Curator's Perspective: Native Photographers Creating a Visual Native American History," *exposure* 29, no. 1 (1993): 15.

AFTERWORD. THEIR SHADOWS BEFORE THEM: PHOTOGRAPHING INDIANS

1. Roland Barthes, *Camera Lucida: Reflections on Photography,* trans. Richard Howard (New York: Hill & Wang, 1981), 110.

2. Ibid., 57, 6.

3. Ibid., 82

4. Susan Sontag, *On Photography* (New York: Farrar, Straus, & Giroux, 1977), 67.

SELECTED BIBLIOGRAPHY

PRIMARY SOURCES

Cumberland County Historical Society Archives, Carlisle, Pa.
Harvard University Archives, Harvard University, Cambridge, Mass.
  Peabody Museum Papers, Pusey Library
Humboldt State University Special Collections, Arcata, Calif.
Huntington Library, San Marino, Calif.
  Grace Nicholson Collection
Idaho State Historical Society, Boise
  Jane Gay Photograph Collection
Manuscripts Division, Library of Congress, Washington, D.C.
  Frances Benjamin Johnston Papers
Museum of Northern Arizona, Flagstaff
  Kate Cory Photography Collection
National Archives, Washington, D.C.
  Alice Fletcher correspondence
Newberry Library, Chicago
  Edward E. Ayer Collection
Peabody Museum of Archaeology and Ethnology, Harvard University, Cambridge, Mass.
  F. W. Putnam Papers
  C . C. Willoughby Papers
San Bruno Federal Archives, San Bruno, Calif.
Schlesinger Library on the History of Women in America, Radcliffe Institute, Harvard University, Cambridge, Mass.
  Jane Gay Dodge Collection
Sharlot Hall Museum, Prescott, Ariz.
  Kate Cory Collection
Smoki Museum, Prescott, Ariz.
  Kate Cory photograph album
  Photocopy of Kate Cory diary
  Paintings by Kate Cory
  Photograph negatives and miscellany
Whyte Museum of the Canadian Rockies, Archives and Library, Banff, Alberta
  Mollie Adams Fonds
  Elliot Barnes Fonds
  Byron Harmon Fonds
  Mary Schäffer Fonds

SECONDARY SOURCES

Aadland, Dan. *Women and Warriors of the Plains: The Pioneer Photography of Julia E. Tuell.* Missoula, Mont.: Mountain Press Publishing, 2000.

Albers, Patricia, and William James. "Illusion and Illumination: Visual Images of American Indian Women in the West." In *The Women's West,* edited by Susan Armitage and Elizabeth Jameson, 35–50. Norman: University of Oklahoma Press, 1987.

Albright, Peggy. *Crow Indian Photographer: The Work of Richard Throssel.* Albuquerque: University of New Mexico Press, 1997.

Alison, Jane, ed. *Native Nations: Journeys in American Photography.* London: Barbican Art Gallery, 1998.

Anderson, George E., W. H. Ellison, and Robert F. Heizer. *Treaty Making and Treaty Rejection by the Federal Government in California, 1850–52.* Socorro, N.Mex.: Bellena Press, 1978.

Anzaldúa, Gloria. *Borderlands/La Frontera.* San Francisco: Aunt Lute Books, 1987.

Apess, William. *A Son of the Forest and Other Writings.* Edited by Barry O'Connell. Amherst: University of Massachusetts Press, 1997.

Arnold, Mary Ellicott, and Mabel Reed. *In the Land of the Grasshopper Song: Two Women in the Klamath Indian River Country in 1908–1909.* 1957. Reprint, Lincoln: University of Nebraska Press, 1980.

Austin, Mary. "The Basket Maker." In *Western Trails: A Collection of Short Stories by Mary Austin,* edited by Melody Graulich, 31–35. Reno: University of Nevada Press, 1987.

———. *Earth Horizon: Autobiography.* 1932. Reprint, Albuquerque: University of New Mexico Press, 1991.

———. "The Walking Woman." In *Western Trails: A Collection of Short Stories by Mary Austin,* edited by Melody Graulich, 91–98. Reno: University of Nevada Press, 1987.

Babbitt, Bruce E. *Color and Light: The Southwest Canvases of Louis Akin.* Flagstaff, Ariz.: Northland Press, 1973.

Babcock, Barbara A., and Nancy J. Parezo, eds. *Daughters of the Desert: Women Anthropologists and the Native American Southwest, 1880–1980.* Albuquerque: University of New Mexico Press, 1988.

Banta, Melissa, and Curtis M. Hinsley. *From Site to Sight: Anthropology, Photography, and the Power of Imagery.* Cambridge, Mass.: Peabody Museum Press, 1986.

Barthes, Roland. *Camera Lucida: Reflections on Photography.* Translated by Richard Howard. New York: Hill & Wang, 1981.

Batchen, Geoffrey. *Burning with Desire: The Conception of Photography.* Cambridge, Mass.: MIT Press, 1997.

Bederman, Gail. *Manliness and Civilization: A Cultural History of Race and Gender in the United States, 1880–1917.* Chicago: University of Chicago Press, 1996.

Berger, John. *About Looking.* 1980. Reprint, New York: Vintage Books, 1991.

Berger, John, and Jean Mohr. *Another Way of Telling.* 1982. Reprint, New York: Vintage Books, 1995.

Berlo, Janet Catherine. "Introduction." In *The Early Years of Native American Art History: The Politics of Scholarship and Collecting,* edited by Janet Catherine Berlo, 1–21. Seattle: University of Washington Press, 1992.

Bernstein, Bruce. "A Native Heritage Returns: The Wilcomb-Sheedy Collection." In

Natives and Settlers: Indian and Yankee Culture in Early California: The Collections of Charles P. Wilcomb, edited by Melinda Young Frye, 69–87. Oakland, Calif.: Oakland Museum, 1979.

"Big Times/Little Times." *News from Native California* 12, no. 2 (1998–1999): 36.

Biolsi, Thomas, and Larry J. Zimmerman. "Introduction." In *Indians and Anthropologists: Vine Deloria Jr. and the Critique of Anthropology,* edited by Thomas Biolsi and Larry J. Zimmerman, 3–23. Tucson: University of Arizona Press, 1997.

Birkenhead, Lord. *Rudyard Kipling.* New York: Random House, 1978.

Breitbart, Eric. *A World on Display: Photographs from the St. Louis World's Fair, 1904.* Albuquerque: University of New Mexico Press, 1997.

Brovarney, Dot. "From the Inside Out: The Native American History Project." *News from Native California* 10, no. 1 (1996): 32–34.

Brown, Stewardson. *Alpine Flora of the Canadian Rocky Mountains.* New York: Putnam, 1907. Illustrated with water-colour drawings and photographs by Mrs. Charles Schäffer.

Brumbaugh, Lee Philip. "Shadow Catchers or Shadow Snatchers? Ethical Issues for Photographers of Contemporary Native Americans." *American Indian Culture and Research Journal* 20 (1996): 33–49.

Bush, Alfred L., and Lee Clark Mitchell. *The Photograph and the American Indian.* Princeton, N.J.: Princeton University Press, 1994.

Butcher, Harold. "Seven Years with the Hopis." *Desert Magazine* 14, no. 4 (1951): 16–19.

Calloway, Colin G. *First Peoples: A Documentary Survey of American Indian History.* Boston: St. Martin's Press, 1999.

Carrington, Charles E. *The Life of Rudyard Kipling.* New York: Doubleday, 1955.

Churchill, Ward, and Glenn T. Morris. "Table: Key Indian Laws and Cases." In *The State of Native America: Genocide, Colonization, and Resistance,* edited by M. Annette Jaimes, 14. Boston: South End Press, 1992.

Clemmer, Richard O. *Roads in the Sky: The Hopi Indians in a Century of Change.* Boulder, Colo.: Westview Press, 1995.

Clifford, James. "Introduction: Partial Truths." In *Writing Culture: The Poetics and Politics of Ethnography,* edited by James Clifford and George E. Marcus, 1–26. Berkeley: University of California Press, 1986.

———. *Routes: Travel and Translation in the Late Twentieth Century.* Cambridge, Mass.: Harvard University Press, 1997.

Cohodas, Marvin. *Basket Weavers for the California Curio Trade: Elizabeth and Louise Hickox.* Tucson: University of Arizona Press, 1997.

———. "Louisa Keyser and the Cohns: Mythmaking and Basket Making in the American West." In *The Early Years of Native American Art History: The Politics of Scholarship and Collecting,* edited by Janet Catherine Berlo, 88–133. Seattle: University of Washington Press, 1992.

Cole, Douglas. "Tricks of the Trade: Some Reflections on Anthropological Collecting." *Arctic Anthropology* 28 (1991): 48–52.

Cory, Kate T. *Children of Hopiland.* Kate Cory Collection, Sharlot Hall Museum. Prescott, Ariz.

———. "Life and Its Living in Hopiland—Good-Bye to Steam-Cars." *The Border: A Monthly Magazine of Politics, News, and Stories of the West* 1, no. 7 (1909): 1.

————. "Life and Its Living in Hopiland—The Hopi Women." *The Border: A Monthly Magazine of Politics, News, and Stories of the West* 1, no. 11 (1909): 1–2.

————. "Life and Its Living in Hopiland—The Races." *The Border: A Monthly Magazine of Politics, News, and Stories of the West* 1, no. 9 (1909): 4.

————. *People of the Yellow Dawn.* Kate Cory Collection, Sharlot Hall Museum. Prescott, Ariz.

————. "A Realistic Story of the Great Hopi Indians." *The Yavapai Magazine* 13, no. 5 (1925): 7–12.

————. "The Snake Dance and It's [sic] Origin." *Arizona* 13, no. 7 (1923).

Crag and Canyon (Banff National Park), 27 January 1939, 1–2.

Cronon, William, George Miles, and Jay Gitlin, eds. *Under an Open Sky: Rethinking America's Western Past.* New York: Norton, 1992.

Cuch, Forrest S., ed. *The Indians of Utah: A History of Utah's American Indians.* Logan: Utah State University Press, 2000.

Cushing, Frank Hamilton. "My Adventures in Zuñi." *Century Magazine* 25 (December 1882): 191–207; 25 (February 1883): 500–511; and 26 (May 1883): 28–47.

Davidov, Judith Fryer. *Women's Camera Work: Self/Body/Other in American Visual Culture.* Durham, N.C.: Duke University Press, 1998.

Davis, Carolyn O'Bagy. *Hopi Quilting: Stitched Traditions from an Ancient Community.* Tucson, Ariz.: Sanpete Publications, 1997.

Davis, Lee. "California Tribes." In *Encyclopedia of North American Indians,* edited by Frederick E. Hoxie, 94–98. Boston: Houghton Mifflin, 1996.

Davis, Lee, and Niccolo Caldararo. "The Repatriation Dilemma: Museum Objects Are Contaminated with Pesticides." *News from Native California* 13, no. 4 (2000): 46–47.

Davis, Lee, and Don Koué. *Going Home: The California Indian Library Collections Manual.* Berkeley: California Indian Project, 1989.

Davis, Mike. *City of Quartz: Excavating the Future in Los Angeles.* 1990. Reprint, New York: Vintage Books, 1992.

Dawson, Lillian W., comp. *Jane Gay Photograph Collection Catalog.* Boise: Idaho State Historical Society, 1980.

Deloria, Philip J. *Playing Indian.* New Haven, Conn.: Yale University Press, 1998.

De Mallie, Raymond J., ed. *Plains.* Vol. 13 of *Handbook of North American Indians,* edited by William C. Sturtevant. Washington, D.C.: Smithsonian Institution Press, 1996.

De Witt, Jennifer. "'When They Are Gone . . .': The Smoki People of Prescott and the Preservation of Indian Culture." *Journal of Arizona History* 37 (1996): 319–336.

Dilworth, Leah. *Imagining Indians in the Southwest: Persistent Visions of a Primitive Past.* Washington, D.C.: Smithsonian Institution Press, 1996.

Dodge, Jane Gay. "Brief Biography of E. Jane Gay." Unpublished manuscript in possession of the Schlesinger Library, Radcliffe Institute, Harvard University, ca. 1939.

————. "Sketch of My First Meeting with Alice C. Fletcher in 1888." Unpublished manuscript in possession of the Schlesinger Library, Radcliffe Institute, Harvard University, ca. 1939.

Durham, Jimmie. "Geronimo!" In *Partial Recall,* edited by Lucy R. Lippard, 53–58. New York: New Press, 1992.

Edwards, Elizabeth. "Introduction." In *Anthropology and Photography, 1860–1920*, edited by Elizabeth Edwards, 3–17. New Haven, Conn.: Yale University Press, 1992.

———. "The Resonance of Anthropology." In *Native Nations: Journeys in American Photography*, edited by Jane Alison, 187–204. London: Barbican Art Gallery, 1998.

Elkins, James. *The Object Stares Back: On the Nature of Seeing*. New York: Harcourt Brace, 1996.

Evans, Brad. "Cushing's Zuni Sketchbooks: Literature, Anthropology, and American Notions of Culture." *American Quarterly* 49 (1997): 717–745.

Faris, James C. *Navajo and Photography: A Critical History of the Representation of an American People*. Albuquerque: University of New Mexico Press, 1996.

Fleming, Paula Richardson, and Judith Lynne Luskey. *Grand Endeavors of American Indian Photography*. Washington, D.C.: Smithsonian Institution Press, 1993.

Fry, Winifred S. "Humboldt Indians: A Sketch." *Out West* 21, no. 6 (1904): 511.

Gaede, Marnie. "Kate Cory: Artist of Arizona." *Arizona Highways*, August 1987, 22–27.

Gasser, Maria Del Carmen, ed. *"My Dear Miss Nicholson": Letters and Myths by William R. Benson, a Pomo Indian*. Pasadena, Calif.: Bickley Printing Company, 1996.

[Gay, E. Jane]. "A Brave Woman Allotting Lands to Indians in Idaho. Novel and Interesting Experiences, as told by the Companion of Miss Fletcher." *The Red Man* 10, no. 4 (April 1890): 2–3, 6–7.

Gay, E. Jane. "Camp Life Experiences: Miss Gay's Interesting Description of Miss Fletcher's Allotting Lands to the Nez Perces, Continued from the July and August Number." *The Red Man* 12, no. 2 (September 1891): 8.

———. *Choup-nit-ki: With the Nez Percés*. Washington, D .C., and North Chelmsford, Mass.: Gay and Gay, n. d. Handwritten manuscript, produced London, 1909. In possession of the Schlesinger Library, Radcliffe Institute, Harvard University.

[———]. "Miss Fletcher and Miss Gay. Incidental Experiences in Allotting Indian Lands." *The Red Man* 3, no. 6 (1890): 3.

———. *With the Nez Perces: Alice Fletcher in the Field, 1889–1892*. Edited by Frederick E. Hoxie and Joan T. Mark. Lincoln: University of Nebraska Press, 1981.

[———]. "A Woman Allotting Lands to Indians. A Rich and Racy View of a Trying Situation." *The Red Man* 9, no. 11 (November 1889): 5, 8.

Gidley, Mick. "A Hundred Years in the Life of American Indian Photographs." In *Native Nations: Journeys in American Photography*, edited by Jane Alison, 153–167. London: Barbican Art Gallery, 1998.

Gilbert, Elliot L., ed. *"O Beloved Kids": Rudyard Kipling's Letters to His Children*. New York: Harcourt Brace Jovanovich, 1983.

Gilmour, David. *The Long Recessional: The Imperial Life of Rudyard Kipling*. New York: Farrar, Straus & Giroux, 2002.

Gordon, Deborah. "Among Women: Gender and Ethnographic Authority of the Southwest, 1930–1980." In *Hidden Scholars: Women Anthropologists and the Native American Southwest*, edited by Nancy J. Parezo, 129–145. Albuquerque: University of New Mexico Press, 1993.

Gover, C. Jane. *The Positive Image: Women Photographers in Turn of the Century America*. Albany: State University of New York Press, 1988.

Graves, Laura. *Thomas Varker Keam, Indian Trader*. Norman: University of Oklahoma Press, 1998.

Green, Rayna. "Repatriating Images: Indians and Photography." In *Benedicte Wrensted: An Idaho Photographer in Focus*, edited by Joanna Cohan Scherer, 151–160. Pocatello: Idaho State University Press, 1993.

———. "Rosebuds of the Plateau: Frank Matsura and the Fainting Couch Aesthetic." In *Partial Recall*, edited by Lucy R. Lippard, 47–54. New York: New Press, 1992.

Haraway, Donna J. "Situated Knowledges: The Science Question in Feminism and the Privilege of Partial Perspective." In *Simians, Cyborgs, and Women: The Reinvention of Nature*, 183–201. New York: Routledge, 1991.

Harlan, Theresa. "Creating a Visual History: A Question of Ownership." In *Strong Hearts: Native American Visions and Voices*, edited by Peggy Roalf, 20–33. New York: Aperture, 1995.

———. "A Curator's Perspective: Native Photographers Creating a Visual Native American History." *exposure* 29, no. 1 (1993): 12–22.

———. "Indigenous Photographies: A Space for Indigenous Realities." In *Native Nations: Journeys in American Photography*, edited by Jane Alison, 233–246. London: Barbican Art Gallery, 1998.

Hart, E. J., ed. *A Hunter of Peace: Mary T. S. Schäffer's Old Indian Trails of the Canadian Rockies*. Banff, Alberta: Whyte Museum of the Canadian Rockies, 1980.

Hedges, James Blaine. *Building the Canadian West: The Land and Colonization Policies of the Canadian Pacific Railroad*. New York: Macmillan, 1939.

Helm, June, ed. *Pioneers of American Anthropology: The Uses of Biography*. Seattle: University of Washington Press, 1966.

Hilden, Patricia Penn. "Readings from the Red Zone: Cultural Studies, History, Anthropology." *American Literary History* 10 (1998): 524–543.

Hirsch, Marianne. *Family Frames: Photography, Narrative and Postmemory*. Cambridge, Mass.: Harvard University Press, 1997.

Hoxie, Frederick E., ed. *Encyclopedia of North American Indians*. Boston: Houghton Mifflin, 1996.

Hyde, Anne Farrar. *An American Vision: Far Western Landscape and National Culture, 1820–1920*. New York: New York University Press, 1990.

Indian Helper 3, no. 52 (10 August 1888): n.p.

Israel, Claudia, ed. *Elizabeth Hickox; Baskets and Weavers*. Eureka, Calif.: Clarke Memorial Museum, 1996.

Iverson, Peter. *Barry Goldwater: Native Arizonan*. Norman: University of Oklahoma Press, 1997.

Jacknis, Ira. "Alfred Kroeber and the Photographic Representation of California Indians." *American Indian Culture and Research Journal* 20 (1996):15–32.

———. "Alfred Kroeber as Museum Anthropologist." *Museum Anthropology* 17 (1993): 27–32.

———. "Franz Boas and Photography." *Studies in the Anthropology of Visual Communication* 10 (1984): 2–60.

———. "In Search of the Image-Maker: James Mooney as an Ethnographic Photographer." *Visual Anthropology* 3 (1990): 179–212.

———. "Preface." *American Indian Culture and Research Journal* 20 (1996): 1–14.

Jackson, Zig. "Indian Photographing Tourist Photographing Indian." In *Strong Hearts: Native American Visions and Voices*, edited by Peggy Roalf, 34–37. New York: Aperture, 1995.

Jacobs, Margaret D. *Engendered Encounters: Feminism and Pueblo Cultures, 1879–1934.* Lincoln: University of Nebraska Press, 1999.

James, Caroline. *Nez Perce Women in Transition, 1877–1990.* Moscow: University of Idaho Press, 1996.

James, Elizabeth. "The Allotment Period on the Nez Perce Reservation: Encroachments, Obstacles, and Reactions." *Idaho Yesterdays* 37 (1993): 11–23.

James, George Wharton. *In and Out of the Old Missions of California: An Historical and Pictorial Account of the Franciscan Missions.* 1886. Reprint, Boston: Little, Brown, 1922.

———. "Indian Basketry in House Decoration." *Chautauquan* 33, no. 6 (September 1901).

———. *Through Ramona's Country.* Boston: Little, Brown, 1908.

———. *What the White Race May Learn from the Indian.* Chicago: Forbes & Company, 1908.

James, Harry C. *Pages from Hopi History.* 1974. Reprint, Tucson: University of Arizona Press, 1996.

Johnson, Ron, and Colleen Kelley Marks. *Her Mind Made Up: Weaving Caps the Indian Way.* Arcata, Calif.: Reese Bullen Gallery and Humboldt State University, 1998.

Josephy, Alvin M., Jr. *500 Nations: An Illustrated History of North American Indians.* New York: Knopf, 1994.

———. *The Nez Perce Indians and the Opening of the Northwest.* New Haven, Conn.: Yale University Press, 1965.

Kaplan, Amy. "Manifest Domesticity." *American Literature* 70 (1998): 581–606.

Kaplan, E. Ann. *Looking for the Other: Feminism, Film, and the Imperial Gaze.* New York: Routledge, 1997.

Kemp, Mrs. Edward H. "Photographing in the Hopi Land." In *Camera Fiends and Kodak Girls: Fifty Selections by and about Women in Photography, 1840–1930,* edited by Peter E. Palmquist, 147–155. New York: Midmarch Arts Press, 1989.

Kent, Kate Peck. *Navajo Weaving: Three Centuries of Change.* Santa Fe, N.Mex.: School of American Research Press, 1985.

Kipling, Rudyard. *Letters to the Family: Notes on a Trip to Canada 1907,* in *From Sea to Sea and Other Sketches.* New York: Doubleday, 1925.

Koutnik, Auriana. "Remembering Indian Island." *News from Native California* 9, no. 2 (1995–1996): 39.

Krupat, Arnold. *The Turn to the Native: Studies in Criticism and Culture.* Lincoln: University of Nebraska Press, 1996.

Lang, Julian, ed. and trans. *Ararapíkva: Creation Stories of the People, Traditional Karuk Indian Literature from Northwestern California.* Berkeley, Calif.: Heyday Books, 1994.

Lears, T. J. Jackson. *No Place of Grace: Antimodernism and the Transformation of American Culture, 1880–1920.* Chicago: University of Chicago Press, 1984.

Limerick, Patricia Nelson. *The Legacy of Conquest: The Unbroken Past of the American West.* New York: Norton, 1988.

Lippard, Lucy R. "Introduction." In *Partial Recall,* edited by Lucy R. Lippard, 13–45. New York: New Press, 1992.

———, ed. *Partial Recall.* New York: New Press, 1992.

Luna, James. "I've Always Wanted to be an American Indian." In *Strong Hearts: Native*

American Visions and Voices, edited by Peggy Roalf, 38–41. New York: Aperture, 1995.

Lurie, Nancy Oestreich. "Women in Early American Anthropology." In *Pioneers of American Anthropology: The Uses of Biography,* edited by June Helm, 31–81. Seattle: University of Washington Press, 1966.

Lyman, Christopher M. *The Vanishing Race and Other Illusions: Photographs of Indians by Edward S. Curtis.* Washington, D.C.: Smithsonian Institution Press, 1982.

McClintock, Anne. *Imperial Leather: Race, Gender and Sexuality in the Colonial Conquest.* London: Routledge, 1995.

McGreevy, Susan Brown. "Daughters of Affluence: Wealth, Collecting, and Southwestern Institutions." In *Hidden Scholars: Women Anthropologists and the Native American Southwest,* edited by Nancy J. Parezo, 76–100. Albuquerque: University of New Mexico Press, 1993.

McLaughlin, Michael R. "The Dawes Act, or Indian General Allotment Act of 1887: The Continuing Burden of Allotment. A Selective Annotated Bibliography." *American Indian Culture and Research Journal* 20, no. 2 (1996), 59–105.

McLendon, Sally. "Collecting Pomoan Baskets, 1889–1939." *Museum Anthropology* 17 (1993): 49–60.

———. "Preparing Museum Collections for Use as Primary Data in Ethnographic Research." In *The Research Potential of Anthropological Museum Collections,* edited by Anne-Marie Cantwell, James B. Griffin, and Nan A. Rothschild, 201–227. New York: New York Academy of Sciences, 1981.

McMaster, Gerald. "Colonial Alchemy: Reading the Boarding School Experience." In *Partial Recall,* edited by Lucy R. Lippard, 76–87. New York: New Press, 1992.

McWilliams, Carey. *North from Mexico: The Spanish-Speaking People of the United States.* 1949. Reprint, New York: Praeger, 1990.

———. *Southern California: An Island on the Land.* 1947. Reprint, Salt Lake City, Utah: Peregrine Smith, 1973.

Mark, Joan. *A Stranger in Her Native Land: Alice Fletcher and the American Indians.* Lincoln: University of Nebraska Press, 1988.

Marks, Colleen Kelley. "Preservation through Mutual Respect." *News from Native California* 9, no. 1 (1995): 17–21.

Marr, Carolyn J. "Marking Oneself: Use of Photographs by Native Americans of the Southern Northwest Coast." *American Indian Culture and Research Journal* 20 (1996): 51–64.

———. "Taken Pictures: On Interpreting Native American Photographs of the Southern Northwest Coast." *Pacific Northwest Quarterly* 80, no. 2 (1989): 52–61.

Masayesva, Victor, Jr. "Kwikwilyaqua: Hopi Photography." In *Hopi Photographers/ Hopi Images,* compiled by Victor Masayesva, Jr., and Erin Younger, 10–12. Tucson: University of Arizona Press, 1983.

Masayesva, Victor, Jr., and Erin Younger, comps. *Hopi Photographers/Hopi Images.* Tucson: University of Arizona Press, 1983.

Masteller, Richard N. "Western Views in Eastern Parlors: The Contribution of the Stereograph Photographer to the Conquest of the West." *Prospects* 6 (1981): 55–71.

Michaels, Barbara. *Gertrude Käsebier: The Photographer and Her Photographs.* New York: Abrams, 1992.

Miller, Angela. *The Empire of the Eye: Landscape Representation and American Cultural Politics, 1825–1875.* Ithaca, N.Y.: Cornell University Press, 1993.

Milner, Clyde A., ed. *A New Significance: Re-envisioning the History of the American West.* New York: Oxford University Press, 1996.

Minh-ha, Trinh T. *When the Moon Waxes Red: Representation, Gender, and Cultural Politics.* New York: Routledge, 1991.

Morrill, Allen Conrad, and Eleanor Dunlap Morrill. *Out of the Blanket: The Story of Sue and Kate McBeth, Missionaries to the Nez Perces.* Moscow: University Press of Idaho, 1978.

Mullin, Molly H. *Culture in the Marketplace: Gender, Art, and Value in the American Southwest.* Durham, N.C.: Duke University Press, 2001.

Nestor, Sarah. "Weaving: The Woven Spirit." In *Harmony by Hand: Art of the Southwest Indians, Basketry, Weaving, Pottery,* by Patrick Hoolihan, Jerold L. Collings, Sarah Nestor, and Jonathan Batkin, 50–74. San Francisco: Chronicle Books, 1987.

Nez Perce Reservation Allotment Book, Prepared by Alice Fletcher, 1889–1892. Photocopy held by Idaho State Historical Society. Original in possession of Ralph Williams, Gifford, Idaho.

Northrup, Jim. *Walking the Rez Road.* Stillwater, Minn.: Voyageur Press, 1993.

Norton, Jack. *Genocide in Northwestern California: When Our Worlds Cried.* San Francisco: Indian Historian Press, 1979.

Norwood, Vera, and Janice Monk, eds. *The Desert Is No Lady: Southwestern Landscapes in Women's Writing and Art.* New Haven, Conn.: Yale University Press, 1987.

O'Connell, Barry. "Introduction." In *A Son of the Forest and Other Writings,* edited by Barry O'Connell. Amherst: University of Massachusetts Press, 1997.

O'Neale, Lila M. *Yurok-Karuk Basket Weavers.* Berkeley: Phoebe Apperson Hearst Museum of Anthropology and the University of California, 1995.

Otis, D. S. *The Dawes Act and the Allotment of Indian Lands.* Edited by Francis Paul Prucha. Norman: University of Oklahoma Press, 1973.

Owens, Louis. *Mixedblood Messages: Literature, Film, Family, Place.* Norman: University of Oklahoma Press, 1998.

Palmquist, Peter E., ed. *Camera Fiends and Kodak Girls: Fifty Selections by and about Women in Photography, 1840–1930.* New York: Midmarch Arts Press, 1989.

———. "Capture the Shadow 'ere the Substance Fly." In *Silver Shadows: A Directory and History of Early Photography in Chico and Twelve Counties of Northern California,* edited by Ira H. Latour, 19–27. Chico, Calif.: Chico Museum Association and Chico Art Center, 1993.

——— (with Lincoln Kilian). *The Photographers of the Humboldt Bay Region: A. W. Ericson.* Arcata, Calif.: Peter E. Palmquist, 1989.

———. *Shadowcatchers: A Directory of Women in California Photography, before 1901.* Eureka, Calif.: Eureka Printing Company, 1990.

———. *Shadowcatchers 2: A Directory of Women in California Photography, 1900–1920.* Eureka, Calif.: Eureka Printing Company, 1991.

———. *With Nature's Children: Emma B. Freeman (1880–1928)—Camera and Brush.* Eureka, Calif.: Interface California Corporation, 1976.

———. "Women Photographers and the American Indian." In *Benedicte Wrensted: An Idaho Photographer in Focus,* edited by Joanna Cohan Scherer, 121–133. Pocatello: Idaho State University Press, 1993.

Parezo, Nancy J., ed. *Hidden Scholars: Women Anthropologists and the Native American Southwest.* Albuquerque: University of New Mexico Press, 1993.

———. "Matilda Coxe Stevenson: Pioneer Ethnologist." In *Hidden Scholars: Women*

Anthropologists and the Native American Southwest, edited by Nancy J. Parezo, 38–62. Albuquerque: University of New Mexico Press, 1993.

Parker, Charles Franklin. "Sojourn in Hopiland." *Arizona Highways,* May 1943, 10–13, 41.

Payment, Diane Paulette. "Plains Metis." In *Plains,* edited by Raymond J. De Mallie, 601–676. Vol. 13 of *Handbook of North American Indians,* edited by William C. Sturtevant. Washington, D.C.: Smithsonian Institution Press, 1996.

Poolaw, Linda. "Spirit Capture: Observations of an Encounter." In *Spirit Capture: Photographs from the National Museum of the American Indian,* edited by Tim Johnson, 166–178. Washington, D.C.: Smithsonian Institution Press, 1998.

Powell, John Wesley. "The Ancient Province of Tusayan." *Scribner's Monthly* 11 (November 1875–April 1876): 193–213.

Pratt, Mary Louise. *Imperial Eyes: Travel Writing and Transculturation.* New York: Routledge, 1992.

Price, Monroe E., and Robert N. Clinton, eds. *Law and the American Indian: Readings, Notes and Cases.* 2d ed. Charlottesville, Va.: Michie, 1983.

Prucha, Francis Paul. *American Indian Policy in Crisis: Christian Reformers and the Indian, 1865–1900.* Norman: University of Oklahoma Press, 1976.

———. "Introduction." In *Americanizing the American Indians: Writings by the "Friends of the Indian," 1880–1900,* edited by Francis Paul Prucha, 1–10. Cambridge, Mass.: Harvard University Press, 1973.

———, ed. "Introduction." *The Dawes Act and the Allotment of Indian Lands,* by D. S. Otis, ix–xvii. Norman: University of Oklahoma Press, 1973.

Raphael, Ray. *Little White Father: Redick McKee on the California Frontier.* Eureka, Calif.: Humboldt County Historical Society, 1993.

Rawls, James J. *Indians of California: The Changing Image.* Norman: University of Oklahoma Press, 1984.

The Red Man 9, no. 11 (November 1889): 1.

"Report of the Field Matron," 1915. Record of Employees, Box 155, Series 63, Record Group 75. Hoopa Valley Agency, San Bruno Federal Archives, San Bruno, Calif.

Reynolds, Larry J. "American Cultural Iconography: Vision, History, and the Real." *American Literary History* 9 (1997): 381–395.

Rickard, Jolene. "Cew Ete Haw I Tih: The Bird That Carries Language Back to Another." In *Partial Recall,* edited by Lucy R. Lippard, 105–111. New York: New Press, 1992.

———. "The Occupation of Indigenous Space as 'Photograph.'" In *Native Nations: Journeys in American Photography,* edited by Jane Alison, 57–71. London: Barbican Art Gallery, 1998.

———. "Sovereignty: A Line in the Sand." In *Strong Hearts: Native American Visions and Voices,* edited by Peggy Roalf, 50–59. New York: Aperture, 1995.

Riley, Glenda. *Woman and Nature: Saving the "Wild" West.* Lincoln: University of Nebraska Press, 1999.

Ring, Mildred. "Kodaking the Indians." In *Camera Fiends and Kodak Girls: Fifty Selections by and about Women in Photography, 1840–1930,* edited by Peter E. Palmquist, 227–231. New York: Midmarch Arts Press, 1989.

Roalf, Peggy, ed. *Strong Hearts: Native American Visions and Voices.* New York: Aperture, 1995.

Roberts, David R. "Sacred Sights." *American Photo* 6, no. 6 (1995): 44, 106, 109.

Rosaldo, Renato. *Culture and Truth: The Remaking of Social Analysis.* Boston: Beacon Press, 1993.

Rosenberg, Rosalind. *Beyond Separate Spheres: Intellectual Roots of Modern Feminism.* New Haven, Conn.: Yale University Press, 1982.

Rosenblum, Naomi. "Women in Photography: An Historical Overview." *exposure* 24, no. 4 (1986): 6–26.

Royster, Judith V. "The Legacy of Allotment." *Arizona State Law Journal* 27 (1995): 1–78.

Rudnick, Lois [Palken]. "Re-naming the Land: Anglo Expatriate Women in the Southwest." In *The Desert Is No Lady: Southwestern Landscapes in Women's Writing and Art,* edited by Vera Norwood and Janice Monk, 10–26. New Haven, Conn.: Yale University Press, 1987.

———. *Utopian Vistas: The Mabel Dodge Luhan House and the American Counterculture.* Albuquerque: University of New Mexico Press, 1996.

Rugoff, Ralph. *Scene of the Crime.* Cambridge, Mass.: MIT Press, 1997.

Ryan, Mary. *The Empire of the Mother: American Writing about Domesticity.* New York: Haworth Press, 1982.

Sakiestewa, Ramona. "Weaving for Dance." In *Partial Recall,* edited by Lucy R. Lippard, 73–75. New York: New Press, 1992.

Samuels, Shirley, ed. *The Culture of Sentiment: Race, Gender, and Sentimentality in Nineteenth-Century America.* New York: Oxford University Press, 1992.

Sandweiss, Martha A. *Laura Gilpin: An Enduring Grace.* Ft. Worth, Tex.: Amon Carter Museum, 1986.

———. "Laura Gilpin and the Tradition of American Landscape Photography." In *The Desert Is No Lady: Southwestern Landscapes in Women's Writing and Art,* edited by Vera Norwood and Janice Monk, 62–73. New Haven, Conn.: Yale University Press, 1987.

———. "Undecisive Moments: The Narrative Tradition in Western Photography." In *Photography in Nineteenth-Century America,* edited by Martha A. Sandweiss, 99–129. New York: Abrams, 1991.

Schäffer, Mary T. S. *Old Indian Trails of the Canadian Rockies.* New York: Putnam, 1911.

Scherer, Joanna Cohan. "You Can't Believe Your Eyes: Inaccuracies in Photographs of North American Indians," *exposure* 16, no. 4 (1978): 6–19.

Seton-Thompson, Grace Gallatin. *A Woman Tenderfoot.* New York: Doubleday, 1900.

Shi, David E. *The Simple Life: Plain Living and High Thinking in American Culture.* New York: Oxford University Press, 1985.

Silko, Leslie Marmon. *Almanac of the Dead.* New York: Simon & Schuster, 1991.

———. *Storyteller.* New York: Seaver, 1981.

———. *Yellow Woman and A Beauty of the Spirit: Essays on Native American Life Today.* New York: Simon & Schuster, 1996.

Silverberg, Helene, ed. *Gender and American Social Science: The Formative Years.* Princeton, N.J.: Princeton University Press, 1998.

———. "Introduction: Toward a Gendered Social Science History." In *Gender and American Social Science: The Formative Years,* edited by Helene Silverberg, 3–32. Princeton, N.J.: Princeton University Press, 1998.

Silversides, Brock V. *The Face Pullers: Photographing Native Canadians, 1871–1939.* Saskatoon, Saskatchewan: Fifth House, 1994.

Slickpoo, Allen P., Sr., and Deward E. Walker, Jr. *Noon-Nee-Me-Poo (We, the Nez Perces): Culture and History of the Nez Perces.* Vol. 1. N.p.: Nez Perce Tribe of Idaho, 1973.

Smith, Paul Chaat. "Ghost in the Machine." In *Strong Hearts: Native American Visions and Voices,* edited by Peggy Roalf, 6–9. New York: Aperture, 1995.

Smith, Shawn Michelle. *American Archives: Gender, Race, and Class in Visual Culture.* Princeton, N.J.: Princeton University Press, 1999.

Smith, Sherry L. *Reimagining Indians: Native Americans through Anglo Eyes, 1880–1940.* New York: Oxford University Press, 2000.

Sontag, Susan. *On Photography.* New York: Farrar, Straus & Giroux, 1977.

Stegner, Wallace. *Angle of Repose.* Garden City, N.Y.: Doubleday, 1971.

———. *Beyond the Hundredth Meridian: John Wesley Powell and the Second Opening of the West.* 1954. Reprint, New York: Penguin Books, 1992.

Stoll, Horatio F. "'Digger' Indians and the Camera: An Amateur Photographer's Experience." *Camera Craft* (February 1903): 155–161.

Stowe, Harriet Beecher. *Uncle Tom's Cabin; or, Life among the Lowly.* 1852. Reprint, Boston: Houghton Mifflin, 1892.

Strickland, Rennard. *Tonto's Revenge: Reflections on American Indian Culture and Policy.* Albuquerque: University of New Mexico Press, 1997.

Tabah, Agnes. *Native American Collections and Repatriation.* Washington, D.C.: Technical Information Service, American Association of Museums, 1993.

Tagg, John. *The Burden of Representation: Essays on Photographies and Histories.* Amherst: University of Massachusetts Press, 1988.

Tapahonso, Luci. "The Way It Is." In *Sign Language: Contemporary Southwest Native America,* 13–17, photographs by Skeet McAuley. New York: Aperture, 1989.

Thompson, Lucy. *To the American Indian: Reminiscences of a Yurok Woman.* 1916. Reprint, Berkeley, Calif.: Heyday Books, 1976.

Trachtenberg, Alan. *Reading American Photographs: Images as History, Mathew Brady to Walker Evans.* New York: Hill & Wang, 1989.

Tremblay, Gail. "Constructing Images, Constructing Reality: American Indian Photography and Representation." *Views: A Journal of Photography in New England* 13–14 (1993): 7–14.

Trumbull, Truman, A.M. [pseud. E. Jane Gay]. *The New Yankee Doodle: Being an Account of the Little Difficulty in the Family of Uncle Sam.* New York: Bourne, 1868.

Tsinhnahjinnie, Hulleah J. "Compensating Imbalances." *exposure* 29, no. 1 (1993): 29–30.

———. "When Is a Photograph Worth a Thousand Words?" In *Native Nations: Journeys in American Photography,* edited by Jane Alison. London: Barbican Art Gallery, 1998.

Turner, Frederick Jackson. "The Significance of the Frontier in American History." *Annual Report of the American Historical Association for the Year 1893.* Readex Microprint, 1966.

Visweswaran, Kamala. "'Wild West' Anthropology and the Disciplining of Gender." In *Gender and American Social Science: The Formative Years,* edited by Helene Silverberg, 86–123. Princeton, N.J.: Princeton University Press, 1998.

Vizenor, Gerald. *Darkness in St. Louis Bearheart.* St. Paul, Minn.: Truck Press, 1978. Reprinted as *Bearheart: The Heirship Chronicles.* Minneapolis: University of Minnesota Press, 1990.

———. *Fugitive Poses: Native American Indian Scenes of Absence and Presence.* Lincoln: University of Nebraska Press, 1998.

———. *Manifest Manners: Postindian Warriors of Survivance.* Hanover, N.H.: University Press of New England, 1994.

Wexler, Laura. "Seeing Sentiment: Photography, Race, and the Innocent Eye." In *Female Subjects in Black and White: Race, Psychoanalysis, Feminism,* edited by Elizabeth Abel, Barbara Christian, and Helen Moglen, 159–186. Berkeley: University of California Press, 1997.

———. *Tender Violence: Domestic Visions in an Age of U.S. Imperialism.* Chapel Hill: University of North Carolina Press, 2000.

———. "Tender Violence, Literary Eavesdropping, Domestic Fiction, and Educational Reform." In *The Culture of Sentiment: Race, Gender, and Sentimentality in Nineteenth-Century America,* edited by Shirley Samuels, 9–38. New York: Oxford University Press, 1992.

Whiteley, Peter. "The End of Anthropology (at Hopi)?" In *Indians and Anthropologists: Vine Deloria, Jr. and the Critique of Anthropology,* edited by Thomas Biolsi and Larry J. Zimmerman, 177–207. Tucson: University of Arizona Press, 1997.

Whyte, Jon. *Indians in the Rockies.* Banff, Alberta: Altitude Publishing, 1985.

Wilson, Angus. *The Strange Ride of Rudyard Kipling: His Life and Works.* New York: Viking, 1977.

Wright, Barton, Marnie Gaede, and Marc Gaede. *The Hopi Photographs: Kate Cory: 1905–1912.* 1986. Reprint, Albuquerque: University of New Mexico Press, 1988.

Wright, Nancy Kirkpatrick. "Kate Thompson Cory: Camera and Paintbrush." *Cactus and Pine* 9, no. 1 (1997): 2–19.

Yellow Bird, Michael. "What We Want to Be Called: Indigenous Peoples' Perspectives on Racial and Ethnic Identity Labels." *American Indian Quarterly* 23, no. 2 (1999): 21–28.

Younger, Erin. "Changing Images: A Century of Photography on the Hopi Reservation (1880–1980)." In *Hopi Photographers/Hopi Images,* compiled by Victor Masayesva, Jr., and Erin Younger, 14–39. Tucson: University of Arizona Press, 1983.

INDEX

Note: Page numbers in italics indicate illustrations.

ABOUT THE AUTHORS

Susan Bernardin is an assistant professor of English at SUNY College at Oneonta, where she teaches American Indian and postcolonial literatures. She has published articles on foundational and contemporary Native writers. She is currently editing a book, *More Stories from the Grasshopper Song: The Restored Text of "In the Land of the Grasshopper Song: Two Women in Klamath River Indian Country, 1908-09,"* in collaboration with Karuk tribal historians and Humboldt County (California) Historical Society members.

Melody Graulich is a professor of English and the director of graduate American Studies at Utah State University. She is also the editor of *Western American Literature.* Over the past twenty years, she has published numerous articles and books focusing on western writers and artists. Recent books include two co-edited collections, *Exploring Lost Borders: A Collection of Essays on Mary Austin* (University of Nevada Press) and *Reading "The Virginian" in the New West: Centennial Essays* (University of Nebraska Press). Another essay on photography, "'Cameras and Photographs Were Not Permitted in the Camps': Developing Photographic Absences in Japanese American Internment Narratives," is forthcoming in a collection titled *True West,* edited by William Handley and Nat Lewis (University of Nebraska Press).

Lisa MacFarlane is an associate professor of English and American Studies at the University of New Hampshire, where she directs the American Studies Program. She writes and teaches courses on nineteenth-century writers, American photography, and American literature and culture from the Civil War to World War II. She is the editor of *This World Is Not Conclusion: Faith in Nineteenth-Century New England Fiction* (University Press of New England) and, with Susan Juster, of *A Mighty Baptism: Race, Gender, and the Creation of American Protestantism* (Cornell University Press), as well as the Penguin edition of Henry Adams's *Esther.*

Louis Owens (1948–2002) was a celebrated critic, fiction writer, and teacher. Among his numerous publications are *Other Destinies: Understanding the American Indian Novel, Mixedblood Messages: Literature, Film, Family, and Place,* and *I Hear the Train: Reflections, Inventions, and Refractions,* as well as several novels, including *The Sharpest Sight, Bone Game,* and *Dark River.* With his death in 2002, American Indian literature lost one of its most perceptive and generous voices.

Nicole Tonkovich is an associate professor of nineteenth-century U.S. literatures and cultures at the University of California, San Diego. She writes and teaches about nineteenth-century literatures and cultures, women's history and literatures, and photography and visual culture. She is the author of *Domesticity with a Difference: The Nonfiction of Catharine Beecher, Sarah J. Hale, Fanny Fern, and Margaret Fuller* (University Press of Mississippi) and the editor of *The American Woman's Home* by Catharine Beecher and Harriet Beecher Stowe (Rutgers University Press).